Learning Kendo UI Web Development

An easy-to-follow practical tutorial to add exciting features to your web pages without being a JavaScript expert

John Adams

BIRMINGHAM - MUMBAI

Learning Kendo UI Web Development

First published: May 2013

Production Reference: 1160513

Published by Packt Publishing Ltd.
Livery Place
35 Livery Street
Birmingham B3 2PB, UK.

ISBN 978-1-84969-434-6

www.packtpub.com

Cover Image by Parag Kadam (paragvkadam@gmail.com)

Credits

Author
John Adams

Reviewers
Ricardo Covo
Long Le

Acquisition Editor
Kartikey Pandey

Lead Technical Editor
Mayur Hule

Technical Editors
Vrinda Amberkar Bhosale
Dominic Pereira

Project Coordinator
Anugya Khurana

Proofreader
Dan McMahon
Lesley Harrison

Indexer
Hemangini Bari

Production Coordinator
Melwyn D'sa

Cover Work
Melwyn D'sa

About the Author

John Adams currently works as an application development consultant in the Dallas/Fort Worth area for a fantastic company called RBA. He has been developing custom business applications with the Microsoft .NET platform for 6 years and has specialized in development with ASP.NET MVC. He loves writing code and creating solutions. Above all, he loves his wife and children and the lord Jesus Christ.

This book is dedicated to Michell, Samuel, and Sophie whose patience with my late nights made this project possible.

I would also like to thank RBA, especially my manager Will, who introduced me to the project and kicked everything off.

Finally, I would like to thank Kartikey Pandey, Anugya Khurana, Mayur Hule, Ricardo Covo, and Long Le for their oversight and editing skills. Their work has been exceptional and valuable throughout.

About the Reviewers

Ricardo Covo has more than a decade of international experience in the Software Development field, with experience in Latin America, California, and Canada. He has a wealth of experience in delivering data-driven enterprise solutions across various industries.

With a Bachelor's degree in Systems Engineering, complemented with a certification in Advanced Project Management, he has the right combination of technical and leadership skills to build development teams and set them up for efficient execution.

In 2007 he founded (and is the principal of) Web Nodes – Software Development (`http://webnodes.ca`); a custom software development company, with clients big and small in Canada, United States, and South America.

Prior to Web Nodes, Ricardo spent some years in the corporate world both in Canada and in the U.S., being part of companies such as Loblaws Inc., Trader Corporation, UNX (`http://www.unix.com`) and Auctiva (`http://www.auctiva.com`).

Ricardo's passion for technology goes beyond work; he normally works on personal projects in an effort to always remain on top of the changes in technology. These projects include: `http://ytnext.com`, `http://serversok.com`, and `http://toystrunk.com`.

Long Le is a senior .NET Architect and Principal ALM Practitioner at CBRE. He also serves as principal consultant for Thinklabs and spends most of his time developing frameworks and application blocks, providing guidance for best practices and patterns, and standardizing the enterprise technology stack. He has been working with Microsoft technologies for over 10 years.

Le has focused on a wide spectrum of server-side and web technologies, such as ASP.NET Web Forms, ASP.NET MVC, Windows Workflow, LINQ and Entity Framework, DevExpress, and Kendo UI. In his spare time, he enjoys blogging (`http://blog.longle.net`) and playing Call of Duty on his XBOX. He's recently became a proud father of his new born daughter Khloe Le. You can reach and follow him on Twitter `@LeLong37`.

Special thanks to my significant other Tina Le for all your love and support throughout this project and to my wonderful newborn daughter Khloe Le. I love you.

---

www.PacktPub.com

Support files, eBooks, discount offers and more

You might want to visit www.PacktPub.com for support files and downloads related to your book.

Did you know that Packt offers eBook versions of every book published, with PDF and ePub files available? You can upgrade to the eBook version at www.PacktPub.com and as a print book customer, you are entitled to a discount on the eBook copy. Get in touch with us at service@packtpub.com for more details.

At www.PacktPub.com, you can also read a collection of free technical articles, sign up for a range of free newsletters and receive exclusive discounts and offers on Packt books and eBooks.

http://PacktLib.PacktPub.com

Do you need instant solutions to your IT questions? PacktLib is Packt's online digital book library. Here, you can access, read and search across Packt's entire library of books.

Why Subscribe?

- Fully searchable across every book published by Packt
- Copy and paste, print and bookmark content
- On demand and accessible via web browser

Free Access for Packt account holders

If you have an account with Packt at www.PacktPub.com, you can use this to access PacktLib today and view nine entirely free books. Simply use your login credentials for immediate access.

Table of Contents

Preface

Web development today requires real expertise in HTML5, JavaScript, and CSS. These technologies are not completely new, but there has been so much growth around this programming model that it can be difficult to find your bearings when trying to create a new website. It seems like every popular website has a different, special trick in rendering attractive layouts or in creating responsive and dynamic experiences. A beginner can feel hopeless in trying to learn how to program like this.

Fortunately, many JavaScript libraries have arisen to meet this intense demand. Most of these libraries enable client-side functionality through special shortcuts so that a developer can utilize very powerful functionality without writing, or even understanding, complicated JavaScript code. The jQuery libraries are a very good example of this; they provide rich functionality and UI controls with only a few lines of code, hiding the complicated programming underneath.

Telerik has taken this model one step further. They have built a powerful JavaScript framework called Kendo UI that is built on top of jQuery, but can create complete widgets with even simpler code. Not only this, it also includes server-side code libraries that enable developers to create widgets on the server, and all JavaScript is generated automatically! This is an enormous productivity boost, and enables both experienced web developers and beginners to operate on the same playing field. This book will take you on an initial journey through the Kendo UI Framework and show you how to create an entire set of useful and powerful widgets that will make your web pages shine like the best sites on the Internet.

What this book covers

Chapter 1, Interacting with Data: DataSource, Templates, and Grid, teaches the foundation of the Kendo UI DataSource and Template JavaScript objects. Learn the basics of these tools and the most important widget of all—the Grid. These concepts will form the basis for all of your creations with the Kendo UI framework.

Chapter 2, The *AutoComplete Widget and its Usage*, shows how to use Kendo UI to create a word wheel, or auto-complete, effect on a textbox so that word suggestions appear as the user types. Learn how to use this widget and how to connect it to different data sources.

Chapter 3, *Using and Customizing Calendar*, shows how to create a full-featured calendar control on a web page with very little required code. Learn how to use the Kendo UI framework to customize this widget to tailor it to your needs.

Chapter 4, *The Kendo MVVM Framework*, introduces you to Model-View-ViewModel (MVVM) development with Kendo UI. JavaScript MVVM frameworks are powerful systems that allow you to bind dynamic data to web pages through declaring HTML attributes. These systems can be complicated, but the Kendo UI MVVM framework is as easy as this can get. Learn how to use this to enable powerful dynamic web pages.

Chapter 5, *HTML Editor and Custom Tools*, demonstrates the Kendo UI Editor widget. This HTML editor widget allows you to give users a useful area to format text input with styles and layout. This is a perfect feature for blogs, forums, and review sites. Learn how to use and customize this widget for your own web pages.

Chapter 6, *Menu and ListView*, introduces you to the Menu and ListView widgets from Kendo UI so you can effectively format and display data on your web pages. The Menu widget creates a dynamic menu that opens with hover effects and allows for custom animation and behaviors. The ListView is a very flexible widget that allows you to format and template data however you like. Learn how to use these widgets to display data on your own pages.

Chapter 7, *Implementing PanelBar and TabStrip*, illustrates how to build accordion controls and tabs on your web pages. Accordion controls provide a useful way to include a lot of content on a page without making the page grow in size. It can show only a single section of content at a time while still providing instant access to the rest. Tabs are very useful for creating navigation bars on a page that show what other areas of your site that a user can visit. You will learn how to create accordion controls with the PanelBar widget and how to create tabs using the TabStrip widget. See how using these widgets can make your web pages look better.

Chapter 8, *Slider Essentials*, will teach you how to use the Kendo UI Slider widgets to display number ranges with an attractive twist. This widget is a very convenient method of collecting numerical input from web forms with graphical bars that can slide and move in steps. Learn how to add these widgets to your web pages to make your web forms really shine.

Chapter 9, Implementing the Splitter and TreeView Widgets, will illustrate how to lay out resizable content areas on your web pages and how to visualize hierarchical data with a simple widget. The Splitter widget helps organize web pages into resizable zones. The TreeView widget creates dynamic displays for hierarchical data. Learn how to create these widgets and connect them to data sources.

Chapter 10, The Upload and Window Widgets, provides instructions on how to build powerful file upload pages and interactive dialog boxes into your web site. The Upload widget creates a powerful file upload utility that works with AJAX and even allows drag-and-drop functionality. The Window widget creates modal dialog boxes that make areas of your web pages appear when necessary on top of other content. Learn how to make these widgets and add them to your pages.

Chapter 11, Web API Examples, takes what you have learned about the Kendo UI widgets and introduces you into a more advanced area of development using the ASP.NET Web API framework. Web API provides a powerful server-side backend for your Kendo UI widgets and opens up the possibilities for creative custom development. Learn how to manage this technology in your own web applications with ASP.NET MVC.

What you need for this book

To complete the examples in this book, you will first need Visual Studio 2012. You can download a free trial of Visual Studio from `www.microsoft.com/visualstudio` if you do not already have it installed. You will also need the Kendo UI Complete for ASP.NET MVC install package from Telerik which you can get at `http://www.kendoui.com/download.aspx`.

Who this book is for

This book is designed for beginner web developers, who are starting to learn how to utilize JavaScript libraries to create rich and interactive web applications. The user should be familiar with JavaScript, HTML, and CSS. Some knowledge of ASP.NET MVC is helpful, but not required.

Conventions

In this book, you will find a number of styles of text that distinguish between different kinds of information. Here are some examples of these styles, and an explanation of their meaning.

Code words in text, database table names, folder names, filenames, file extensions, pathnames, dummy URLs, user input, and Twitter handles are shown as follows: "The `both` tick placement option will place the tick marks on both sides of a slider."

A block of code is set as follows:

```
<style>
    #stateOrTerritory {
      width:200px;
    }
</style>

<h2>AutoCompletePage</h2>
<input type="text" name="stateOrTerritory" id="stateOrTerritory" />

<script type="text/javascript">
```

When we wish to draw your attention to a particular part of a code block, the relevant lines or items are set in bold:

```
new StateTerritory{ Name = "Washington", IsContiguous = true,
IsState = true, IsTerritory = false },
new StateTerritory{ Name = "West Virginia", IsContiguous = true,
IsState = true, IsTerritory = false },
new StateTerritory{ Name = "Wisconsin", IsContiguous = true,
IsState = true, IsTerritory = false },
new StateTerritory{ Name = "Wyoming", IsContiguous = true,
IsState = true, IsTerritory = false }
```

New terms and **important words** are shown in bold. Words that you see on the screen, in menus or dialog boxes for example, appear in the text like this: "Notice that the content of the Kendo UI Window widget is not yet shown, it must first be activated through an event; in this case that event is clicking on the **Show Window** button."

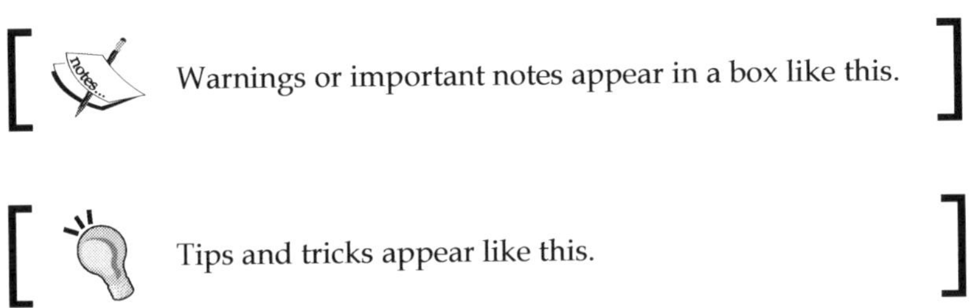

Warnings or important notes appear in a box like this.

Tips and tricks appear like this.

Reader feedback

Feedback from our readers is always welcome. Let us know what you think about this book—what you liked or may have disliked. Reader feedback is important for us to develop titles that you really get the most out of.

To send us general feedback, simply send an e-mail to `feedback@packtpub.com`, and mention the book title via the subject of your message.

If there is a topic that you have expertise in and you are interested in either writing or contributing to a book, see our author guide on `www.packtpub.com/authors`.

Customer support

Now that you are the proud owner of a Packt book, we have a number of things to help you to get the most from your purchase.

Downloading the example code

You can download the example code files for all Packt books you have purchased from your account at `http://www.packtpub.com`. If you purchased this book elsewhere, you can visit `http://www.packtpub.com/support` and register to have the files e-mailed directly to you.

Errata

Although we have taken every care to ensure the accuracy of our content, mistakes do happen. If you find a mistake in one of our books—maybe a mistake in the text or the code—we would be grateful if you would report this to us. By doing so, you can save other readers from frustration and help us improve subsequent versions of this book. If you find any errata, please report them by visiting `http://www.packtpub.com/submit-errata`, selecting your book, clicking on the **errata submission form** link, and entering the details of your errata. Once your errata are verified, your submission will be accepted and the errata will be uploaded on our website, or added to any list of existing errata, under the Errata section of that title. Any existing errata can be viewed by selecting your title from `http://www.packtpub.com/support`.

Piracy

Piracy of copyright material on the Internet is an ongoing problem across all media. At Packt, we take the protection of our copyright and licenses very seriously. If you come across any illegal copies of our works, in any form, on the Internet, please provide us with the location address or website name immediately so that we can pursue a remedy.

Please contact us at `copyright@packtpub.com` with a link to the suspected pirated material.

We appreciate your help in protecting our authors, and our ability to bring you valuable content.

Questions

You can contact us at `questions@packtpub.com` if you are having a problem with any aspect of the book, and we will do our best to address it.

1

Interacting with Data: DataSource, Templates, TabStrip, and Grid

Today is an exciting time to be a web developer. Web browsers and web standards have matured to the point that today's programmer has rich frameworks available to boost productivity and to reach wide audiences with less code and fewer headaches. HTML, CSS, and JavaScript have converged into a powerful and coherent unit that allows web applications to be both aesthetically and architecturally beautiful and elegant. Kendo UI, from Telerik, is a modern framework that embraces these advances and provides a set of tools to enable rich web development and configurable widgets, all with a familiar and accessible syntax.

Along these same lines, development tools have been improving as well and Visual Studio 2012 from Microsoft is a good example. JavaScript is now a first-class citizen in the Microsoft world and there are many improvements for JavaScript development in the IDE, along with improved support for HTML5 and CSS3. This is largely to support a new programming model in Windows 8 that allows web developers to take their skills to the Windows 8 desktop, but these improvements also directly benefit ASP.NET development —especially ASP.NET MVC. This is the programming environment that we will use throughout this book to demonstrate and learn the Kendo UI framework for the web.

Setting up the sample project

Kendo UI for web development is a client-side, jQuery-powered JavaScript framework that is not dependent on any specific server technology or platform. This means that you can type and run the client-side examples in this book using your choice of tools and debugging/testing environment. However, Telerik has also released a great set of server-side extensions for the Microsoft ASP.NET MVC framework that can significantly boost productivity. To take advantage of both of these models, I will be using Visual Studio 2012 and the ASP.NET MVC 4 project template for all my demonstrations and I invite you to follow along with me. Visual Studio 2012 Express is a freely available download from `http://www.microsoft.com/visualstudio/eng/products/visual-studio-overview`, if you do not already have it installed.

Rather download completed samples?

The samples that are displayed in this book are available for download and you can start from the completed code if you do not want to follow all of the steps of setting it up yourself.

Once you have Visual Studio 2012 installed, click on **New Project** either from the Start page or from the **File** menu. Then choose **ASP.NET MVC 4 Web Application** from the **Web** group of project choices. As you can see from the following screenshot, I have named my project `LearningKendoUIWeb`:

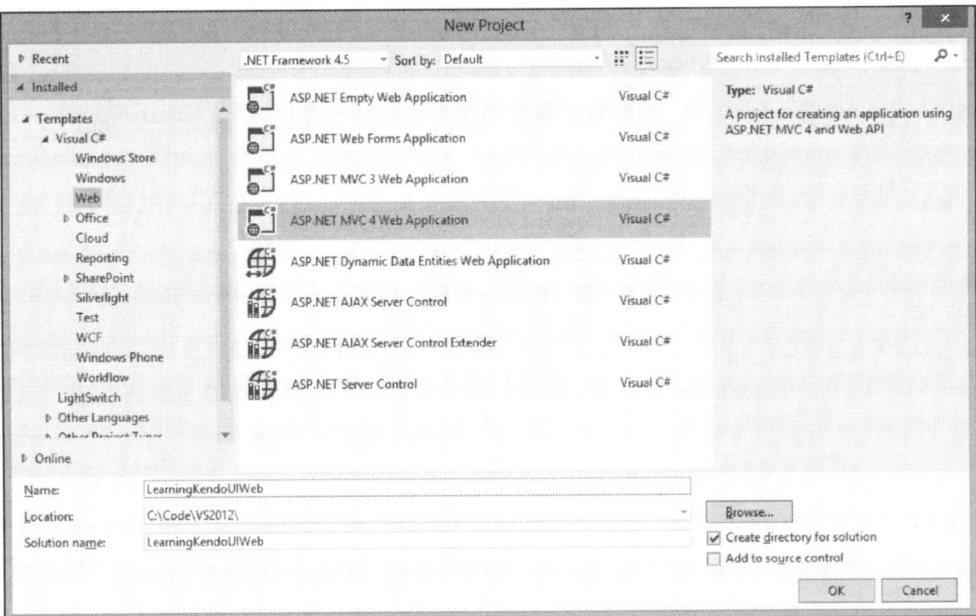

Select this and click on **OK**. The next window will display some selections for the type of template you want to use. I chose the basic template, but you can choose any of the templates other than the empty template in order to follow along with the examples. You do not need to create a unit test project for the purposes of this book.

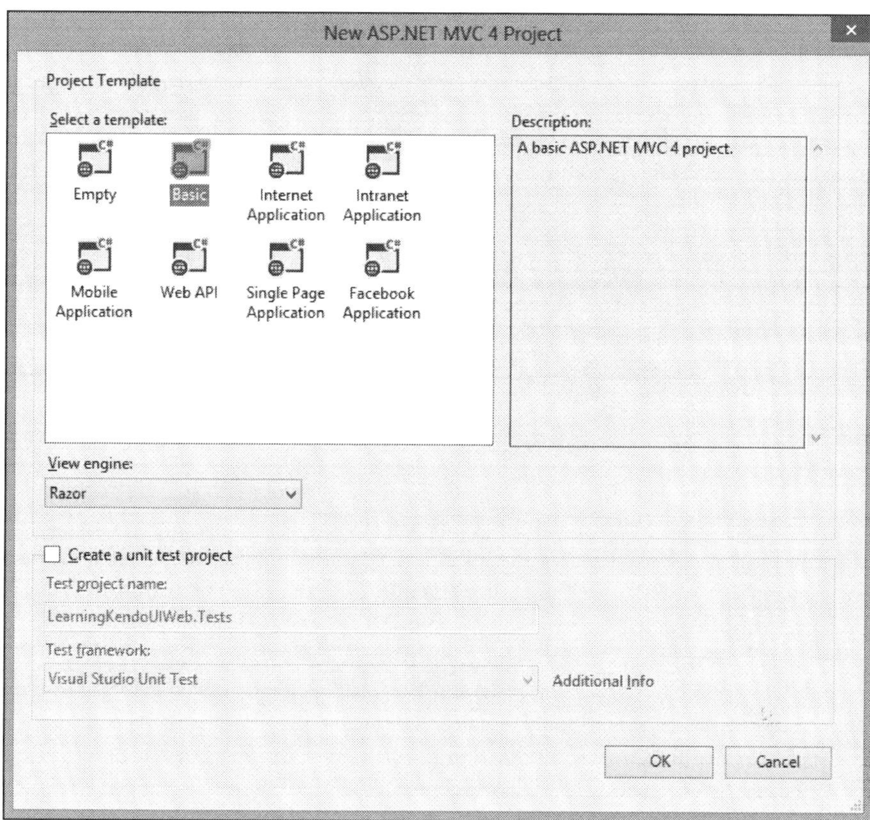

Downloading the example code

You can download the example code files for all Packt books you have purchased from your account at `http://www.packtpub.com`. If you purchased this book elsewhere, you can visit `http://www.packtpub.com/support` and register to have the files e-mailed directly to you.

Visual Studio will create the folder structure for your new project, and will copy all of the necessary files into that structure so that you can run your project in the debugger. Once this is complete, you will see your project tree in the **Solution Explorer** section of the Visual Studio IDE.

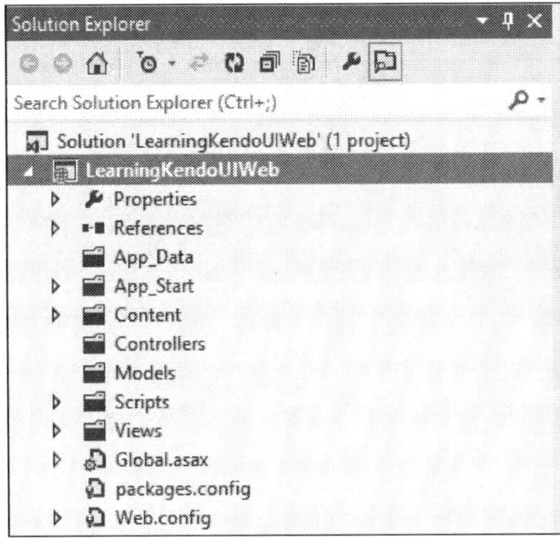

Now that we have our structure, it is time to download the Telerik Kendo UI files and place them in their proper location. Navigate to the Telerik Kendo UI website at `http://www.kendoui.com/download.aspx` and download the 30-day free trial of the Kendo UI Complete package that includes the server wrappers for ASP.NET MVC. It will arrive as a ZIP file containing everything that you need for development with Kendo UI. Extract the contents of the ZIP file somewhere you will remember since you will need to reference these files throughout the rest of the book. This screenshot shows what the ZIP file should contain:

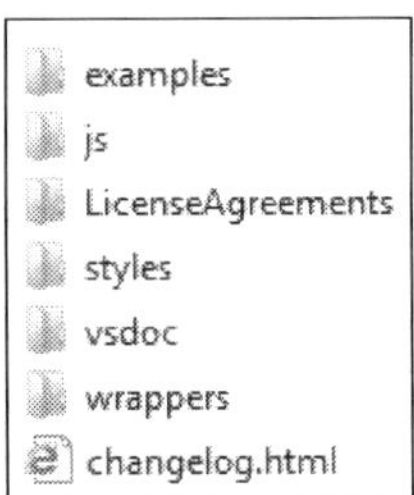

Now, follow these steps:

1. Go back to Visual Studio and right-click on the `Content` folder in the **Solution Explorer** and choose **Add, New Folder**. Name the new folder `kendo`.

2. Right-click on the `kendo` folder that you just created and create two more folders—`Default` and `textures`. Now, right-click on the `Default` folder and choose **Add, Existing Item**.
3. In the file dialog that displays, navigate to the folder with the unzipped Kendo files, then open the `Styles` folder and then the `Default` folder inside it.
4. Select all of the files in this folder and click on the **Add** button. This will add all of these items to the Visual Studio project so that they show in **Solution Explorer** and can be managed from the Visual Studio IDE.
5. Next, follow these same steps to add all of the items to the `textures` folder. Once you have these files in place, right click on the `kendo` folder in **Solution Explorer** again and choose **Add, Existing Item**.

In the dialog that displays, choose these two specific files from the `Styles` folder of the unzipped kendo files and add them as well:

- `kendo.common.min.css`
- `kendo.default.min.css`

Once these two files appear in **Solution Explorer**, rename them by removing the `.min` portion of their file names (`kendo.default.min.css` becomes `kendo.default.css`); this will be explained in greater detail in next few paragraphs. The `Content` folder in **Solution Explorer** should look something like this when you are finished:

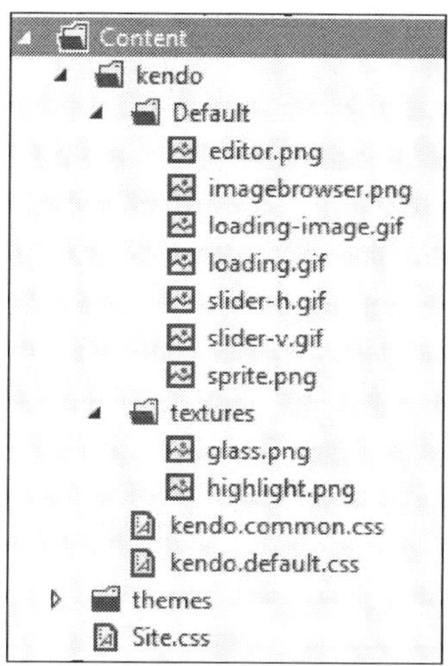

Next, we will prepare the `Scripts` folder by following some very similar steps. Create a `kendo` folder inside of the `Scripts` folder in **Solution Explorer** and then copy these files from the `js` folder of the downloaded Kendo files:

- `jquery.min.css`
- `kendo.all.min.js`
- `kendo.aspnetmvc.min.jskendo.web.min.js`

Once again, remove the `.min` portion of their filenames. We will, however, need two versions of the `kendo.aspnetmvc.js` file as will be explained later. Go ahead and copy the file, but only remove the <code>.min</code> portion of the filename from one copy. This way you will have one copy of the file with a `.min` filename and another copy of the file without the `.min` file name. The completed `kendo` folder in **Solution Explorer** should look something like this:

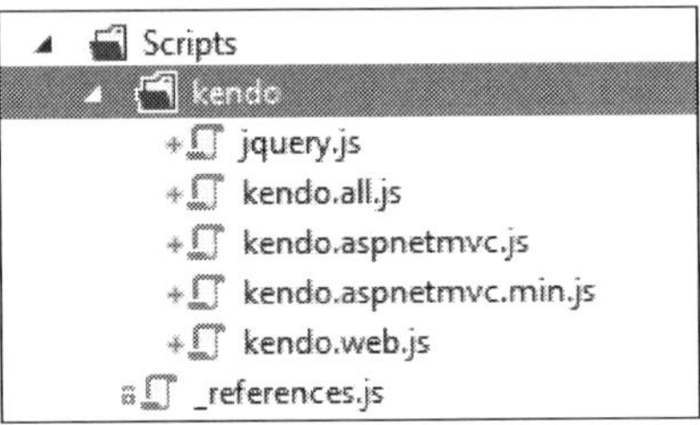

As a web developer, you are surely familiar with the exercise of referencing scripts and styles in the head portion of your web pages. ASP.NET MVC 4 comes with a great feature that enables bundling and minimization of these scripts, along with built-in caching, so that the browser can download these files faster and thereby increase the performance of your site with very little effort on your part. This feature also works with CDN locations, so that you can run with local files during debugging and still reference CDN hosted scripts or style sheets when your site is deployed. To enable this functionality for our sample project, you will need to add the following code to the `BundleConfig.cs` file in the `App_Start` folder of the project. First, add this code at the top of the file to enable CDN functionality and to save the paths of the CDN locations that we want to use:

```
// Enable CDN
bundles.UseCdn = true;

// CDN paths for kendo stylesheet files
var kendoCommonCssPath = "http://cdn.kendostatic.com/2013.1.319/
styles/kendo.common.min.css";
var kendoDefaultCssPath = "http://cdn.kendostatic.com/2013.1.319/
styles/kendo.default.min.css";
```

```
// CDN paths for kendo javascript files
var kendoWebJsPath = "http://cdn.kendostatic.com/2012.2.710/js/kendo.
web.min.js";
```

Then, add this code at the bottom of the file to create the bundles for your Kendo files. By passing the CDN location as the second parameter of the `ScriptBundle` constructor, Visual Studio will build your solution using your local files when debugging and will build your solution using the CDN location files when building in release mode. This is also where I should explain why we removed the `.min` portion of the JavaScript and stylesheet filenames. The bundling and minification features of ASP.NET MVC intentionally ignore files that include `.min` in their filenames during debugging. This means that none of your script references from the Kendo download will work during debugging because we do not have the pre-minified files included in our project. There are several documented ways to deal with this problem floating around the Internet, but the easiest way to address this for our project is just to rename to files to avoid the entire issue.

```
// Create the CDN bundles for kendo javascript files
bundles.Add(new ScriptBundle("~/bundles/kendo/web/js", kendoWebJsPath)
.Include("~/Scripts/kendo/kendo.web.js"));
// The ASP.NET MVC script file is not available from the Kendo Static
CDN,
// so we will include the bundle reference without the CDN path.
bundles.Add(new ScriptBundle("~/bundles/kendo/mvc/js")
.Include("~/Scripts/kendo/kendo.aspnetmvc.js"));

// Create the CDN bundles for the kendo styleshseet files
bundles.Add(new StyleBundle("~/bundles/kendo/common/css",
kendoCommonCssPath)
    .Include("~/Content/kendo/kendo.common.css"));
bundles.Add(new StyleBundle("~/bundles/kendo/default/css",
kendoDefaultCssPath)
    .Include("~/Content/kendo/kendo.default.css"));
```

Now that we have the `BundleConfig.cs` file properly configured, we can adjust the references in the head portion of our `_Layout.cshtml` file. The `_Layout.cshtml` file acts as our default master page by creating a uniform head structure for all of our pages and a default layout within which all the other pages place their specific content. Open the `_Layout.cshtml` file in the `Views`, `Shared` folder and make some changes. By default, it will have some script references that appear in the body portion of the page and some that appear in the head portion.

There are undoubtedly some good reasons for doing this, but since we will have references to Kendo scripts in the body of our page before these script references would appear, we need to move everything to the head portion. Since this file is not very long, I have included my finished version here so that you can copy it:

```
@using Kendo.Mvc.UI;
<!DOCTYPE html>
<html>
<head>
<meta charset="utf-8" />
<meta name="viewport" content="width=device-width" />
<title>@ViewBag.Title</title>
@Styles.Render("~/Content/css")
@Styles.Render("~/bundles/kendo/common/css")
@Styles.Render("~/bundles/kendo/default/css")
@Scripts.Render("~/bundles/jquery")
@Scripts.Render("~/bundles/kendo/web/js")
@Scripts.Render("~/bundles/kendo/mvc/js")
</head>
<body>
@RenderBody()

@RenderSection("scripts", required: false)
</body>
</html>
```

Note also that I have added an `@using` statement at the top of the file, make sure you copy that as well since it will enable **Intellisense** on all of your pages. Intellisense is a feature of Visual Studio that auto-completes code as you write and is a great productivity booster. To fully enable this, you will also need to add a reference to the `Kendo.Mvc.dll` file to your Visual Studio project:

1. First, right-click on the **LearningKendoUIWeb** project in the Visual Studio **Solution Explorer** and choose **Add Reference**.

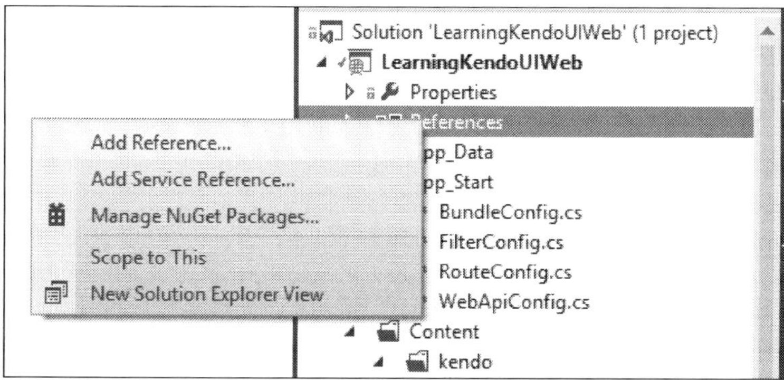

2. Next, click on **Browse** and navigate the file dialog to the location where you downloaded the Kendo files.
3. Find the folder named `aspnetmvc`, open the folder named `Binaries` inside it, and then open the folder named `Mvc3` inside that.
4. Here you will find the `Kendo.Mvc.dll` file; click on it and choose **Add**.

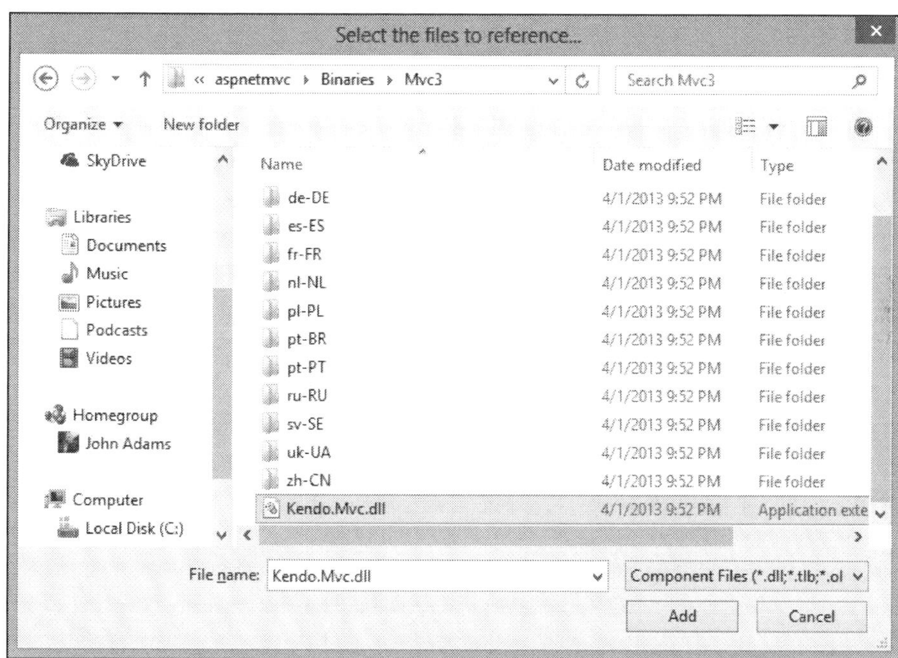

5. With this reference added, you can make the code inside it available to all of your web pages by adding a special entry in a file called `web.config`.

6. This file is located in the root of your **LearningKendoUIWeb** project. Open `web.config` and locate the section called `namespaces`. Add the `Kendo.Web.UI` namespace to the list like this:

   ```
   <pages>
   <namespaces>
     <add namespace="System.Web.Helpers" />
     <add namespace="System.Web.Mvc" />
     <add namespace="System.Web.Mvc.Ajax" />
     <add namespace="System.Web.Mvc.Html" />
     <add namespace="System.Web.Optimization" />
     <add namespace="System.Web.Routing" />
     <add namespace="System.Web.WebPages" />
     <add namespace="Kendo.Mvc.UI" />
   </namespaces>
   </pages>
   ```

Now create a folder to hold static content in the project. Right-click the project name in **Solution Explorer**, choose **Add, New Folder**. Call the new folder `static`. This will be the location where we place all of our client-side examples that run apart from the MVC framework.

Visual Studio 2012 includes some good improvements in JavaScript Intellisense and it is going to help us as we write our code. Open the file called `"_references.js"` in the scripts folder and delete all of the text in it. This is the entire contents of my `"_references.js"` file, copy this into yours as well:

```
/// <reference path="kendo/jquery.js" />
/// <reference path="kendo/kendo.web.js" />
/// <reference path="kendo/kendo.aspnetmvc.js" />
```

Visual Studio 2012 uses this file as the list of JavaScript libraries that it should use for Intellisense in the editor. I have included the jQuery file included with the Kendo zipped package and two JavaScript files that we will be using in the majority of our web pages. Once you have this in place, you will get some very helpful coding assistance in your JavaScript files like this:

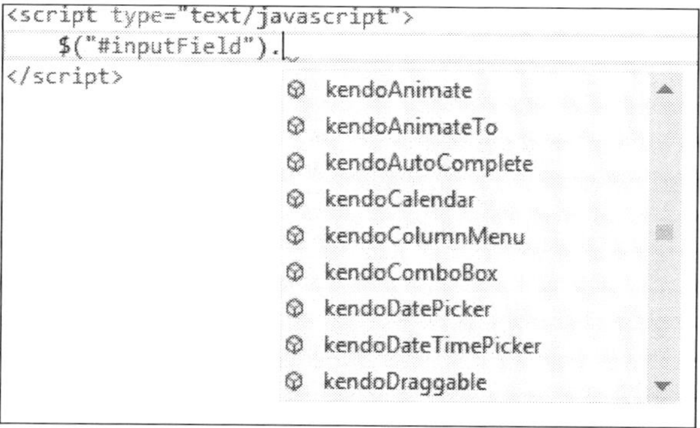

Notice how all of the Kendo options show up as you type JavaScript code in the editor? As you program the examples throughout this book, this will become something that you will help you.

OK, now we are ready!

KendoUI syntax styles

When using the KendoUI framework in your web pages, you will find that there are two ways to add the widgets to your content. The standard method is to use a jQuery syntax within script elements like this:

```
<input type="date" id="makeMeADatePicker" />
<script type="text/javascript">
    $("#makeMeADatePicker").kendoDatePicker();
</script>
```

The convention, as shown, is to select the elements through jQuery and then apply a JavaScript method from the Kendo namespaces that alters the content into an interactive Kendo UI widget.

There is another way, now available through HTML5, to add Kendo UI widgets to your content through a method known as declarative initialization. This is a practice where you typically add special attributes to your elements that start with "data-" and then call an initializer that reads these attributes and then applies the appropriate changes. See this code as an example:

```
<input type="date" id="makeMeADatePicker" data-role="datepicker" />
<script type="text/javascript">
kendo.init($("#makeMeADatePicker"));
</script>
```

This type of syntax allows for a cleaner separation between JavaScript and mark-up, and is important in the MVVM pattern that we will cover later in the book. It is also powerfully expressive and can make the code more readable, since relevant attributes are contained directly within the elements to which they pertain. Script blocks containing code do not necessarily appear beside the code actually being affected, which can make things difficult to trace in a complicated project.

Kendo UI MVC – basics

Since we will be using ASP.NET MVC quite a bit in this book, I should define some important terms so that there isn't any confusion later. **MVC** stands for **Model-View-Controller**; so let's establish a common terminology around these. First, a web page is referred to as a *view* and, when using Razor syntax with C#, the web pages have a file extension, `cshtml`. There is also the option of using Visual Basic in which case the web pages have a file extension, `vbhtml`, but we will be using C# in this book so you won't see this in the examples.

Second, the *controller* is a server-side classfile that is responsible for all of the logic used in generating the content included in a web page (view). The controller, along with the route table, is also responsible for establishing the publicly accessible URLs to which the server will respond, and enforcing which HTTP verbs are required to access them. In general, a controller is responsible for contacting any external dependencies, such as a database or web server, performing any necessary logic and calculations on the data retrieved from those external dependencies, and then packaging up all of that processed data into an object called the *model*.

The model, then, is an object container that contains the data that the web page (view) needs in order to display itself. In a properly separated system, the controller is the engine that performs all logic, data manipulation, user-input handling, authorization, and security. The view is the data presenter and is concerned only with the graphical representation of the data it has been given; no logic apart from what is required for presentation (not to say that presentation can't be complex). The model is the standard data format that the controller uses to send its final product to the view to be presented to the user.

When programming in the ASP.NET MVC environment, Kendo UI offers a rich set of server-side extensions for creating its widgets. Instead of typing out an HTML element, specifying its attributes and wiring it up to Kendo UI JavaScript, the entire process can be done using server-side objects that appear in the view. For example, creating a `DatePicker` widget in MVC Razor syntax looks like this:

```
@(Html.Kendo().DatePicker().Name("datePickerField"))
```

No HTML, no JavaScript, just extension methods on the HTML class. When the page is generated, however, you can see what was sent to the browser:

```
<input class="k-input" id="datePicker" name="datePicker" type="date"
/>
<script>
jQuery(function(){jQuery("#datePicker").kendoDatePicker({format:"M/d/
yyyy",
min:new Date(1900,0,1,0,0,0,0),max:new Date(2099,11,31,0,0,0,0)});});
</script>
```

The extension methods create all the HTML, JavaScript, and CSS information dynamically. You can see how the final output uses the jQuery method of selecting the input element and using `.kendoDatePicker(...)` to create the widget through JavaScript. So, although the programmer didn't type out the JavaScript, it was still necessary for Kendo UI to work; the MVC extensions are only wrappers around the normal Kendo UI client-side framework.

I should also explain that even though the view is what generates the final web page sent to the user's browser, it is processed on the server first. The Razor syntax (everything that starts with `@`) never appears in the final page markup, it is processed on the server in order to generate the final markup. This means that the Kendo MVC extension methods are really a server-side shortcut to creating the final markup needed to make them work as they normally would in JavaScript.

Programming in the MVC framework allows for a very clean separation of concerns within the web server itself and this, in turn, allows for a great deal of flexibility around how the views run and how dependent they are on server-side logic. For example, widgets that use data can receive this data either as embedded material in the view itself (a dependency on server-side logic), or they can query for data from the client-side by calling action methods that return JSON (less dependency on server-side logic).

As an example of a server-dependent implementation, here is a strongly-typed view with embedded model data that can then be used by widgets on the page. A strongly-typed view is a view page that specifies a specific type of object that contains its model data. You can see the strongly-typed model object in this sample on the first line starting with `@model`:

```
@model IEnumerable<LearningKendoUIWeb.Models.StateTerritory>
<textarea id="serverData" style="display:none">
@Html.Raw(ViewBag.serverData)
</textarea>
<script type="text/javascript">
varserverData = eval($("#serverData").html());
```

```
for (var i = 0; i<serverData.length; i++) {
console.log(serverData[i].Name);
    }
</script>
```

`ViewBag` is a dynamic object that is available to you within controller action methods and view pages. It is a dictionary object that can contain any data or objects that you need in your view pages. The controller can add anything that you need to `ViewBag`, and your view pages will then have access to that data or object just as this sample code has shown. In this case, the controller has attached an object called `serverData` that contains a JSON representation of its model data. We are using the JavaScript function called `eval()` to parse it into a JavaScript object and then showing on the JavaScript console what was inside. This is merely an example of how to embed data into the view itself without having to use additional network requests, such as the jQuery functions `$.get` or `$.ajax`, to retrieve data to display on the page; it may prove beneficial in some cases where network traffic needs to be weighed against immediate data availability that the server can provide up front.

The `ViewBag.serverData` property is filled in the controller like this:

```
publicActionResultAutoCompletePage()
{
var repository = new SampleRepository();
var data = repository.GetStatesAndTerritories();
ViewBag.serverData = new JavaScriptSerializer().Serialize(data);
return View(data);
}
```

Note that in this example the controller is both filling in this `ViewBag` property and sending the same data to the view as a strongly-typed model; this isn't necessary, but it is handy here since we can leverage the server's `JavaScriptSerializer` class to create JSON for us before we send it to the view. Here is what the JavaScript console shows when we fill `ViewBag.serverData` with the JSON representation of an array of objects that have a **Name** property:

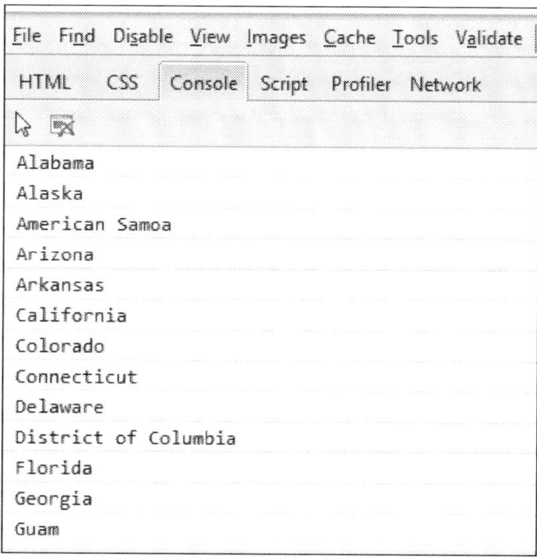

It is far more common to request data from a separate endpoint and then use it once it has been retrieved. This allows for data from external sources, and breaks the dependency on the server to provide the data inside the page, which in turn means the specific server implementation is likely less important and less complex. jQuery provides several common and friendly ways of retrieving JSON data such as `$.ajax`, `$.get`, and `$.getJSON`. Kendo also provides standard ways of retrieving external data through configuration options on its widgets, often through the property method `transport.read`. We will see more about this in the rest of this chapter as we discuss DataSource and Grid, and throughout the rest of the book.

Managing data

The Kendo UI framework consists of two parts—the framework components and the user interface (UI) widgets. Most of the content that we will cover in this book relates to the user interface widgets and how to use them, but we will begin with the important topic of how to manage data within Kendo UI. The DataSource component and Templates provide a good starting place and will build a foundation that we will use throughout the rest of this book.

Templates

Kendo UI Templates are script blocks that contain a small section of page markup that is used by other Kendo UI widgets to display repeating content. We will cover these first, since they will be used throughout the rest of our examples. Here is an example of a simple template:

```
var template = kendo.template("<span>#= horseColor #</span>");
$("#horseDiv").html(template({
  horseColor: 'brown}));
```

Running this code would set the HTML content of the `horseDiv` to a span element that contained the `horseColor` value that was passed into the template function object. It would produce the following code output:

```
<div id='horseDiv'><span>brown</span></div>
```

Templates can also be written within a special type of HTML script block so that their layout appears more naturally within the HTML content.

```
<script type="text/x-kendo-template" id="template">
<tr>
<td>#= rank #</td>
<td>#= rating #</td>
<td>#= title #</td>
<td>#= year #</td>
</tr>
</script>
```

In this template sample, note the lines containing the code fragments `#= variable_name #`. These indicate the sections of code that are interpreted by the Kendo UI Template engine. The variable names inside these code blocks are supplied to the template when it is used. The JavaScript property names that you use inside of a template need to be properties on the object that is passed to the template when it is called. Note also that the script type is `x-kendo-template` instead of `javascript`, this is important so that the browser will not attempt to execute the script block on its own. This is a code sample showing this template being initialized in JavaScript:

```
<script type="text/javascript">
var template = kendo.template($("#template").html());

functionshowMovies() {
$("#moviesTable").html(template(
          {rank: 1, rating: 9.2, title: 'Prometheus', year: 2012}
      ));
   }
```

```
showMovies();
</script>
```

Notice how the template is created through a call to `kendo.template()`. This method takes the literal template code as its parameter, which is why the example shows a call to the jQuery statement `$("#template").html()` since this code returns the literal content of the template script block as it appears in the web page. So, in this example, it is equivalent to calling `kendo.template('<tr><td>#= rank #</td>...')`. This means that templates can also be created in-line by typing out the exact template code directly in the constructor.

When the template object is called as a method, it needs the data passed in as a parameter. When the example code above runs, it produces this output:

```
<table id="moviesTable">
<tr>
<td>1</td>
<td>9.2</td>
<td>Prometheus</td>
<td>2012</td>
</tr>
</table>
```

Templates can also include JavaScript which makes it possible to do more advanced operations, such as iterating over an array and rendering the template for each item in that array individually. In this case, you supply the template with an array of objects instead of a single object as before. This time, using the explicit parameter name `data` is critical. Note how JavaScript code is surrounded by single # signs like `# javascript code #` and variable statements are surrounded by #= and then # as in #= `variable statement` #. Note also that the space between the # signs and the content inside is important.

```
<script type="text/x-kendo-template" id="template">
# for(vari=0; i<data.length; i++) { #
<tr>
<td>#= data[i].rank #</td>
<td>#= data[i].rating #</td>
<td>#= data[i].title #</td>
<td>#= data[i].year #</td>
</tr>
    # } #
</script>
```

Templates are an important part of building functional Kendo UI widgets, and they become even more useful when used in tandem with the DataSources and Grids as we will see later.

DataSource

The Kendo UI DataSource is a JavaScript object that gives data a common interface for the various Kendo UI widgets. The full documentation for the DataSource object can be found on the Kendo UI website at this address: `http://docs.kendoui.com/api/framework/datasource`. The DataSource is a fairly complicated object and relies on some building blocks that deserve explanations of their own. These building blocks are the Kendo objects known as Schema, Transport, and Model. Let's address these first and then continue exploring the DataSource itself.

It is important to note that when creating a DataSource object, you should use the `new` keyword to instantiate a new object instead of just using an object literal:

```
var dataSource = new kendo.data.DataSource({...<properties>...});
```

Model

The Model object is from the namespace `kendo.data.Model` and inherits from Kendo's `ObservableObject`. It provides a known structure, or model, to the data that is used by a DataSource and can also be used to enable some more advanced functionality such as change tracking. To create a new model, you must do so through the method `kendo.data.Model.define()`. In this method, you pass an object that defines the structure of the model and sets configurable options on the data elements within. Here is an example of a model:

```
var Service = kendo.data.Model.define( {
id: "serviceId", // the identifier of the model
fields: {
"serviceName": {
type: "string"
        },
"unitPrice": {
type: "number"
        },
"serviceId": {
type: "number"
  }
    }
});

var currentService = new Service( {
serviceName: "Rotate Tires",
unitPrice: 29.95,
serviceId: 400
```

```
});

console.log(currentService.get("serviceName")); // outputs "Rotate
Tires"
console.log(currentService.get("unitPrice")); // outputs 29.95
```

In this example, we have created a model with three properties and we set the data type for each of them. We then created a new model object from our model definition and demonstrated how to access its properties through the `model.get()` method. We just demonstrated that the ID of the model object is defined through the property called `id`, and that the fields are defined through a property called `fields`. Within the `fields` property, these are the options that can be set to configure each data element:

```
fields: {
"serviceName": {     // Property name for a field
type: "string", // "string"(default), "number", "boolean", or "date"
defaultValue: "Inspection", // Default value for field when model is
                             / created. Default for string is "", number
                           // is 0, and date is new Date() (.i.e. today)
editable: true, // Specifies whether field is editable
nullable: false, // Specifies if default value should be used when
empty
parse: function(){...} // Specifies custom parser for field value
validation: {...} // Specifies the validation options used by Kendo
                        // Validator such as 'required', 'min', and
'max'.
    },...
}
```

These are not all required, but they are available when you want a very specific configuration. Here is an example from the Kendo UI site:

```
var Product = kendo.data.Model.define( {
id: "id", // the identifier is the "id" field (declared below)
fields: {
  /* name of the field */
name: {
type: "string", // the field is a string
validation: { // validation rules
required: true // the field is required
    },
defaultValue: "<empty>" // default field value
  },

  /* name of the field */ price: {
type: "number", // the field is a number
```

```
validation: { // validation rules
required: true, // the field is required
min: 1 // the minimum value is 1
    },
defaultValue: 99.99 // default field value
  },

  /* name of the field */ id: {
editable: false, // this field is not editable
nullable: true // a default value will not be assigned
        }
    }
});
```

Since the properties within a model are observable, you need to use special getter and setter methods to properly trigger the behaviors that other functions and objects are observing. To retrieve the current value of one of these properties, use `model_name.get()` such as `currentService.get('unitPrice')`. To set the value of the property and thereby change it, use `model_name.set()` such as `currentService.set('unitPrice', 14.95)`. The concept of observable objects is a key feature of the MVVM framework that we will cover in a later chapter.

Two other methods available on model objects are `isNew` and `toJSON`. The `isNew` method checks if the model is new or not. This is determined by whether or not the `id` field is still set at the default value. If the `id` field is not set at the default value, the model object is not considered new. The `toJSON` method returns a JSON representation of the complete model's properties and values.

Since, as I mentioned, the model inherits from `ObservableObject`, it exposes three events to which you can attach custom behaviors — `change`, `get`, and `set`. The syntax for these is to use `model.bind()` with the name of the event and a function to handle it:

```
currentService.bind('change', function(e){
alert(e.field + " just changed its value to " +
currentService.get([e.field]));
});
```

Schema

The `schema` object within a DataSource is responsible for describing the raw data format. It functions at a higher level than the model, and can even contain a model definition within it. The Schema's job is to instruct the DataSource on where to find information on errors, aggregates, data, groups, and total records within the raw data object that the DataSource is using. Each of these pieces of information exists as a property within the `schema` object like this:

```
schema: {
  errors: function(response) {
    return response.errors;
  },
  aggregates: function(response) {
    return response.aggregates;
  },
  data: function(response) {
    return response.data;
  },
  total: function(response) {
    return response.totalCount;
  }
}
```

In the preceding code sample, each of the properties has been set to a function which, when passed the raw data object, will return the appropriate data from within that object. These properties can also be set to text fields, in which case the field name given must exist at the top level of the object and already contain the appropriate data in the appropriate format:

```
schema: {
  errors: "errors_field_name",
  aggregates: "aggregates_field_name",
  data: "data_field_name",
  total: "total_field_name"
}
```

The `aggregates` property needs data returned in an object format with a structure something like this. Each property name inside the **aggregates** object can contain information on its aggregate values, such as the maximum value (**max**), minimum value (**min**), or the total **count**:

```
{
unitPrice: {   // Field Name
  max: 100,     // Aggregate function and value
  min: 1     // Aggregate function and value
```

```
    },
  productName: {  // Field Name
    count: 42     // Aggregate function and value
    }
  }
```

In this case, the data has a **max** and **min** defined on the **unitPrice** field and a **count** defined on the **productName** field. The DataSource object has not calculated these values; rather they are already present in the raw data sent from the remote server, and the schema has indicated to the DataSource object where to locate them. It is possible to use a function to calculate aggregate values, but it is normal for the raw data to already contain these values within it as returned by a remote server.

As I said earlier, the schema can contain a model definition within it. If this is the case, the DataSource will call `kendo.data.Model.define` on the model definition for you, in order to create the model objects from the raw data:

```
var dataSource = new kendo.data.DataSource({
schema: {
  model: {
    id: "ProductID",
    fields: {
    ProductID: {
      editable: false,
      nullable: true
      },
      ...
```

If you have already defined a Model definition, you can simply reference it and the DataSource will use it just the same:

```
vardataSource = new kendo.data.DataSource({
schema: {
model: Product // Use the existing Product model
    }
});
```

The `schema` object has a `parse` property, which you can set to a function that will be called before the raw data is processed. This gives you a chance to do any pre-processing if you need it. There is also a `type` property that can be set to either `json` or `xml`.

Transport

The `transport` object contains properties that a DataSource can use to communicate with a remote server for any of its normal data functions. Those data functions are `create`, `destroy`, `read`, and `update` (corresponding to the different actions that can be taken on a record). Each of these data functions exists as a property object within the `transport` object and follows the same pattern of configuration options. I should note that not all of the data functions are required; only those functions that your DataSource should perform need to be defined within your `transport` object.

This is the basic configuration structure for the `transport` object.

```
transport: {
  create: { // this sets configuration for creating new records
            // on the remote server
  },
  destroy: { // this sets configuration for deleting records
             // on the remote server
  },
  read: {  // this sets configuration for reading records
           // from the remote server
  },
  update: { // this sets configuration for updating records
            // on the remote server
  },
  autoSync: false, // set true to automatically sync all changes
  batch: false     // set true to enable batch mode
}
```

Here are the different options for configuring the transport object's remote data operations. Each of the four properties follows the same configuration pattern, but in this code sample I have shown different ways of configuring them for the sake of example. In this first code sample, I have configured the **create** operation to simply send the value of an HTML element to the remote server.

```
create: { // for creating data records on remote source.
url: "/orders/create", // the url to the create service.
data: {  // data to send to the create service as part of the request.
// this can also be specified as a function call.
orderId: $("#input").val()
},
cache: true, // make false to force fresh requests every time.
contentType: "application/json", // default is
  // "application/w-www-form-urlencoded"
dataType: "json", // "jsonp" is also common.
type: "POST" // which http verb to use.
  }
```

In this example, we have set the destroy method to use a jQuery `$.ajax` function to send data to the remote server instead of configuring it directly on the **destroy** configuration object. You can do this if you prefer the jQuery syntax and want to easily attach callback functions to the results of the operation.

```
destroy: {  // same options as "create", with some alternatives shown.
      // this is how you use $.ajax() to run this remote service call.
          // this option can be used with "create", "destroy", "read",
              // and "update"
    $.ajax( {
url: "/orders/destroy",
data: options.data, // the data field contains paging, sorting,
                          // filtering, and grouping data
success: function(result) {
               // notify the DataSource that the operation is complete
Options.success(result);
}
});
}
```

In this example, we have created a function to serve as the source of data for the read operation. This might be useful if you need to perform some custom logic before receiving remote data, or if you need to bypass the remote data source entirely for some reason.

```
read: {  // same options as above in "create" and "destroy".
data: function() {  // this is how you specify data as a function.
return {
id: 42,
name: "John Doe"
};
}
}
```

Remember that the configuration options you just saw are valid for any of the transport operations, I simply showed different operations as an example for each configuration. When a DataSource is configured with a transport configuration like this, it will use the properties and functions within these options to perform the related actions. It will call `read` when it is loading data, `update` when a record has been changed, `destroy` when a record has been deleted, and `create` when a new record is added.

Other DataSource properties

When reading from local data, you need to reference it by using the property called `data` like this:

```
var someData = [{ title: 'Prometheus', year: 2012, rating: 9, rank: 25
}];

var dataSource = new kendo.data.DataSource({
data: someData
});
```

Some other properties of DataSource that we have not yet seen are more for data manipulation—`aggregate`, `filter`, `group`, `sort`, `page`, and `pageSize`. They can work on the data client-side, or they can request that the server do the operations by using the `serverAggregates`, `serverFiltering`, `serverGrouping`, `serverSorting`, and `serverPaging` properties by adding these to the DataSource object properties list and setting them to true.

The `aggregate` property takes an array of fieldnames and aggregate function names:

```
aggregate: [{ field: 'title', aggregate: 'count' }]
```

The `filter` property can take a simple object, an array of simple objects, or a configurable object with some more logic to specify filtering that should be done on the data:

```
// simple object
filter: { field: 'title', operator: 'startswith', value: 'Shawshank' }

// ...or array...
filter: [{field: 'year', operator: 'eq', value: '1998'}, {field: ...

// ...or configurable object...
filter:{
logic: "or",
filters: [
{ field: 'title', operator: 'startswith', value: 'Shawshank' }]
}
```

These are the different operators that can be used with the filter object. They can also be used when asking the server for filtering by using the `serverFiltering` property.

- **Equality**: `eq`, `==`, `isequalto`, `equals`, `equalto`, `equal`
- **Inequality**: `neq`, `!=`, `isnotequalto`, `notequals`, `notequalto`, `notequal`, `ne`
- **Less**: `lt`, `<`, `islessthan`, `lessthan`, `less`

- **Less or Equal**: `lte`, `<=`, `islessthanorequalto`, `lessthanequal`, `le`
- **Greater**: `gt`, `>`, `isgreaterthan`, `greaterthan`, `greater`
- **Greater or Equal**: `gte`, `>=`, `isgreaterthanorequalto`, `greaterthanequal`, `ge`
- **Starts With**: `startswith`
- **Ends With**: `endswith`
- **Contains**: `contains`

The `group` and `sort` properties can take either an object or an array of objects to specify grouping:

```
group: { field: 'year', dir: 'asc' }
sort: { field: 'title', dir: 'desc' }
```

The `page` and `pageSize` properties both take numbers to indicate the page number and records per page respectively.

DataSource methods

The DataSource methods are used to either change or retrieve certain elements of the DataSource object. Several of them are related to the same data manipulation properties that we just talked about—`aggregate`, `aggregates`, `filter`, `group`, `page`, `pageSize`, and `sort`. In each of these cases, calling the method without parameters will return the current value of the like-named property within the DataSource; calling the method with a parameter value will set the value of the like-named property of the DataSource to the new value passed in:

```
// get the current group descriptors
var g = dataSource.group();

// set a new value for filtering
dataSource.filter({ field: 'year', operator: 'gt', value: 1990 });
```

There are also methods for adding and removing records. The methods `add` and `insert` both add a new record to the DataSource. The `add` method simply takes a model object or an object literal matching the current data format of the items in the DataSource. The `insert` method takes the same object as `add`, but also specifies an `index` property indicating the zero-based location at which to insert the new record. The `remove` method takes a model object and removes it from the DataSource:

```
// add a new item
dataSource.add({ year: 1997, title: 'The Fifth Element', rating: 10
});
```

```
// insert an item at the 6th position in the DataSource
dataSource.insert(5, {year: 1995, title: 'Twelve Monkeys', rating
9.5});

// remove an item from the DataSource
var movie = dataSource.at(5);
dataSource.remove(movie);
```

The `at`, `get`, and `getByUid` methods retrieve specific records from the DataSource:

```
// get the 3rd item in the DataSource
var movie = dataSource.at(2);

// get the model instance with an id of 5
// (id is determined by the value of the schema.model.id property)
var movie = dataSource.get(5);

// get the model instance, or ObservableObject if no model has been
set
// uid is a property inherited from ObservableObject
varuid = $("tr").data("uid");
var movie = dataSource.getByUid(uid);
```

The `fetch`, `query`, `read`, `sync`, `cancelChanges`, and `view` methods are used for managing the current contents and structure of the DataSource:

```
// fetches data using the current filter/sort/group/paging
information.
// will fetch data from transport if data is not already available in
memory.
dataSource.fetch(); // can optionally take a callback function which
                    // is executed once the data is ready.

// executes a query over the data (i.e. paging/sorting/filtering/
grouping)
// this effects what the call to dataSource.view() will return.
dataSource.query({ page: 5, pageSize: 20, group:{field:'year',dir:'a
sc'}});

// read data into the DataSource using the transport.read setting
dataSource.read();  // also conveniently causes the change event to
fire
```

```
// synchronizes changes through the transport for any pending CRUD
operations.
// if batch mode is enabled, it uses only one call per operation type
(create,
//   read, update, destroy)
dataSource.sync();

// discards all un-synced changes made to the DataSource
dataSource.cancelChanges();

// returns the current state of the items in the DataSource with all
applied
//settings such as paging, sorting, filtering, and grouping.
// to ensure that data is available, this method should be used from
//within the change event of the DataSource
change: function(e){
    ...
kendo.render(template, dataSource.view());
}
```

To finish up the list, we will look at `data`, `total`, and `totalPages`:

```
// retrieve an observable array of items (the current data within the
DataSource)
var movies = dataSource.data();

// set the DataSource to some new data
datSource.data([{year: 2009, title: 'Cargo', rating: 6.8}, {year: ...
]);

// get, but not set, the total number of items in the DataSource
var total = dataSource.total();

// get, but not set, the total number of pages of items in the
DataSource
var pages = dataSource.totalPages();
```

It is important to note that you must call `dataSource.read()` in order for the DataSource object to initiate the read process and populate itself with data. In other words, until you call `dataSource.read()`, there is nothing to read inside your DataSource.

DataSource events

There are three events that are available on the DataSource object—`change`, `error`, and `requestStart`. The `change` event is fired when data is changed or read from the transport. The `error` event is fired any time an error occurs during data read or data sync; it is also fired if `schema.errors` has been set within the DataSource and the response from a server operation contains data in the field specified by `schema.errors`. The `requestStart` event is fired when a data request is about to start. Like other events, these can be set as part of the DataSource definition or later through the `bind` method.

```
// set event handler as part of DataSource definition
var dataSource = new kendo.data.DataSource({
change: function(e){
        // handle event
    }
});

// or set event handler later through the bind method
dataSource.bind("error", function(e){
    // handle event
});
```

As you will see later, the change event can be a good place to put some code in order to generate markup while a DataSource is reading in new records. It is also the appropriate place to put any other code that should respond to changes in the DataSource.

Getting started with basic usage

Now that we have seen the definitions of the components within a DataSource, we will put together our first example page to demonstrate the basic usage of the DataSource object in JavaScript. Add a new HTML file to the static folder of the project and name it `DataSource.html`. Start out by adding this code:

```
<!DOCTYPE html>
<html>
<head>
<title>DataSource</title>
<script src="/Scripts/kendo/jquery.js"></script>
<script src="/Scripts/kendo/kendo.all.js"></script>
<link href="/Content/kendo/kendo.common.css" rel="stylesheet" />
<link href="/Content/kendo/kendo.default.css" rel="stylesheet" />
</head>
<body>
<div id="example" class="k-content">
<table id="movies">
<thead>
<tr>
<th>Rank</th>
<th>Rating</th>
```

```
<th>Title</th>
<th>Year</th>
</tr>
</thead>
<tbody>
<tr>
<td colspan="4"></td>
</tr>
</tbody>
</table>
</div>
</body>
</html>
```

We have referenced jQuery and Kendo UI Web JavaScript files in the head of our page. Now let's add a template block after the `div` tag so that we can script the creation of additional table rows:

```
<script id="template" type="text/x-kendo-template">
<tr>
<td>#= rank #</td>
<td>#= rating #</td>
<td>#= title #</td>
<td>#= year #</td>
</tr>
<script>
```

Now what we need is the ability to take some data and fill out that table using the layout as defined by this template, enter the DataSource. Add this code after the template script block that you just typed in:

```
<script type="text/javascript">
    $(document).ready(function() {
        // create a template using the above definition
var template = kendo.template($("#template").html());

var movies = [
{ "rank": 1, "rating": 9.2, "year": 1994,
"title": "The Shawshank Redemption" },
{ "rank": 2, "rating": 9.2, "year": 1972,
"title": "The Godfather" },
{ "rank": 3, "rating": 9, "year": 1974,
"title": "The Godfather: Part II" },
{ "rank": 4, "rating": 8.9, "year": 1966,
"title": "Il buono, ilbrutto, ilcattivo." },
{ "rank": 5, "rating": 8.9, "year": 1994,
```

```
"title": "Pulp Fiction" },
{ "rank": 6, "rating": 8.9, "year": 1957,
"title": "12 Angry Men" },
{ "rank": 7, "rating": 8.9, "year": 1993,
"title": "Schindler's List" },
{ "rank": 8, "rating": 8.8, "year": 1975,
"title": "One Flew Over the Cuckoo's Nest" },
{ "rank": 9, "rating": 8.8, "year": 2010,
"title": "Inception" },
{ "rank": 10, "rating": 8.8, "year": 2008,
"title": "The Dark Knight" }
        ];

var dataSource = new kendo.data.DataSource({
data: movies,
change: function () {
// subscribe to the CHANGE event of the data source
$("#movies tbody").html(
kendo.render(template, this.view())); // populate the table
              }
        });

// read data from the "movies" array
dataSource.read();
    });
</script>
```

Let's step through this code. You should recognize the first few lines where a Kendo template is created from the script block that you typed just a few paragraphs ago. After that, you see a JavaScript array of objects holding data about various movies. This array is going to be the raw data behind the DataSource object that comes next. The DataSource object is instantiated (note the `new` keyword) into the variable called `dataSource`. It references the `movies` array as its data parameter and then defines a function to handle the `change` event of the DataSource object. Inside this `change` event, we are using jQuery to select the `movies` table and then using `kendo.render()` to generate markup from our `template` variable for each item in our `dataSource` object. Note how the template we are using does not need special JavaScript to iterate over a collection; the DataSource object passes all of the data to the `change` event through `this.view()`. Finally, we call `dataSource.read()` which reads in the data and consequently fires the `change` event, thereby adding the content to our `movies` table.

The `kendo.render()` method takes a template function as its first argument and then an array of data as its second argument. It runs the data through the template, generating the resulting markup and returning it back to the caller. In the case above, we have used jQuery to set the `<tbody>` element's HTML to the result of this `kendo.render()` function.

Binding to remote data

Our last example was a demonstration of using local data (a JavaScript array) with a DataSource. It is also very common and important to use the DataSource with data that exists on a remote system. To simulate this, we will turn to the ASP.NET MVC framework to create a server for our remote data.

In the Visual Studio Solution Explorer window, right-click on the **Controllers** folder and choose **Add, Controller**. Name the new controller **KendoController** and leave the rest of the dialog that opens at its default settings.

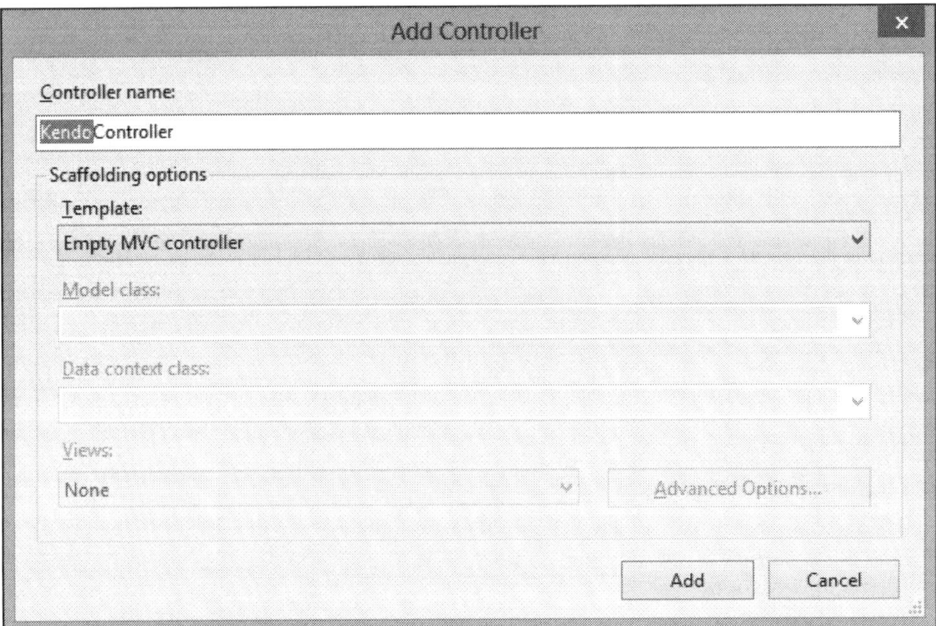

The newly created controller class will appear in the editor portion of Visual Studio and you will see a generic Index() method sitting in the file. This method is known as an **action method** and is used to process an HTML response back to a web browser. The comment above it indicates the route and HTTP verb that are used to locate this action method:

```
// GET: /Kendo/

public ActionResult Index()
{
return View();
}
```

In this case, it shows that typing the route "Kendo", as in http://<server-name>/Kendo/, would match this action method and cause it to return its view to the browser. It would also work to specify http://<server-name>/Kendo/Index and it is usual to supply both the controller name, "Kendo", and the action method name, "Index", in a normal route. As a matter of convention, the MVC framework names all controller classes with the suffix "Controller", but it does not use the suffix when referring to the controller in an actual route (such as the path in the address bar of your web browser). This means that the KendoController class is referred to as "kendo" when it is part of a route. GET is the default HTTP verb that this controller will accept when the browser requests this route.

At the top of KendoController, add a using statement for a namespace that we are about to create—LearningKendoUIWeb.Repository. Also add Kendo.Mvc.UI and Kendo.Mvc.Extensions:

```
using LearningKendoUIWeb.Repository;
using Kendo.Mvc.UI;
using Kendo.Mvc.Extensions;
```

Add a new action method called RemoteData and set it up like this:

```
publicJsonResultRemoteData()
{
var repository = new SampleRepository();
var data = repository.GetAllMovies();
returnJson(result, JsonRequestBehavior.AllowGet);
}
```

This is a simple method that instantiates a repository (which we will create in just a moment), gathers some data from that repository, and then returns it to the client as JSON. The second parameter to the Json() method notifies the controller class that it is acceptable to return JSON data from this method even though the verb is GET.

Right-click on the **Models** folder and click on **Add, Class**. Name the new class `Movie.cs`. This is a very simple class to hold data about a movie:

```
namespace LearningKendoUIWeb.Models
{
public class Movie
  {
public int Rank { get; set; }
public double Rating { get; set; }
public int Year { get; set; }
public string Title { get; set; }
  }
}
```

Add a new folder to the project and call it `Repository`. Add a class to this folder called `SampleRepository.cs`:

```
using LearningKendoUIWeb.Models;

namespaceLearningKendoUIWeb.Repository
{
public class SampleRepository
  {
public List<Movie>GetAllMovies()
    {
var movies = new List<Movie>{
new Movie { Rank = 1, Rating = 9.2,
                    Title = "The Shawshank Redemption", Year = 1994 },
new Movie { Rank = 2, Rating = 9.1,
                    Title = "The Godfather", Year = 1974 }
            };
            Return movies;
      }
   }
}
```

Feel free to add more movies to this list, the more the better. Now we have a simple repository class that can return a list of movie objects, so the action method we created in `KendoController` is finally valid. When the `RemoteData` action method is called, it will return the list of Movie objects as a JSON array of objects like this:

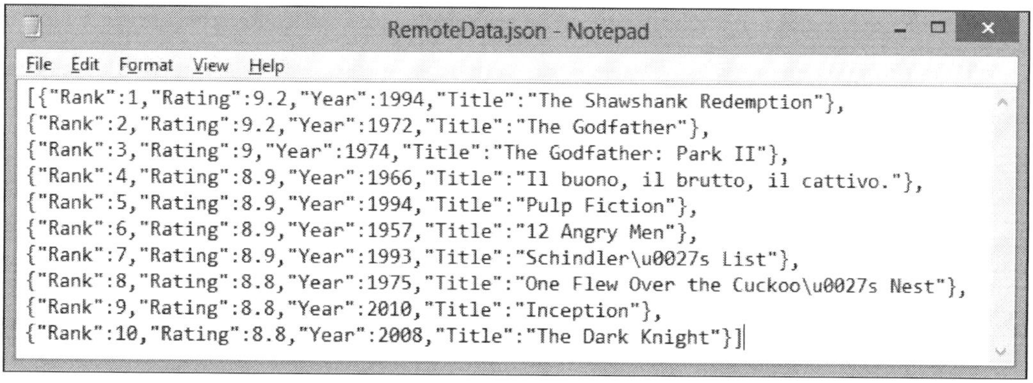

RemoteData.json - Notepad

File Edit Format View Help


```
[{"Rank":1,"Rating":9.2,"Year":1994,"Title":"The Shawshank Redemption"},
{"Rank":2,"Rating":9.2,"Year":1972,"Title":"The Godfather"},
{"Rank":3,"Rating":9,"Year":1974,"Title":"The Godfather: Park II"},
{"Rank":4,"Rating":8.9,"Year":1966,"Title":"Il buono, il brutto, il cattivo."},
{"Rank":5,"Rating":8.9,"Year":1994,"Title":"Pulp Fiction"},
{"Rank":6,"Rating":8.9,"Year":1957,"Title":"12 Angry Men"},
{"Rank":7,"Rating":8.9,"Year":1993,"Title":"Schindler\u0027s List"},
{"Rank":8,"Rating":8.8,"Year":1975,"Title":"One Flew Over the Cuckoo\u0027s Nest"},
{"Rank":9,"Rating":8.8,"Year":2010,"Title":"Inception"},
{"Rank":10,"Rating":8.8,"Year":2008,"Title":"The Dark Knight"}]
```


I have added more movies to my repository, but the structure of the result is the same. This is exactly the sort of data that DataSource knows how to use. Here is how to wire up DataSource to use it, find the line in the `RemoteData.cshtml` file where the `dataSource` variable is created in JavaScript and change the code so that it looks like this:

```
var dataSource = new kendo.data.DataSource({
  transport: {
read: {
url: 'Kendo/RemoteData/'
        }
    },
change: function () {
        $("#movies tbody").html(kendo.render(template, this.view()));
    }
});
```

Instead of the using the `data` property to point to a locally available array of objects, we are using the `transport` property to tell Kendo that we need to request the data from a remote source. In this case, all we have specified is how the DataSource can read remote data and that is all we need, since the only method call we make to the DataSource is in this line:

```
dataSource.read();
```

These examples have only scratched the surface, but it does show the DataSource in action in a real page. It is hard, however, to really demonstrate a DataSource object in isolation. The DataSource is only actually useful when it serves a data-rich widget, like the Kendo UI Grid. In the pages to follow, we will explore this Grid widget and will be able to demonstrate a more fully configured DataSource that the Grid can take full advantage of. We will also see how to configure both the Grid and the DataSource through the MVC Razor syntax within a view page.

Page layout

Now that we have discussed the DataSource and Template features of the Kendo UI framework, we can turn our attention to widgets that provide graphical elements on our web pages. Some of these widgets actually assist you in organizing the content or the data in your page, and the Grid is a very good example of this, which we will cover next.

Grid

The Kendo UI Grid is a very handy widget to be familiar with. It is an easy way to transform data into a usable and interactive grid that would normally take a full-featured server control (as in ASP.NET WebForms) or some complex and time-consuming JavaScript development in the page markup. In fact, it is remarkably easy to set up a simple example. Let's say we have some JavaScript data like this that we want to display within a web page:

```
<script type="text/javascript">
var repairs = [{
name: "State Inspection",
price: 39.75,
labor: 1,
staff: 1
            },
            {
name: "Brake & Clutch System Service",
price: 149.95,
labor: 3,
staff: 1
            },
            {
name: "Power Steering Service",
price: 109.96,
labor: 3,
staff: 1
            },
            {
name: "Cooling System Service",
price: 126.95,
labor: 2,
staff: 1
            },
            {
name: "Oil Change",
```

```
price: 37.77,
labor: 1,
staff: 1
            },
            {
name: "CV Axle Replacement",
price: 271.11,
labor: 5,
staff: 2
            },
            {
name: "Battery Cabling Replacement",
price: 179.97,
labor: 2,
staff: 1
            },
            {
name: "Battery Replacement",
price: 118.38,
labor: 1,
staff: 1
            },
            {
name: "Fuel Induction Service",
price: 168.88,
labor: 3,
staff: 2
            },
            {
name: "Engine Air Filter Replacement",
price: 36.63,
labor: 1,
staff: 1
            },
            {
name: "Timing Belt Replacement",
price: 221.75,
labor: 3,
staff: 2
            },
            {
name: "Drive Belt Replacement",
price: 194.79,
labor: 3,
```

```
staff: 2
                }
            ];
</script>
```

In order to turn this into a well-formatted dynamic table, it would normally require some looping and HTML markup generation, probably through jQuery. With Kendo UI, however, all we have to do is create a `kendoGrid()` function and we can see some magic in action. Take note of how little code is involved to create a grid from this data here:

```
<div id="repairsGrid"></div>
<script type="text/javascript">
        $("#repairsGrid").kendoGrid({
dataSource: repairs
        });
</script>
```

And here is the page output from this simple code:

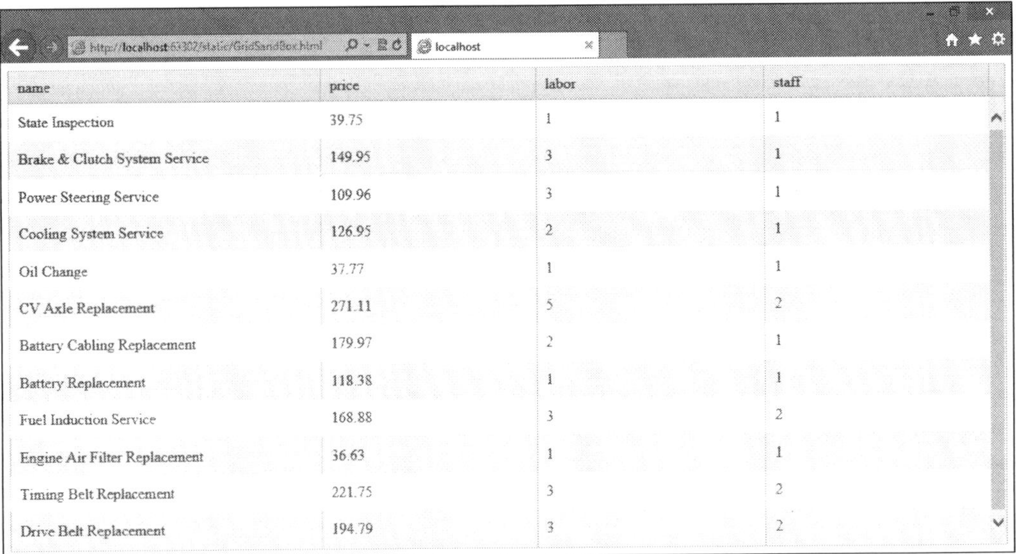

name	price	labor	staff
State Inspection	39.75	1	1
Brake & Clutch System Service	149.95	3	1
Power Steering Service	109.96	3	1
Cooling System Service	126.95	2	1
Oil Change	37.77	1	1
CV Axle Replacement	271.11	5	2
Battery Cabling Replacement	179.97	2	1
Battery Replacement	118.38	1	1
Fuel Induction Service	168.88	3	2
Engine Air Filter Replacement	36.63	1	1
Timing Belt Replacement	221.75	3	2
Drive Belt Replacement	194.79	3	2

See how the code involved didn't even require a table to be present within the web page? Kendo UI generated everything that it needed in order to display this data as a grid on the page. Now we can turn our attention to creating grids that are more interactive and intelligent, and explore what the Kendo UI Grid widget has to offer in displaying data from different sources.

Columns

First of all, we can take control of the formatting of the Grid by specifying properties on a `columns` object array. This object array is used to indicate to the Grid how to display the data appropriately so that it appears as you want on the page. Here is a columns object example using the Grid that we saw just a moment ago to demonstrate the various options available for formatting:

```
$("#repairsGrid").kendoGrid({
...
columns: [{
field: "name",
title: "Service",
width: 300
    },
    {
field: "price",
title: "Price",
width: 50,
format: "${0:##.##}"
    },
    {
field: "labor",
title: "Labor",
width: 50,
template: "#= labor# hour(s)"
    },
    {
field: "staff",
title: "Staff",
width: 50,
template: "#= staff # tech(s)"
    }]
```

Here is the effect on the output:

There are also simple options for enabling some dynamic interactive behaviors by specifying which columns are filterable or sortable. Note that these are only useful if the Grid, as a whole, has `pageable` and/or `sortable` set to `true`.

```
$("#repairsGrid").kendoGrid({
    ...
columns: [{
field: "name",
title: "Service",
width: 300,
sortable: true,
filterable: true
    },
    {
field: "price",
title: "Price",
width: 50,
format: "${0:##.##}",
sortable: true,
filterable: true
    },
    {
field: "labor",
title: "Labor",
width: 50,
template: "#= labor # hour(s)",
sortable: true,
filterable: true
```

```
        },
        {
    field: "staff",
    title: "Staff",
    width: 50,
    template: "#= staff # tech(s)",
    sortable: false,
    filterable: false
        }],
    sortable: true,
    filterable: true
```

Note in the following screenshot, how the **Service** column has been sorted alphabetically and I have clicked the filter icon, which enables me to input a filter on the data to be displayed on the page. You can see the filter icon right above the open window on the screen, it looks like a small funnel. Kendo UI takes care of actually doing the sorting and the filtering by means of the `dataSource` property that we set on the Grid. This means that settings you have put in place on the `dataSource` that you supply to the Grid will be used by the Grid for sorting and filtering:

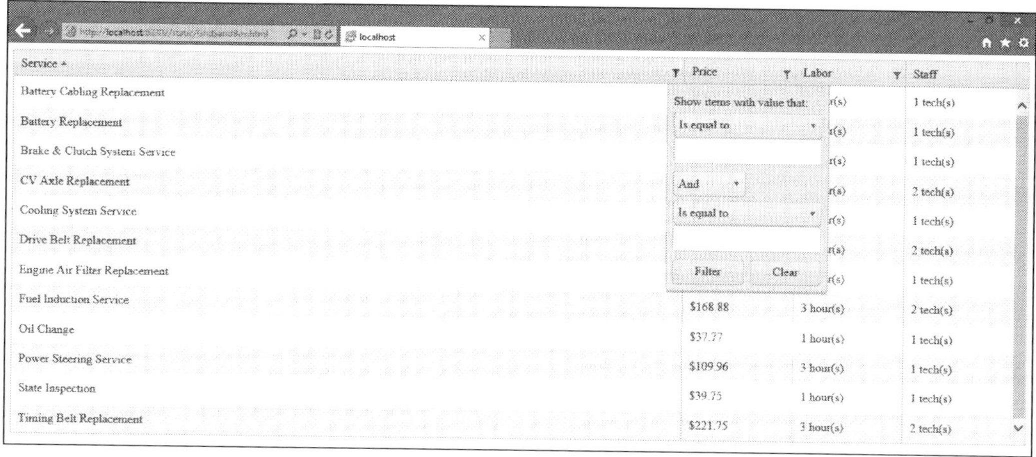

When the Grid has been configured to allow editing of data, the `columns` property allows you to specify a custom editor function that can be used when changing data in that column. This can be a useful way of giving the user an easier way to input a change, or even to control the sort of changes that can be made. For example, this updated code sample shows adding an editor function to the `Labor` column so that it displays a drop-down list when edited, giving the user a specific set of options to choose from. There are a couple of other changes here that we will talk about next:

```
$("#repairsGrid").kendoGrid({
dataSource: repairs,
columns: [
  {
title: "Action",
width: 75,
command: ["edit"]
  },
{
field: "name",
title: "Service",
width: 300,
sortable: true,
filterable: true
  },
{
field: "price",
title: "Price",
width: 50,
format: "${0:##.##}",
sortable: true,
filterable: true
  },
{
field: "labor",
title: "Labor",
width: 50,
template: "#= labor # hour(s)",
sortable: true,
filterable: true,
editor: function (container, options) {
varselectEditor = $("<select name=" + options.field +
"></select>");
selectEditor.append(new Option("1", 1));
selectEditor.append(new Option("2", 2));
selectEditor.append(new Option("3", 3));
```

```
selectEditor.append(new Option("4", 4));
selectEditor.append(new Option("5", 5));
selectEditor.appendTo(container);
        }
    },
    {
field: "staff",
title: "Staff",
width: 50,
template: "#= staff # tech(s)",
sortable: false,
filterable: false
    }],
sortable: true,
filterable: true,
editable: "inline"
```

Here is the output of the `editor` function, showing the drop-down list that appears when a row enters the edit mode. It is important to set the `name` attribute of the `<select>` element so that Kendo can bind the user's choice back to the `dataSource` when the edit is saved.

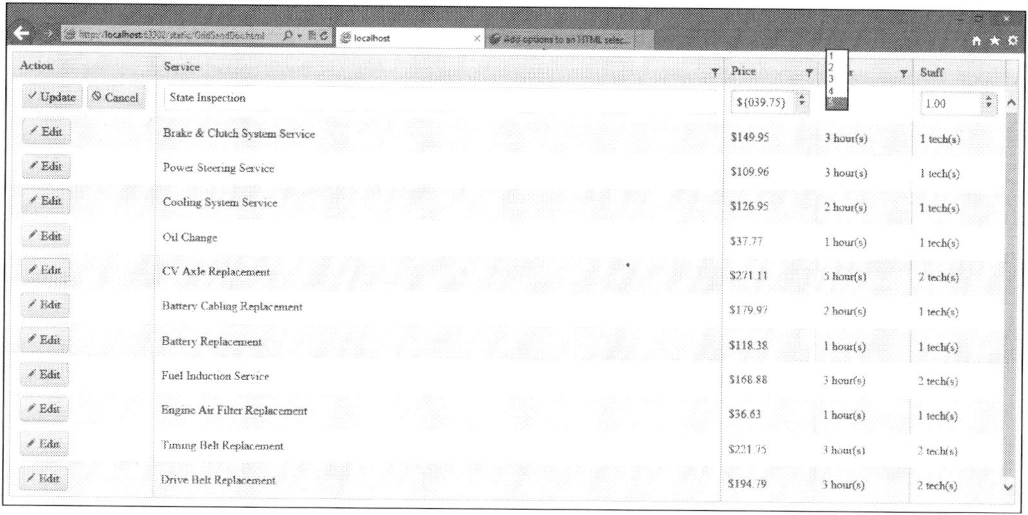

When using a custom editor function like this, the `container` and `options` objects that are passed in have some specific properties available to them that can be useful to you when writing your function. The `container` object is the page element to which you should add any new mark-up, as we did in our example. The `options` object contains two properties: `options.field` and `options.model`. The `options.field` property contains the name of the field that you should use in your new mark-up so that Kendo can bind everything properly. The `options.model` property contains a reference to the actual model of the data being edited if one was specified in the `dataSource`; this gives you access to data that could be important when creating your custom logic.

Additional changes that appeared in the code sample were the `editable: "inline"` property on the Grid definition (required for editing to work; the alternative to `inline` is `popup`, which opens a special window for editing the record), and the new column that includes command buttons. The command property of a column object takes an array of command buttons to generate within each row. The available options for this array include `edit`, `create`, `destroy`, `save`, and `cancel`. We will return to this topic soon when we go into more detail on how to bind a Grid to CRUD operations.

Note that all that was necessary to add these command buttons to the Grid was to specify the `command` property of the column object. I did not add any `<button>` elements to the column, nor did I create JavaScript event handlers. Kendo UI generated all of this necessary markup for me through the Grid widget's existing functionality.

A significant portion of Grid functionality can be enabled through properties that describe the Grid's current capabilities. Each of them end in -able. These properties are `editable`, `filterable`, `groupable`, `navigatable`, `pageable`, `scrollable`, `selectable`, and `sortable`. We have already seen `filterable` and `sortable` and that they take simple true/false values when used. We have also seen `editable`, but there is more that can be done with this option:

```
...
editable: {
confirmation: "Are you sure?", // text displayed to confirm a delete
                                  operation
destroy: true,          // whether or not to delete item when button
                           is clicked
mode: "popup",                    // options are "incell", "inline",
                                     and "popup"
template: "#= ... #",             // template to use for pop-up editing
update: true                      // switch item to edit mode when
                                     clicked?
}
```

The `groupable` property lets the user group columns by dragging them to the top of the screen. The `groupable` option also includes a property, `groupable.messages.empty` that will be displayed in an empty grouping area on a Grid. If you specify this `messages` property, the `groupable: true` value is assumed and does not need to be specified. The `navigatable` property turns on or off keyboard navigation within the Grid. Here is how the bottom of our Grid definition would look with `groupable` and `navigatable` turned on:

```
...
sortable: true,
filterable: true,
editable: "inline",
navigatable: true,
groupable: {
messages: {
empty: "Drag column header here for grouping"
    }
}
```

And the output in the page when rendered with these options:

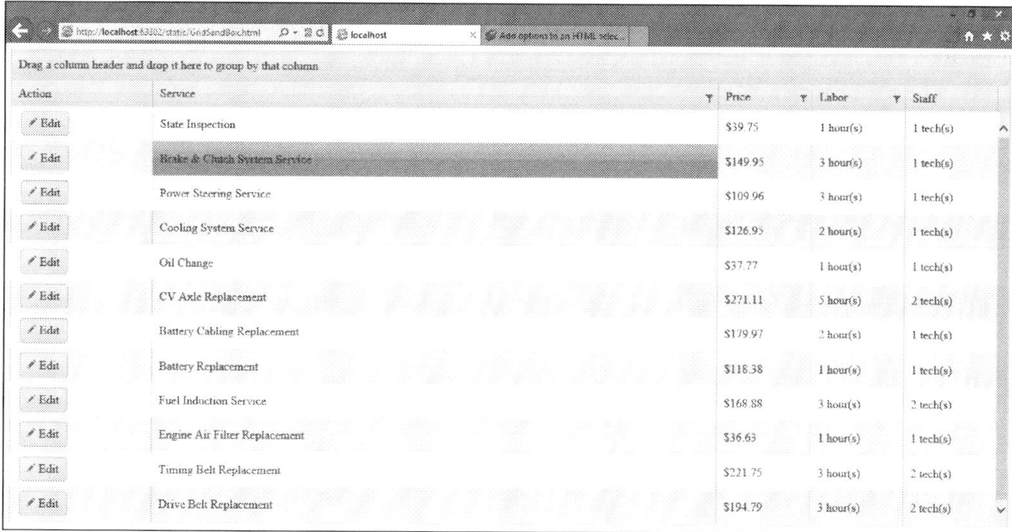

The `pageable` option can be simply set to `true`/`false`, like several of the other options, but it also allows for more fine-grained control if you desire it:

```
...
pageable: {
pageSize: 10,
```

```
previousNext: true, // show buttons navigating to first/last/next/
                        previous
numeric: true, // show numeric portion of the pager in the Grid?
buttonCount: 10, // number of buttons to show in numeric pager
input: true, // create input element allowing user to navigate to page
pageSizes: [5,10,20], //array of page size choices for user
refresh: true, //  show a refresh button in the Grid?
info: true, // show a label with current paging information in it
messages: {
display: "Detail Template - {1} of {2} items", // info text
empty: "No Records", // text to show when there are no records
page: "Page", // first part of text of input option
of: "of Detail Template", // last part of text of input option
itemsPerPage: "items per page", // text for selecting page size
first: "Go to first page", // text of first page button tooltip
previous: "Go to the previous page", // previous page tooltip
next: "Go to next page", // next page tooltip
last: "Go to the last page", // last page tooltip
refresh: "Refresh" // text of refresh button tooltip
  }
}
```

Our example code configured for paging with 10 items per page would appear like this:

```
...
sortable: true,
filterable: true,
editable: "inline",
navigatable: true,
groupable: {
messages: {
empty: "Drag column header here for grouping"
}
},
pageable: {
pageSize: 10
}
```

And the output generated with these options:

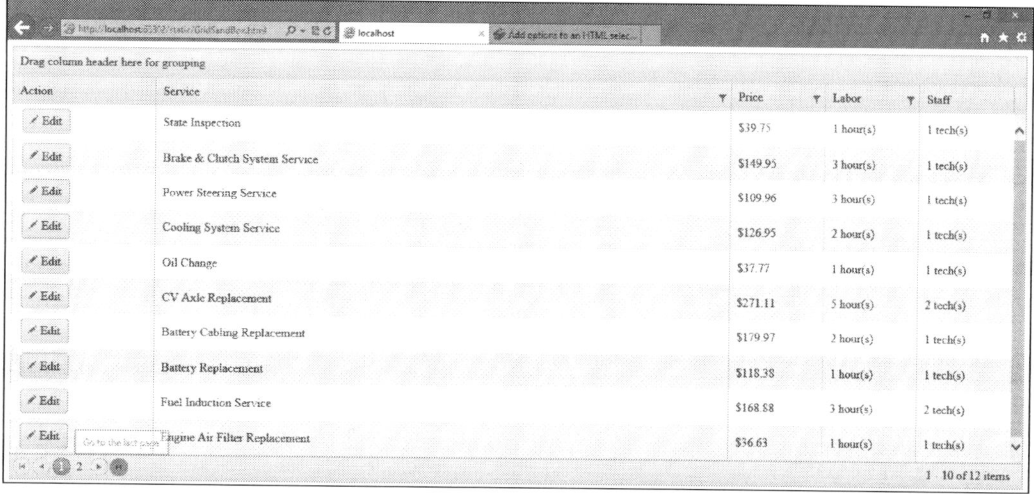

The `scrollable` property configures whether a Grid can have a vertical scroll bar within it, and is usually specified if you have restricted the height of the Grid on your page. It can be set to a simple Boolean value of `true/false`.

The `selectable` property indicates whether selection is enabled or disabled within the Grid. Its possible values are `row`, `cell`, `multiple, row`, and `multiple, cell`. Here is how our example Grid looks with `selectable: "multiple, cell"`.

Note that I have selected some rows for display.

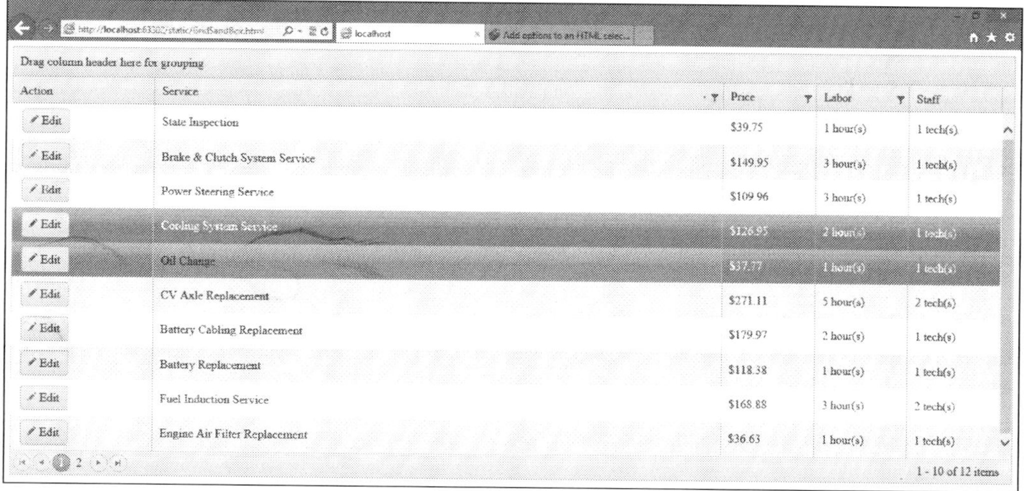

The `toolbar` property enables a toolbar for the Grid with a certain set of commands, similar to the command property of the column objects. Each toolbar within the `toolbar` object array can have a `name`, `template`, and `text` configured:

```
...
toolbar: [
"create",
{ name: "save", text: "Save This Record" },
{ name: "cancel", text: "Cancel Changes: }]
```

Note how a toolbar can be a simple text value indicating which command to implement. You can also specify objects to contain the configuration data that you want (as in the preceding screenshot). Refer to the following screenshot:

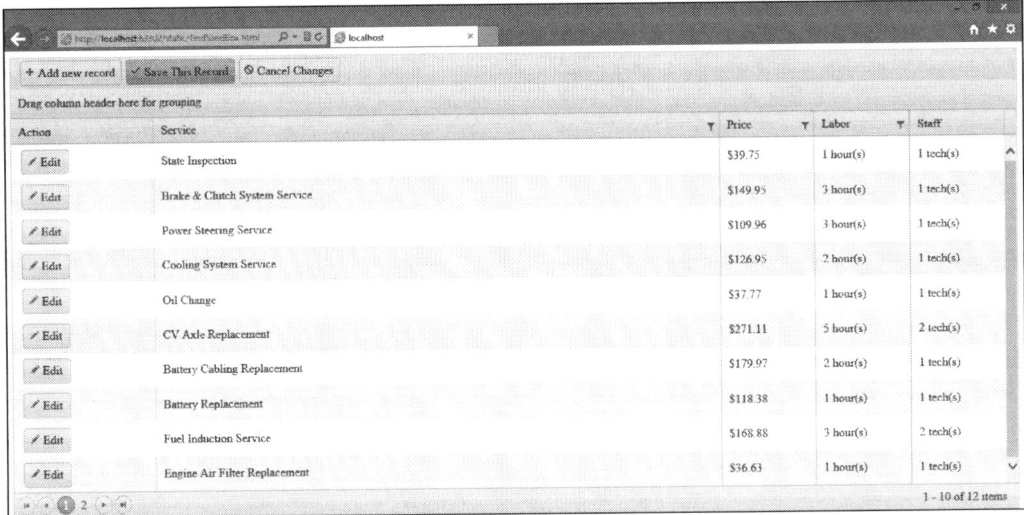

Summary

In this chapter, we have covered a lot of fundamental information so that you can get started creating Kendo UI-enabled web pages properly. It is essential to understand how to use a Template and how to use a DataSource in order to do much at all with the Kendo UI framework. Second to these, the Grid is an essential component of the Kendo UI framework and knowing how to configure it will give you a head start when building pages that need to display tabular data to a user.

In the next chapter, we will learn about the AutoComplete widget. It allows you to add a word-wheel effect to input text boxes, to assist users in typing information that can be looked up from a data source. It is a great tool that many users are drawn to and will add a lot of functionality to your web pages without a lot of effort in writing the code.

2
The AutoComplete Widget and its Usage

The AutoComplete widget from Kendo UI creates the "word wheel" effect on an input box as a user types. A word wheel is an effect where words appear beneath a textbox as a user types that help suggest possible search terms. You often see this on search engines such as Google and Bing. This can be used to give the user a list of approved choices from which he or she can choose, or it can also help the user type specific keywords accurately, since the canonical form of the item appears directly beneath the input box for the user to select. It also saves the user's time if he or she only has to type one or two characters of a potentially long search term. The AutoComplete widget in Kendo UI is very easy to configure and brings this functionality to users of your site with little effort on your part.

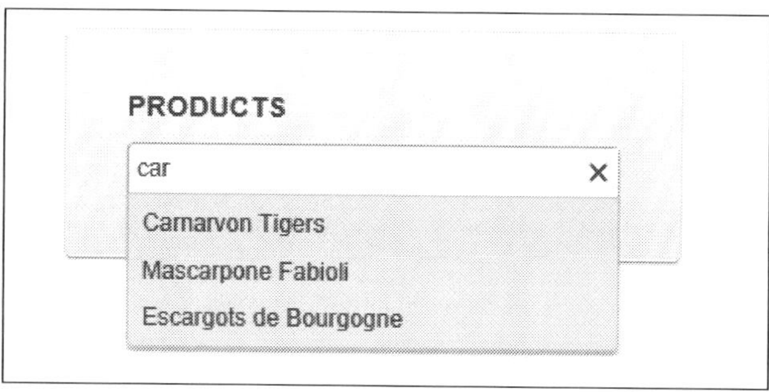

AutoComplete widget – basics

Open the Visual Studio project that you created in the previous chapter and then open the `KendoController.cs` class in the `Controllers` folder. Let's add a new action method for our initial AutoComplete test page.

```
public ActionResult AutoCompletePage()
{
  return View();
}
```

Right-click on the action method's name and choose **Add View**. For now, choose the defaults that appear in the dialog and this will take you to the web page so that we can get started.

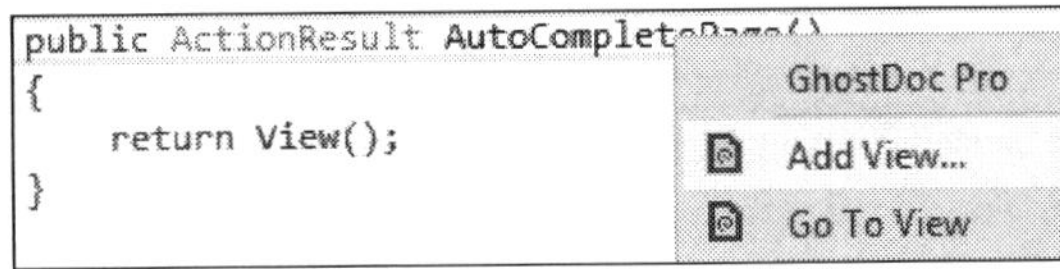

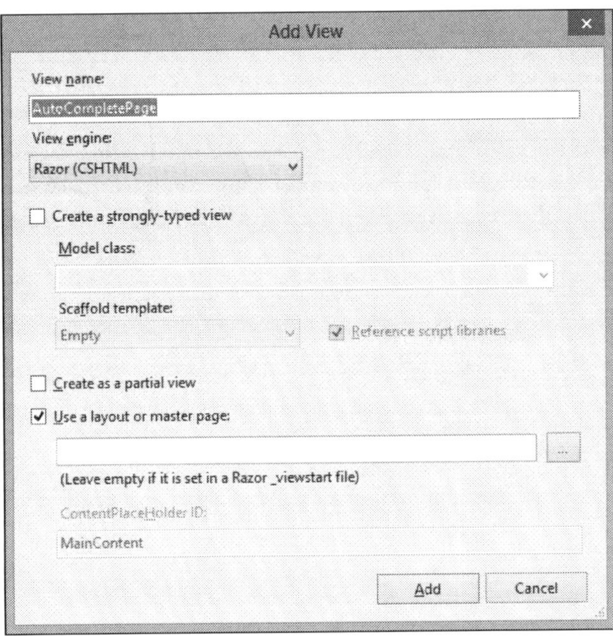

Binding AutoComplete to a local source

Since we are referencing the default layout that we created in the last chapter, we will get all of the Kendo and jQuery files that we need in our page header without having to retype anything.

We will start by demonstrating how to use the AutoComplete widget purely through JavaScript with local data binding. We will need an input element, a JavaScript array, and some jQuery.

```
<style>
    #stateOrTerritory {
      width:200px;
    }
</style>

<h2>AutoCompletePage</h2>
<input type="text" name="stateOrTerritory" id="stateOrTerritory" />

<script type="text/javascript">
varstatesAndTerritories = ["Alabama",
            "Alaska",
            "American Samoa",
            "Arizona",
            "Arkansas",
            ...
            "Washington",
            "West Virginia",
            "Wisconsin",
            "Wyoming"];

    $("#stateOrTerritory").kendoAutoComplete({
      dataSource: statesAndTerritories,
      filter: "startswith",
      placeholder: "Choose state or territory...",
      separator: ", "
    });

</script>
```

We can use a list of the United States and Territories for a nice sampling of the alphabet and a list long enough for a demonstration. All that we have done so far is created some data in JavaScript for the AutoComplete to use, and then wired it up with jQuery and Kendo UI to the input element at the top of the page. We have specified that we want to use the `statesAndTerritories` JavaScript array as our data source, that we wanted the filter to run in "`startswith`" mode, that we want placeholder text in the input element, and that the items in the array are separated by a comma. These properties are explained in more detail at the end of the chapter. Run this and you should see an input box with some nice looking placeholder text in your browser. Type some letters in it and you get an immediate result with some state and territory suggestions.

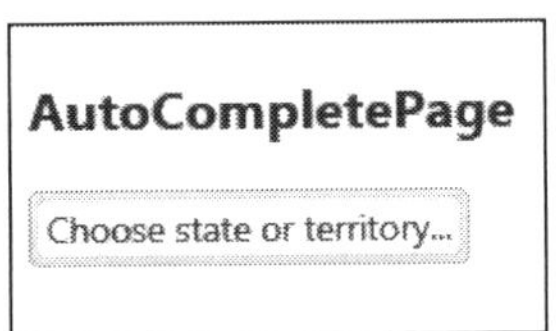

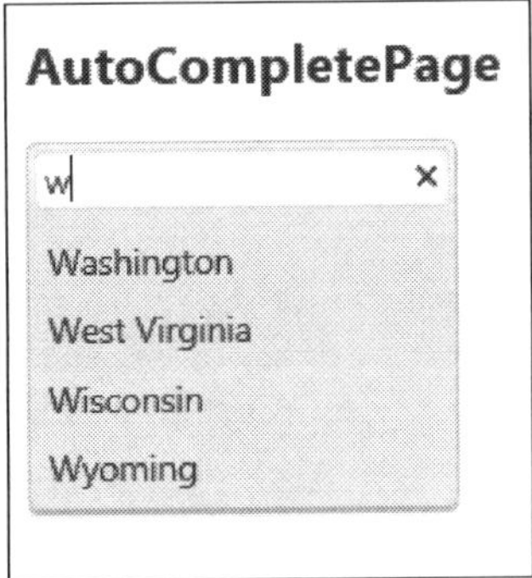

Binding AutoComplete to Remote Data

Now that we have seen how to wire up the AutoComplete widget using local JavaScript data, let's see how to do it with remote data. Add a new class called `StateTerritory.cs` to the `Models` folder in the Visual Studio project. Structure it to hold the relevant data about states and territories so that we can use this in our page.

```
namespace LearningKendoUIWeb.Models
{
  public class StateTerritory
  {
    public string Name { get; set; }
    public bool IsState { get; set; }
    public bool IsTerritory { get; set; }
```

```
        public bool IsContiguous { get; set; }
    }
}
```

Now open the `SampleRepository.cs` class file and add some logic to create a repository of our state and territory data. Note that I have intentionally counted the District of Columbia as both a state and a territory for the purposes of future examples.

```
public List<StateTerritory>GetStatesAndTerritories()
{
var stateTerritories = new List<StateTerritory>{
new StateTerritory{ Name = "Alabama", IsContiguous = true,
IsState = true, IsTerritory = false },
new StateTerritory{ Name = "Alaska", IsContiguous = false,
IsState = true, IsTerritory = false },
new StateTerritory{ Name = "American Samoa", IsContiguous = false,
IsState = false, IsTerritory = false },
new StateTerritory{ Name = "Arizona", IsContiguous = true,
IsState = true, IsTerritory = false },
new StateTerritory{ Name = "Arkansas", IsContiguous = true,
IsState = true, IsTerritory = false },
...
new StateTerritory{ Name = "Washington", IsContiguous = true,
IsState = true, IsTerritory = false },
new StateTerritory{ Name = "West Virginia", IsContiguous = true,
IsState = true, IsTerritory = false },
new StateTerritory{ Name = "Wisconsin", IsContiguous = true,
IsState = true, IsTerritory = false },
new StateTerritory{ Name = "Wyoming", IsContiguous = true,
IsState = true, IsTerritory = false }
    };
return stateTerritories;
}
```

Now we have some server-side data that we can play with, but we still need to expose it across HTTP. Go back to the `KendoController.cs` class file and add a new action method like you see in this code block:

```
public JsonResult AutoCompleteData()
{
  var repository = new SampleRepository();
  var data = repository.GetStatesAndTerritories();
  returnJson(data, JsonRequestBehavior.AllowGet);
}
```

This will expose our collection of states and territories as a JSON array of `StateTerritory` objects. Remember to set the `JsonRequestBehavior.AllowGet` property or this will not work. Now we can modify our `AutoCompletePage.cshtml` file to use the transport property to get its data.

```
$("#stateOrTerritory").kendoAutoComplete({
  dataSource: {
    transport: {
    read: {
      url: "/Kendo/AutoCompleteData/"
          }
    }
  },
  dataTextField: "Name",
  filter: "startswith",
  placeholder: "Choose state or territory...",
});
```

Run the page again and watch it pull data from the server. We have to specify which field contains the data text field, since our JSON data is structured as objects and not simply an array. We also no longer need the separator property.

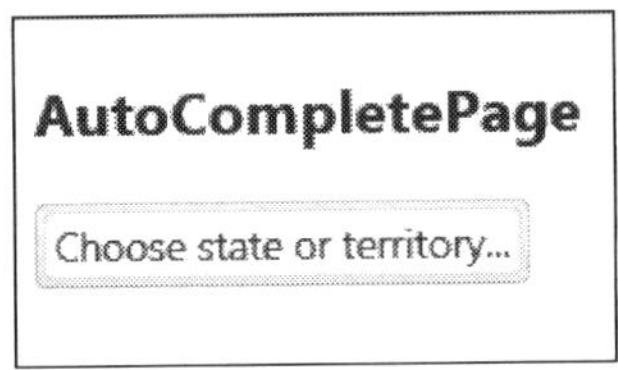

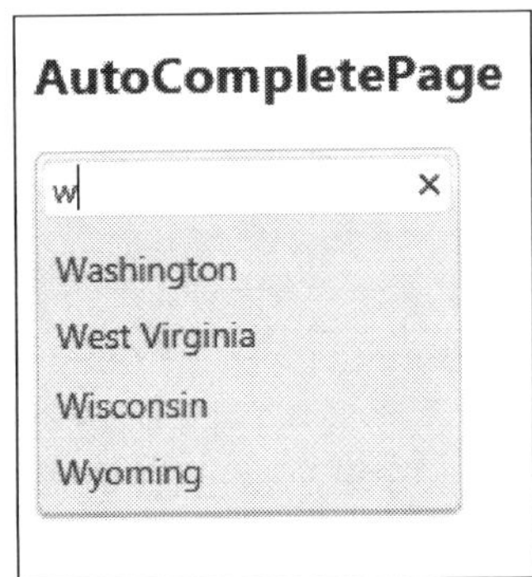

Using AutoComplete with MVC through Models

We can take this one step further and transform our code into Razor syntax with MVC. First, create a controller action method to return data from the server.

```
public ActionResult AutoCompletePage()
{
  var repository = new SampleRepository();
  var data = repository.GetStatesAndTerritories();
  return View(data);
}
```

Next, open `AutoCompletePage.cshtml` and delete everything in it after the `<h2>` tag. At the top of the file, we need to add a declaration so that this **View** page becomes strongly-typed to our new model class `StateTerritory.cs`.

```
@model IEnumerable<LearningKendoUIWeb.Models.StateTerritory>
```

Now add this code that utilizes the HTML helper class and the Kendo extension methods.

```
<h2>AutoCompletePage</h2>
@(Html.Kendo().AutoComplete()
     .Name("statesAndTerritories")
     .DataTextField("Name")
     .BindTo(Model)
     .Filter("startswith")
     .Placeholder("Choose state or territory...")
)
```

Recognize the syntax? Except for the `BindTo(Model)` statement, these method names are the same as the properties we used in JavaScript (except that they start with capital letters, of course). The call to `BindTo(Model)` is how the MVC controller passes data into the MVC view. In this case, we strongly-typed our view to a collection (`IEnumerable`) of `StateTerritory` objects, and here in the code we are telling the Kendo framework that this model contains the data to display in the AutoComplete. The data in this model is used while the page is being created by the server, and is only accessible through the Razor syntax code statements in the **View** page.

Even though we just wired up the AutoComplete to the server through MVC, the method we used isn't really like a call to remote data. It is actually using local data, by saving all of the model data from the server into the JavaScript where the AutoComplete is initialized. There isn't anything wrong with this, so long as we do not attempt to embed so much data into the page that it loads slowly. In fact it is likely a good way to boost performance in some situations, but it is important to know where the data is and how the page is accessing it. If we want the page to request the data from a URL, we need to make some changes to our view.

Using AutoComplete with MVC through Ajax

Open the view and make a change to the `AutoComplete()` extension method call just like this code block.

```
<h2>AutoCompletePage</h2>
@(Html.Kendo().AutoComplete()
    .Name("statesAndTerritories")
    .Placeholder("Choose state or territory...")
    .DataTextField("Name")
    .Filter("startswith")
    .DataSource(source =>
        {
source.Read(read =>
            {
read.Action("AutoCompleteData", "Kendo");
            })
            .ServerFiltering(false);
        })
)
```

We have removed the `BindTo(Model)` and replaced it with a call to `DataSource()` where we use a lambda expression to define how to create the data source. In this case, we have configured it to use the action method that returns the JSON data we configured earlier, and also that the server is not performing any filtering. This effectively sets our web page up in the same way as our original JavaScript page that used the `transport` property to get JSON data from the server.

Sending data to the server

We want to be able to filter the data for the AutoComplete widget on the server side. We can either use the `data` property within the `transport` JavaScript object, or we can continue with our MVC example and specify the data to send inside the `DataSource` lambda expression. Let's say, for example, that we want to be able to choose what type of states and territories show up in the AutoComplete widget. We can accomplish this by sending some data along with the request, then having the server revise the data that it sends back. Replace the contents of `AutoCompletePage.cshtml` with this updated code.

```
<h2>AutoCompletePage</h2>
<label for="stateType">Choose whether to see States:</label>
<select id="stateType" name="stateType">
<option value="true">Show States</option>
<option value="false">Show Only Territories</option>
</select>
<br />
@(Html.Kendo().AutoComplete()
    .Name("statesAndTerritories")
    .Placeholder("Choose state or territory...")
    .DataTextField("Name")
    .Filter("startswith")
    .DataSource(source =>
        {
          source.Read(read =>
          {
              read.Action("AutoCompleteData", "Kendo")
                    .Data("onAdditionalData");
            })
            .ServerFiltering(false);
        })
)
<script type="text/javascript">
var autocomplete = $("#statesAndTerritories").
data("kendoAutoComplete");

functiononAdditionalData() {
  return {
    showStates: $("#stateType").val()
        }
    }
</script>
```

Notice the call to `Data("onAdditionalData")` in the lambda expression and the new JavaScript method `onAdditionalData()` with the same name. When the data source for the AutoComplete is read, it will fire this JavaScript event and send the result to the server with a parameter named `showStates`. In order to receive this data into your action method, you need to add a parameter to it with a matching name.

```
public JsonResult AutoCompleteData(bool showStates = true)
{
  // setting showStates = true means that it is an optional parameter
  // with the default value of true.
  var repository = new SampleRepository();
  var data = repository.GetStatesAndTerritories();
  if (!showStates)
  {
    data = data.Where(s =>s.IsState == false).ToList();
  }
  return Json(data, JsonRequestBehavior.AllowGet);
}
```

Now, when the AutoComplete code sends the `showStates` parameter as part of its web request, the controller will use the value of that to determine whether or not to filter the data that it sends back.

Using Templates to Customize AutoComplete

Kendo templates can be used to customize the appearance of the items in your AutoComplete. This can even get quite fancy with images and special styles. Here is a simple example. Update the Razor portion of the `AutoCompletePage.cshtml` page to look like this:

```
@{
var template = "#= Name # - #= IsState #";
}
@(Html.Kendo().AutoComplete()
    .Name("statesAndTerritories")
    .Placeholder("Choose state or territory...")
    .DataTextField("Name")
    .Filter("startswith")
    .DataSource(source =>
    {
      source.Read(read =>
      {
```

```
            read.Action("AutoCompleteData", "Kendo")
                        .Data("onAdditionalData");
        })
      .ServerFiltering(false);
      })
      .Template(template)
  )
```

Here we have added a variable called `template` that is holding our Kendo template definition. We then referenced that in our `AutoComplete()` setup code. Run the page and take a look.

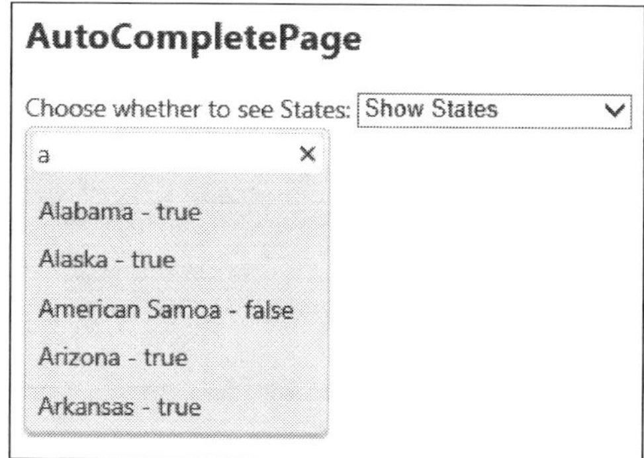

Configuring all of the AutoComplete properties

The AutoComplete widget has several different properties that can be set during its initialization to customize its behavior. Here is a structured code sample to show you what is available on the AutoComplete widget.

```
$("autocomplete").kendoAutoComplete({
dataSource: dataSource, // see chapter 1
  animation: {
  close: {
    effects: "fadeOut",
      duration: 300,
      hide: true,
      show: false
    },
    open: {
    effects: "fadeIn",
      duration: 300,
```

```
        show: true
      }
    },
    dataTextField: "Name", // name of field in data source to display
    delay: 500, // milliseconds before auto complete activates
    enable: true, // set "false" to disable
    filter: "contains", // type of filtration, passed to remote source
    height: 200, // height of drop-down list
    highlightFirst: true, // highlight first item in list?
    ignoreCase: true,
    minLength: 1, // minimum characters before activating drop-down list
    placeHolder: "Enter value...", // placeholder text
    separator: ", ", // separator for completion of search terms.
    //allows for multiple search terms by using comma or
                      //   other delimiter
    suggest: false, // auto-type rest of search term?
    template: template // see chapter 1
  }
```

Hooking into AutoComplete widget events

The AutoComplete widget has several different events that it fires while performing actions on your page. You can bind them after the AutoComplete widget has been initialized like this:

```
varautoComplete = $("#autoComplete").data("kendoAutoComplete");
$("#autoComplete").data("kendoAutoComplete").bind("change",
function(e) {
    // handle event
});
```

Or you can define them within the properties of the AutoComplete widget itself like this:

```
$("#autoComplete").kendoAutoComplete({
close: function(e) {
        // handle event
    }
});
```

In either case, this is the list of events to which you can attach your own code.

Change

The `change` event fires as the selection in the AutoComplete widget changes. You can bind events after initialization.

Close

The `close` event fires when the drop-down list is closed from the AutoComplete widget.

Open

The `open` event fires every time the drop-down list is opened from the AutoComplete widget.

Select

The `select` event fires when any of the elements is selected from the AutoComplete widget. It passes the argument `e.item` to the function that handles it so that you can access the item that was selected.

Using the API AutoComplete methods

To access the AutoComplete widget from within JavaScript code, you can access it through the API by calling it this way through jQuery:

```
var autocomplete = $("autocomplete").data("kendoAutoComplete");
```

Once you have a variable reference to the AutoComplete widget, you will be able to call the API methods and manipulate it through code as you wish. These are the API methods available on the AutoComplete widget.

Close

The `close()` method closes the drop-down list on the AutoComplete widget.

```
// get a reference to the autocomplete widget
var autocomplete = $("autocomplete").data("kendoAutoComplete");

autocomplete.close();
```

DataItem

The `dataItem()` method returns the data record at the specified index. This `dataItem` object will be the specific object from the AutoComplete widget's data source at the specified index. In our examples above, it would be a specific `stateOrTerritory` object.

```
var autocomplete = $("#autocomplete").data("kendoAutoComplete");

// get the dataItem corresponding to the passed index.
var dataItem = autocomplete.dataItem(1);
```

Destroy

The `destroy()` method prepares the AutoComplete widget for safe removal from the DOM. It detaches all event handlers and removes data attributes. It does not actually take the final step of removing it from the DOM; that is an action you must program yourself.

```
var autocomplete = $("#autocomplete").data("kendoAutoComplete");

// detach events
autocomplete.destroy();
```

Enable

The `enable()` method toggles the AutoComplete widget on and off.

```
// get a reference to the autocomplete widget
var autocomplete = $("autocomplete").data("kendoAutoComplete");

// disables the autocomplete
autocomplete.enable(false);

// enables the autocomplete
autocomplete.enable(true);
```

Refresh

The `refresh()` method re-renders the items in the drop-down list of the AutoComplete widget.

```
// get a reference to the Kendo UI AutoComplete
var autocomplete = $("autocomplete").data("kendoAutoComplete");
// re-render the items in drop-down list.
autocomplete.refresh();
```

Search

The `search()` method filters the data source of the AutoComplete widget using the provided parameter and then rebinds the drop-down list.

```
// get a reference to the autocomplete widget
var autocomplete = $("autocomplete").data("kendoAutoComplete");

// Searches for item which has "Inception" in the name.
autocomplete.search("Inception");
```

Select

The `select()` method selects a drop-down list item from the AutoComplete widget and sets the text of the AutoComplete input box.

```
// get a reference to the autocomplete widget
var autocomplete = $("autocomplete").data("kendoAutoComplete");

// selects by jQuery object
autocomplete.select(autocomplete.ul.children().eq(0));
```

Suggest

The `suggest()` method forces a suggestion onto the text of the AutoComplete widget.

```
// note that this suggest is not the same as the configuration method
// suggest which enables/disables auto suggesting for the AutoComplete
//
// get a reference to the Kendo UI AutoComplete
varautoComplete = $("#autoComplete").data("kendoAutoComplete");

// force a suggestion to the item with the name "Inception"
autoComplete.suggest("Inception");
```

Value

The `value()` method gets or sets the value of the AutoComplete widget.

```
// get a reference to the autocomplete widget
var autocomplete = $("autocomplete").data("kendoAutoComplete");

// get the text of the autocomplete.
var value = autocomplete.value();
```

Summary

The AutoComplete widget is a great way to aid users on your site. Any time an input box's values can be predicted, such as when they come from a specific set of values or when searching common terms, an AutoComplete widget will immediately make your site easier to use and your users are sure to notice and appreciate it. Not only that, but the configuration is so straightforward that you can enable it without much effort.

In the next chapter we will learn how to use the Calendar widget. This widget will allow you to display and configure interactive calendar controls in your web pages so that users can easily select dates. It will also give you a way of binding data to calendars to show important dates. The Telerik Kendo UI Calendar widget will help change a complicated JavaScript calendar into a simple-to-use tool for developing great web pages.

3

Using and Customizing Calendar

Calendars have long been a feature of web pages that require some clever JavaScript. HTML5 is working toward making it all much simpler, but browser support still isn't consistent. This is where Kendo UI is a perfect solution, being a framework that combines HTML5 and JavaScript to create cross-browser consistency using the latest standards. Like always, the Kendo UI solution couldn't be simpler to implement.

Calendar widget – basics

The Kendo UI Calendar widget transforms a simple HTML element, such as a `div`, into a specialized HTML table that displays a calendar. It also wires up JavaScript functionality to this table to support all of the Calendar widget events and methods. To see the simplest possible implementation of this widget, create a new action method in the Kendo controller so that we have a URL for "calendar":

```
public ActionResult Calendar()
{
    return View();
}
```

Then add a view for this action method and set up an empty `div` to hold a Kendo calendar widget:

```
@{
    ViewBag.Title = "Calendar";
}

<h2>Calendar</h2>
<div id="calendar">
```

```
</div>
<script type="text/javascript">
    $("#calendar").kendoCalendar();
</script>
```

The output is amazing considering how little code we have written:

Click around on the calendar and observe how much functionality it already has. The arrows at the top of the calendar navigate forward or backward by one month. The text at the top of the calendar, shown as **October 2012** in the preceding screenshot, navigates up to a broader level of dates which makes it easy to select a different year or decade. The date at the bottom of the calendar is a hyperlink that navigates directly to the current date. As we add functionality later in this chapter, we can make the calendar do even more.

Configuring the Calendar widget

Since the Calendar widget only has a few properties, let's start by examining them and then move on to examples in using them. The calendar widget has two different types of properties:

- **Data/template properties**: These properties configure the data behind the calendar widget
- **Display/formatting properties**: These properties configure how the calendar is rendered on the page and how that data is formatted

Here are these properties listed in code format. Add this code to the page and run it:

```
$("#calendar").kendoCalendar({
    culture: 'en-US', // specifies the culture
    depth: 'month',   // specifies navigation depth
                      //(century/decade/month/year)
    max: new Date(2012,11,31), // latest date calendar can show
    min: new Date(1980, 0, 1), // oldest date calendar can show
    start: 'year',    // specifies the start view (century/decade/
month/year)
    value: new Date(2012,9,25), // initially selected date
    format: 'yyyy/MM/dd'  // format string used when the value() of
this
                          //calendar is requested
});
```

The calendar, when configured as above, renders initially by showing a selection of months available within the currently selected year (`start: 'year'`). Since we have configured it to allow a navigation depth into each month (`depth: 'month'`) we can click on a month and then see that month and all of its available days:

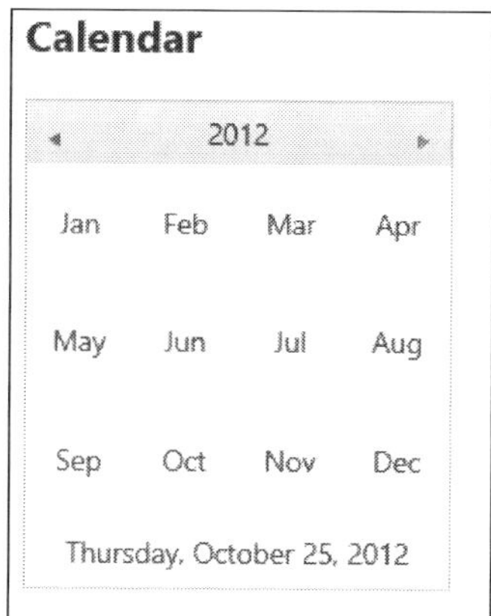

Even though the current view is "year", today's date is still visible within the footer of the calendar.

Speaking of the footer, let's take a look at the data/template properties that the calendar makes available. The three main properties here are `data`, `month`, and `footer` and they are the primary way to customize the calendar widget. To demonstrate a simple example of customizing specific dates in a calendar, add this code to a page and run it:

```
<h2>Calendar</h2>
<div id="calendar">
</div>
<style type="text/css">
    .specialDay {
        color: white;
        background-color: orange;
        border:1px solid black;
    }
</style>
<script type="text/x-kendo-template" id="redDays">
    # if ($.inArray(+data.date, data.dates) != -1) { #
        <div class="specialDay">#= data.value #</div>
    # } else { #
        #= data.value #
    # } #
</script>
<script type="text/javascript">
    var datesArray = [+new Date(2012, 5, 15), +new Date(2012, 5, 21)];

    $("#calendar").kendoCalendar({
        culture: 'en-US', // specifies the culture
        depth: 'month',    // specifies navigation depth
        max: new Date(2012, 5,31), // latest date calendar can show
        min: new Date(2012, 5, 1), // oldest date calendar can show
        start: 'month',    // specifies the start view
        value: new Date(2012,5,11), // initially selected date
        format: 'yyyy/MM/dd',  // format string used to format the
date values
        dates: datesArray,
        month: {
            content: $("#redDays").html(),
            empty: "X"
        },
        footer: "Today is #= kendo.toString(data, 'd') #"
});
</script>
```

Let's step through this code together. First, we have a special style instruction for how special days are to be displayed. In this case, white text on an orange background with a solid black border. We also specify a Kendo UI template block with JavaScript to determine whether the date being rendered is one of our special days. If it is one of the special days, then we want the custom style applied to it; otherwise just render it as usual.

```
<style type="text/css">
    .specialDay {
        color: white;
        background-color: orange;
        border:1px solid black;
    }
</style>
<script type="text/x-kendo-template" id="redDays">
    # if ($.inArray(+data.date, data.dates) != -1) { #
        <div class="specialDay">#= data.value #</div>
    # } else { #
        #= data.value #
    # } #
</script>
```

Next, we define the actual configuration of the calendar widget. This is where the relationship between the `month` property and the `dates` property becomes apparent: the `dates` property supplies the data that the `month` property uses to render the days on the calendar. In the template that we have defined, we check to see if the current date being rendered is included in the `dates` array and then use `data.value` to render the number of the date currently executing. Notice also that we have prepended the dates in the `dateArray` with a plus sign + to force them into a numeric date that we can easily compare with `$.inArray()`. This is not a requirement in every case, but works for this example.

```
<script type="text/javascript">
    var datesArray = [+new Date(2012, 5, 15), +new Date(2012, 5, 21)];

    $("#calendar").kendoCalendar({
        culture: 'en-US', // specifies the culture
        depth: 'month',    // specifies navigation depth
        max: new Date(2012, 5,31), // latest date calendar can show
        min: new Date(2012, 5, 1), // oldest date calendar can show
        start: 'month',    // specifies the start view
        value: new Date(2012,5,11), // initially selected date
        format: 'yyyy/MM/dd',  // format string used to format the
date values
        dates: datesArray,
```

```
            month: {
                content: $("#redDays").html(),
                empty: "X"
            },
            footer: "Today is #= kendo.toString(data, 'd') #"
});
</script>
```

The other things to note are the new property called `footer` that is used to render a template for the footer of the calendar, which has access to today's date through the `data` property passed to it. Also, note that the `month` object has another property called `empty` that is used to render dates that fall outside of the `min` or `max` property value ranges.

With the calendar set up in this way, it looks like this in the browser:

Note the special display of the dates supplied through the `dateArray`, the dates out of range, and the new text used in the footer.

Calendar Widget using MVC

The Calendar widget can also be configured through the ASP.NET MVC extension methods. To imitate the calendar we just created, you can replace the contents of your view with this code:

```
<h2>Calendar</h2>
<style type="text/css">
    .specialDay {
        color: white;
        background-color: orange;
        border:1px solid black;
```

```
    }
</style>
<script type="text/x-kendo-template" id="redDays">
    # if ($.inArray(+data.date, data.dates) != -1) { #
<div class="specialDay">#= data.value #</div>
    # } else { #
        #= data.value #
    # } #
</script>
<script type="text/javascript">
    var datesArray = [+new Date(2012, 5, 15), +new Date(2012, 5, 21)];
</script>
@(Html.Kendo().Calendar()
    .Name("mvcCalendar")
    .Depth(CalendarView.Month)
    .Max(new DateTime(2012, 6, 30))
    .Min(new DateTime(2012, 6, 1))
    .Start(CalendarView.Month)
    .Value(new DateTime(2012, 6, 11))
    .Format("yyyy/MM/dd")
    .MonthTemplate("# if ($.inArray(+data.date, datesArray) != -1) {
#" +
                    "<div class='specialDay'>#= data.value #</div>" +
                    "# } else { #" +
                    "#= data.value #" +
                    "# } #")
    .Footer("Today is #= kendo.toString(data, 'd') #")
    )
```

This is the output when using this new code:

Pretty similar, isn't it? Note that the MVC extension hid the dates below `max` and `min` and didn't give us an empty property on the `month`. There are a few other unique things to note as well. First, notice that we are still using an array of dates through JavaScript inside the view. This is because the `month` template is running in JavaScript, not through MVC extensions, and needs access to this data on the client. Because of this, and because of the fact that the MVC extensions do not provide a `dates` property, we have to change the template from using `data.dates` to the actual name of the JavaScript array—`datesArray`. In this example, I typed out the template code directly into the MVC extension method, but there is also a method called `MonthTemplateId()` where you can pass the HTML `id` of the template already on the page.

Also, remember to always call the `.Name()` method on every Kendo MVC extension object; it is required for the code to work. This is how the MVC extension methods assign a unique `name` and `id` attribute to the rendered HTML output, and how all of the JavaScript methods and events are properly wired up in the web browser. If you do not include the `.Name()` method, you will also see a runtime error when you try to run the page.

Methods available on the Calendar widget

The Calendar widget exposes several methods that can be used to interact with it on the page. These methods can be used to configure the widget by changing its properties or firing specific functionality in real time. Here is a code form of the available methods specific to the Kendo UI Calendar widget:

```
var calendar = $("calendarId").data("kendoCalendar");

// Set a new max date
calendar.max(new Date(2013,11,31));
// Retrieve the current max date
var lastDay = calendar.max();

// Set a new min date
calendar.min(new Date(2011, 11, 31);
// Retrieve the current min date
var oldestDay = calendar.min();

// Navigate to a specific date using a specific view
calendar.navigate(new Date(2012,2,5), "month");
```

```
// Navigate down to a lower view (i.e. goes from "year" to "month")
calendar.navigateDown(new Date(2012,6,7)); // date is optional

// Navigate to the future
calendar.navigateToFuture();

// Navigate to the past
calendar.navigateToPast();

// Navigate up to a higher view (i.e. goes from "year" to "decade")
calendar.navigateUp("year");

// Set a new value (selected date) for the calendar
calendar.value(new Date(2012,4,7));

// Get the current value (selected date) of the calendar
var selectedDate = calendar.value();
```

Let's take an example of some of these and see it in action on our page. Modify the code we just created for the MVC view like this:

```
<h2>Calendar</h2>
<style type="text/css">
    .specialDay {
        color: white;
        background-color: orange;
        border:1px solid black;
    }
</style>
<script type="text/x-kendo-template" id="redDays">
    # if ($.inArray(+data.date, data.dates) != -1) { #
<div class="specialDay">#= data.value #</div>
    # } else { #
        #= data.value #
    # } #
</script>
<script type="text/javascript">
    var datesArray = [+new Date(2012, 5, 15), +new Date(2012, 5, 21)];
</script>
@(Html.Kendo().Calendar()
    .Name("mvcCalendar")
    .Depth(CalendarView.Month).Start(CalendarView.Month)
    .Value(new DateTime(2012, 6, 11))
    .Format("yyyy/MM/dd")
    .MonthTemplate("# if ($.inArray(+data.date, datesArray) != -1) {
```

```
#" +
                        "<div class='specialDay'>#= data.value #</div>" +
                        "# } else { #" +
                        "#= data.value #" +
                        "# } #")
    .Footer("Today is #= kendo.toString(data, 'd') #")
    )
<br />
<button type="button" id="navigateUp">Navigate Up</button><br />
<button type="button" id="navigateDown">Navigate Down</button><br />
<button type="button" id="showValue">Pop-Up Value</button>
<script type="text/javascript">
    $("#navigateUp").click(function () {
        var calendar = $("#mvcCalendar").data("kendoCalendar");
        calendar.navigateUp();
    });
    $("#navigateDown").click(function () {
        var calendar = $("#mvcCalendar").data("kendoCalendar");
        calendar.navigateDown(calendar.value());
    });
    $("#showValue").click(function () {
        var calendar = $("#mvcCalendar").data("kendoCalendar");
        alert(calendar.value());
    });
</script>
```

In order to use the calendar widget as a JavaScript object, we have to call the `.data()` function on the page element that contains the calendar that we created. Click the buttons on the page and see what they do. It should give you some idea of what the calendar widget can offer, and how you could plug your own interactive code into a calendar to improve the user experience.

Events fired by the Calendar widget

The Kendo UI calendar widget has two events—`change` and `navigate`. These events fire when the action after which they are named occurs. The `Change` fires when the selected date is changed, `navigate` fires when the calendar is navigated—such as when the month is changed or the view is moved up from "month" to "year".

What if you wanted the calendar to only appear when a user selected a certain input box on a page, and then place its value into that input element? You could try something like this. Modify the final `script` block of the page that we are working on to look like this example:

```
<script type="text/javascript">
    $(function () {
        $("#mvcCalendar").hide();
    });
    $(document).ready(function () {
        $("#mvcCalendar").data("kendoCalendar").bind("change",
function (e) {
            var date = $("#mvcCalendar").data("kendoCalendar").
value();
            $("#showTheCalendar").val(kendo.toString(date, 'd'));
        });
    });
    $("#showTheCalendar").focusin(function () {
        $("#mvcCalendar").slideDown();
    });
    $("#nameInput").focusin(function () {
        $("#mvcCalendar").slideUp();
    });
    $("#ageInput").focusin(function () {
        $("#mvcCalendar").slideUp();
    });
    $("#navigateUp").click(function () {
        var calendar = $("#mvcCalendar").data("kendoCalendar");
        calendar.navigateUp();
    });
    $("#navigateDown").click(function () {
        var calendar = $("#mvcCalendar").data("kendoCalendar");
        calendar.navigateDown(calendar.value());
    });
    $("#showValue").click(function () {
        var calendar = $("#mvcCalendar").data("kendoCalendar");
        alert(calendar.value());
    });
</script>
```

Here we have some events, wired up by simple jQuery and jQuery UI, that show or hide the calendar and take its value when selected. The `change` event of the calendar is used to determine when to place the new date value into the input element of the page. This is how the page appears when first rendered.

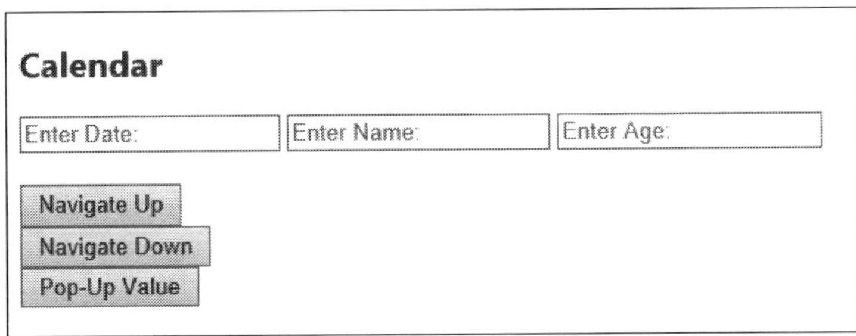

The calendar is hidden until the user clicks into the first textbox. As soon as that happens, the events we wired up cause the calendar to appear so that the use can select the appropriate date for the page.

Summary

The Kendo UI calendar widget is easy to configure, and offers a rich element on your page that can make working with dates a much simpler task. It can be configured from either JavaScript or MVC extensions and makes use of Kendo templates for highly customizable formatting and display. I have only shown basic examples of what can be done with the templates and events; you can take these and run with them to create some very useful interactive content.

In the next chapter we will learn about one of the most powerful features of the Kendo UI framework of all, the Model-View-ViewModel (MVVM) framework. This framework lets you bind data and functionality to your page through simple HTML attributes and enable real-time changes to your data, or to a server, with immediate feedback for the user. The MVVM framework is a great tool that you will want to use in all of your pages.

4
The Kendo MVVM Framework

JavaScript development has come a long way since its inception and the appearance of rich MVVM frameworks is wonderful evidence of that evolution. These allow the developer to separate responsibilities within the code to better handle complexity. They also provide a beautifully simple syntax so that the MVVM framework itself is left to handle the tedious work of binding dynamic data into your web pages. If you have never used a JavaScript MVVM framework before, you are in for a treat with the Kendo MVVM framework.

Understanding MVVM – basics

MVVM stands for **Model** (**M**), **View** (**V**), and **View-Model** (**VM**). It is part of a family of design patterns related to system architecture that separate responsibilities into distinct units. Some other related patterns are **Model-View-Controller** (**MVC**) and **Model-View-Presenter** (**MVP**). These differ on what each portion of the framework is responsible for, but they all attempt to manage complexity through the same underlying design principles. Without going into unnecessary details here, suffice it to say that these patterns are good for developing reliable and reusable code and they are something that you will undoubtedly benefit from if you have implemented them properly. Fortunately, the good JavaScript MVVM frameworks make it easy by wiring up the components for you and letting you focus on the code instead of the "plumbing".

In the MVVM pattern for JavaScript through Kendo UI, you will need to create a definition for the data that you want to display and manipulate (the Model), the HTML markup that structures your overall web page (the View), and the JavaScript code that handles user input, reacts to events, and transforms the static markup into dynamic elements (the View-Model). Another way to put it is that you will have data (Model), presentation (View), and logic (View-Model).

In practice, the Model is the most loosely-defined portion of the MVVM pattern and is not always even present as a unique entity in the implementation. The View-Model can assume the role of both Model and View-Model by directly containing the Model data properties within itself, instead of referencing them as a separate unit. This is acceptable and is also seen within ASP.NET MVC when a View uses the `ViewBag` or the `ViewData` collections instead of referencing a strongly-typed Model class. Don't let it bother you if the Model isn't as well defined as the View-Model and the View. The implementation of any pattern should be filtered down to what actually makes sense for your application.

Simple data binding

As an introductory example, consider that you have a web page that needs to display a table of data, and also provide the users with the ability to interact with that data, by clicking specifically on a single row or element. The data is dynamic, so you do not know beforehand how many records will be displayed. Also, any change should be reflected immediately on the page instead of waiting for a full page refresh from the server. How do you make this happen?

A traditional approach would involve using special server-side controls that can dynamically create tables from a data source and can even wire-up some JavaScript interactivity. The problem with this approach is that it usually requires some complicated extra communication between the server and the web browser either through "view state", hidden fields, or long and ugly query strings. Also, the output from these special controls is rarely easy to customize or manipulate in significant ways and reduces the options for how your site should look and behave. Another choice would be to create special JavaScript functions to asynchronously retrieve data from an endpoint, generate HTML markup within a table and then wire up events for buttons and links. This is a good solution, but requires a lot of coding and complexity which means that it will likely take longer to debug and refine. It may also be beyond the skill set of a given developer without significant research. The third option, available through a JavaScript MVVM like Kendo UI, strikes a balance between these two positions by reducing the complexity of the JavaScript but still providing powerful and simple data binding features inside of the page.

Creating the view

Here is a simple HTML page to show how a view basically works:

```
<!DOCTYPE html>
<html xmlns="http://www.w3.org/1999/xhtml">
<head>
<title>MVVM Demo 1</title>
<script src="/Scripts/kendo/jquery.js"></script>
<script src="/Scripts/kendo/kendo.all.js"></script>
<link href="/Content/kendo/kendo.common.css" rel="stylesheet" />
<link href="/Content/kendo/kendo.default.css" rel="stylesheet" />
<style type="text/css">
th {
width: 135px;
   }
</style>
</head>
<body>
<table>
<caption>People Data</caption>
<thead>
<tr>
<th>Name</th>
<th>Hair Color</th>
<th>Favorite Food</th>
</tr>
</thead>
<tbody data-template="row-template"
data-bind="source: people"></tbody>
</table>
</body>
</html>
```

Here we have a simple `table` element with three columns but instead of the `body` containing any `tr` elements, there are some special HTML5 `data-*` attributes indicating that something special is going on here. These `data-*` attributes do nothing by themselves, but Kendo UI reads them (as you will see below) and interprets their values in order to link the View with the View-Model. The `data-bind` attribute indicates to Kendo UI that this element should be bound to a collection of objects called `people`.

The `data-template` attribute tells Kendo UI that the `people` objects should be formatted using a Kendo UI template. Here is the code for the template:

```
<script id="row-template" type="text/x-kendo-template">
<tr>
<td data-bind="text: name"></td>
<td data-bind="text: hairColor"></td>
<td data-bind="text: favoriteFood"></td>
</tr>
</script>
```

This is a simple template that defines a `tr` structure for each row within the table. The `td` elements also have a `data-bind` attribute on them so that Kendo UI knows to insert the value of a certain property as the "text" of the HTML element, which in this case means placing the value in between `<td>` and `</td>` as simple text on the page.

Creating the Model and View-Model

In order to wire this up, we need a View-Model that performs the data binding. Here is the View-Model code for this View:

```
<script type="text/javascript">
var viewModel = kendo.observable({
people: [
            {name: "John", hairColor: "Blonde", favoriteFood:
"Burger"},
            {name: "Bryan", hairColor: "Brown", favoriteFood:
"Steak"},
            {name: "Jennifer", hairColor: "Brown", favoriteFood:
"Salad"}
        ]
    });
kendo.bind($("body"), viewModel);
</script>
```

A Kendo UI View-Model is declared through a call to `kendo.observable()` which creates an **observable object** that is then used for the data-binding within the View. An observable object is a special object that wraps a normal JavaScript variable with events that fire any time the value of that variable changes. These events notify the MVVM framework to update any data bindings that are using that variable's value, so that they can update immediately and reflect the change. These data bindings also work both ways so that if a field bound to an observable object variable is changed, the variable bound to that field is also changed in real time.

In this case, I created an array called `people` that contains three objects with properties about some people. This array, then, operates as the Model in this example since it contains the data and the definition of how the data is structured. At the end of this code sample, you can see the call to `kendo.bind($("body"), viewModel)` which is how Kendo UI actually performs its MVVM wiring. I passed a jQuery selector for the `body` tag to the first parameter since this `viewModel` object applies to the full body of my HTML page, not just a portion of it.

With everything combined, here is the full source for this simplified example:

```
<!DOCTYPE html>
<html xmlns="http://www.w3.org/1999/xhtml">
<head>
<title>MVVM Demo 1</title>
<scriptsrc="/Scripts/kendo/jquery.js"></script>
<scriptsrc="/Scripts/kendo/kendo.all.js"></script>
<link href="/Content/kendo/kendo.common.css" rel="stylesheet" />
<link href="/Content/kendo/kendo.default.css" rel="stylesheet" />
<style type="text/css">
th {
width: 135px;
        }
</style>
</head>
<body>
<table>
<caption>People Data</caption>
<thead>
<tr>
<th>Name</th>
<th>Hair Color</th>
<th>Favorite Food</th>
</tr>
</thead>
<tbody data-template="row-template"
data-bind="source: people"></tbody>
</table>
<script id="row-template" type="text/x-kendo-template">
<tr>
<td data-bind="text: name"></td>
<td data-bind="text: hairColor"></td>
<td data-bind="text: favoriteFood"></td>
</tr>
</script>
```

```
<script type="text/javascript">
var viewModel = kendo.observable({
people: [
        {name: "John", hairColor: "Blonde", favoriteFood: "Burger"},
        {name: "Bryan", hairColor: "Brown", favoriteFood: "Steak"},
{ name: "Jennifer", hairColor: "Brown", favoriteFood: "Salad" }
            ]
        });
kendo.bind($("body"), viewModel);
</script>
</body>
</html>
```

Here is a screenshot of the page in action. Note how the data from the JavaScript `people` array is populated into the table automatically:

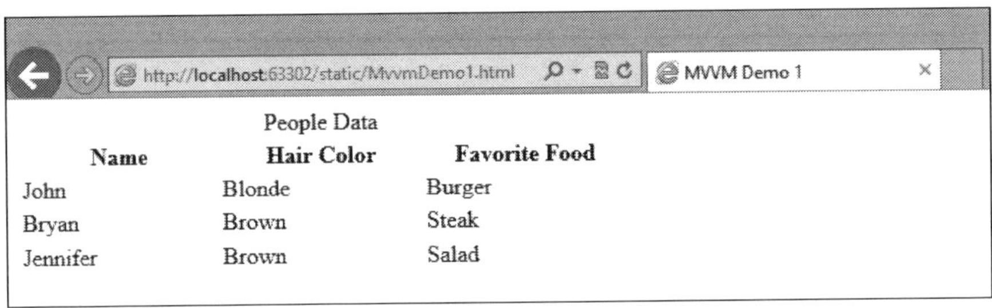

Even though this example contains a Model, a View, and a View-Model, all three units appear in the same HTML file. You could separate the JavaScript into other files, of course, but it is also acceptable to keep them together like this. Hopefully you are already seeing what sort of things this MVVM framework can do for you.

Observable data binding

Binding data into your HTML web page (View) using declarative attributes is great, and very useful, but the MVVM framework offers some much more significant functionality that we didn't see in the last example. Instead of simply attaching data to the View and leaving it at that, the MVVM framework maintains a running copy of all of the View-Model's properties, and keeps references to those properties up to date in real time. This is why the View-Model is created with a function called "observable". The properties inside, being observable, report changes back up the chain so that the data-bound fields always reflect the latest data. Let's see some examples.

Adding data dynamically

Building on the example we just saw, add this horizontal rule and form just below the table in the HTML page:

```
<hr />
<form>
<header>Add a Person</header>
<input type="text" name="personName" placeholder="Name"
data-bind="value: personName" /><br />
<input type="text" name="personHairColor" placeholder="Hair Color"
data-bind="value: personHairColor" /><br />
<input type="text" name="personFavFood" placeholder="Favorite Food"
data-bind="value: personFavFood" /><br />
<button type="button" data-bind="click: addPerson">Add</button>
</form>
```

This adds a form to the page so that a user can enter data for a new person that should appear in the table. Note that we have added some `data-bind` attributes, but this time we are binding the `value` of the input fields not the `text`. Note also that we have added a `data-bind` attribute to the `button` at the bottom of the form that binds the `click` event of that `button` with a function inside our View-Model. By binding the `click` event to the `addPerson` JavaScript method, the `addPerson` method will be fired every time this button is clicked.

These bindings keep the value of those input fields linked with the View-Model object at all times. If the value in one of these input fields changes, such as when a user types something in the box, the View-Model object will immediately see that change and update its properties to match; it will also update any areas of the page that are bound to the value of that property so that they match the new data as well.

The binding for the button is special because it allows the View-Model object to attach its own event handler to the click event for this element. Binding an event handler to an event is nothing special by itself, but it is important to do it this way (through the `data-bind` attribute) so that the specific running View-Model instance inside of the page has attached one of its functions to this event so that the code inside the event handler has access to this specific View-Model's data properties and values. It also allows for a very specific context to be passed to the event that would be very hard to access otherwise.

Here is the code I added to the View-Model just below the `people` array. The first three properties that we have in this example are what make up the Model. They contain that data that is observed and bound to the rest of the page:

```
personName: "",        // Model property
personHairColor: "",   // Model property
personFavFood: "",     // Model property
addPerson: function () {
this.get("people").push({
name: this.get("personName"),
hairColor: this.get("personHairColor"),
favoriteFood: this.get("personFavFood")
});
this.set("personName", "");
this.set("personHairColor", "");
this.set("personFavFood", "");
}
```

The first several properties you see are the same properties that we are binding to in the input form above. They start with an empty value because the form should not have any values when the page is first loaded. It is still important to declare these empty properties inside the View-Model in order that their value can be tracked when it changes.

The function after the data properties, `addPerson`, is what we have bound to the click event of the button in the input form. Here in this function we are accessing the `people` array and adding a new record to it based on what the user has supplied in the form fields. Notice that we have to use the `this.get()` and `this.set()` functions to access the data inside of our View-Model. This is important because the properties in this View-Model are special observable properties so accessing their values directly may not give you the results you would expect.

The most significant thing that you should notice about the `addPerson` function is that it is interacting with the data on the page through the View-Model properties. It is not using jQuery, `document.querySelector`, or any other DOM interaction to read the value of the elements! Since we declared a `data-bind` attribute on the values of the input elements to the properties of our View-Model, we can always get the value from those elements by accessing the View-Model itself. The values are tracked at all times. This allows us to both retrieve and then change those View-Model properties inside the `addPerson` function and the HTML page will show the changes right as it happens. By calling `this.set()` on the properties and changing their values to an empty string, the HTML page will clear the values that the user just typed and added to the table. Once again, we change the View-Model properties without needing access to the HTML ourselves.

Here is the complete source of this example:

```
<!DOCTYPE html>
<html xmlns="http://www.w3.org/1999/xhtml">
<head>
<title>MVVM Demo 2</title>
<scriptsrc="/Scripts/kendo/jquery.js"></script>
<scriptsrc="/Scripts/kendo/kendo.all.js"></script>
<link href="/Content/kendo/kendo.common.css" rel="stylesheet" />
<link href="/Content/kendo/kendo.default.css" rel="stylesheet" />
<style type="text/css">
th {
width: 135px;
        }
</style>
</head>
<body>
<table>
<caption>People Data</caption>
<thead>
<tr>
<th>Name</th>
<th>Hair Color</th>
<th>Favorite Food</th>
</tr>
</thead>
<tbody data-template="row-template" data-bind="source: people"></
tbody>
</table>
<hr />
<form>
<header>Add a Person</header>
<input type="text" name="personName" placeholder="Name" data-
bind="value: personName" /><br />
<input type="text" name="personHairColor" placeholder="Hair Color"
data-bind="value: personHairColor" /><br />
<input type="text" name="personFavFood" placeholder="Favorite Food"
data-bind="value: personFavFood" /><br />
<button type="button" data-bind="click: addPerson">Add</button>
</form>
<script id="row-template" type="text/x-kendo-template">
<tr>
<td data-bind="text: name"></td>
<td data-bind="text: hairColor"></td>
<td data-bind="text: favoriteFood"></td>
```

```
</tr>
</script>
<script type="text/javascript">
var viewModel = kendo.observable({
people: [
                {name: "John", hairColor: "Blonde", favoriteFood:
"Burger"},
                {name: "Bryan", hairColor: "Brown", favoriteFood:
"Steak"},
                {name: "Jennifer", hairColor: "Brown", favoriteFood:
"Salad"}
            ],
personName: "",
personHairColor: "",
personFavFood: "",
addPerson: function () {
this.get("people").push({
name: this.get("personName"),
hairColor: this.get("personHairColor"),
favoriteFood: this.get("personFavFood")
                });
this.set("personName", "");
this.set("personHairColor", "");
this.set("personFavFood", "");
            }
        });
kendo.bind($("body"), viewModel);
</script>
</body>
</html>
```

And here is a screenshot of the page in action. You will see that one additional person has been added to the table by filling out the form. Try it out yourself to see the immediate interaction that you get with this code:

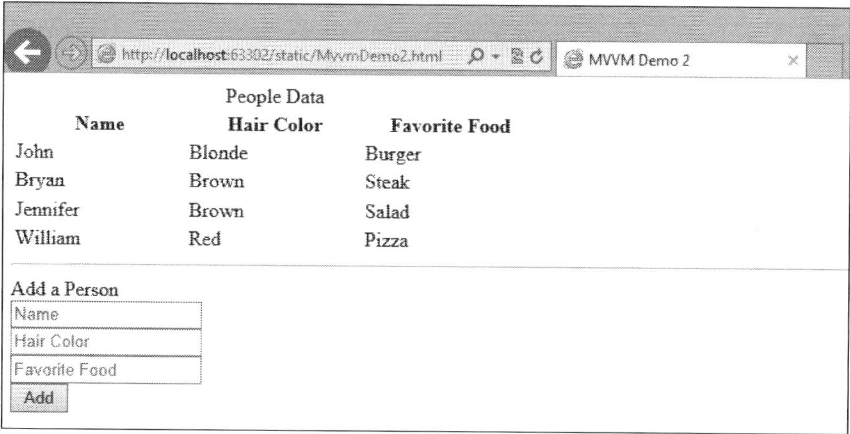

Using observable properties in the View

We just saw how simple it is to add new data to observable collections in the View-Model, and how this causes any data-bound elements to immediately show that new data. Let's add some more functionality to illustrate working with individual elements and see how their observable values can update content on the page.

To demonstrate this new functionality, I have added some columns to the table:

```
<table>
<caption>People Data</caption>
<thead>
<tr>
<th>Name</th>
<th>Hair Color</th>
<th>Favorite Food</th>
<th></th>
<th>Live Data</th>
</tr>
</thead>
<tbody data-template="row-template" data-bind="source: people"></
tbody>
</table>
```

The first new column has no heading text but will contain a button on the page for each of the table rows. The second new column will be displaying the value of the "live data" in the View-Model for each of the objects displayed in the table.

Here is the updated row template:

```
<script id="row-template" type="text/x-kendo-template">
<tr>
<td><input type="text" data-bind="value: name" /></td>
<td><input type="text" data-bind="value: hairColor" /></td>
<td><input type="text" data-bind="value: favoriteFood" /></td>
<td><button type="button"
data-bind="click: deletePerson">Delete</button></td>
<td><span data-bind="text: name"></span> - 
<span data-bind="text: hairColor"></span> - 
<span data-bind="text: favoriteFood"></span></td>
</tr>
</script>
```

Notice that I have replaced all of the simple `text data-bind` attributes with input elements and `valuedata-bind` attributes. I also added a button with a `clickdata-bind` attribute and a column that displays the text of the three properties so that you can see the observable behavior in real time.

The View-Model gets a new method for the delete button:

```
deletePerson: function (e) {
var person = e.data;
var people = this.get("people");
var index = people.indexOf(person);
people.splice(index, 1);
}
```

When this function is called through the binding that Kendo UI has created, it passes an event argument, here called `e`, into the function that contains a data property. This data property is a reference to the model object that was used to render the specific row of data. In this function, I created a `person` variable for a reference to the person in this row and a reference to the `people` array; we then use the index of this person to splice it out of the array. When you click on the **Delete** button, you can observe the table reacting immediately to the change.

Here is the full source code of the updated View-Model:

```
<script id="row-template" type="text/x-kendo-template">
<tr>
<td><input type="text" data-bind="value: name" /></td>
```

```
<td><input type="text" data-bind="value: hairColor" /></td><td><input
type="text" data-bind="value: favoriteFood" /></td>
<td><button type="button" data-bind="click:
deletePerson">Delete</button></td>
<td><span data-bind="text: name"></span> - 
<span data-bind="text: hairColor"></span> - 
<span data-bind="text: favoriteFood"></span></td></tr>
</script><script type="text/javascript">
var viewModel = kendo.observable({
people: [
        {name: "John", hairColor: "Blonde", favoriteFood: "Burger"},
        {name: "Bryan", hairColor: "Brown", favoriteFood: "Steak"},
        {name: "Jennifer", hairColor: "Brown", favoriteFood: "Salad"}
            ],
personName: "",
personHairColor: "",
personFavFood: "",
addPerson: function () {
this.get("people").push({
name: this.get("personName"),
hairColor: this.get("personHairColor"),
favoriteFood: this.get("personFavFood")
                });
this.set("personName", "");
this.set("personHairColor", "");
this.set("personFavFood", "");
            },
deletePerson: function (e) {
var person = e.data;
var people = this.get("people");
var index = people.indexOf(person);
people.splice(index, 1);
            }
        });
kendo.bind($("body"), viewModel);
</script>
</body>
</html>
```

Here is a screenshot of the new page:

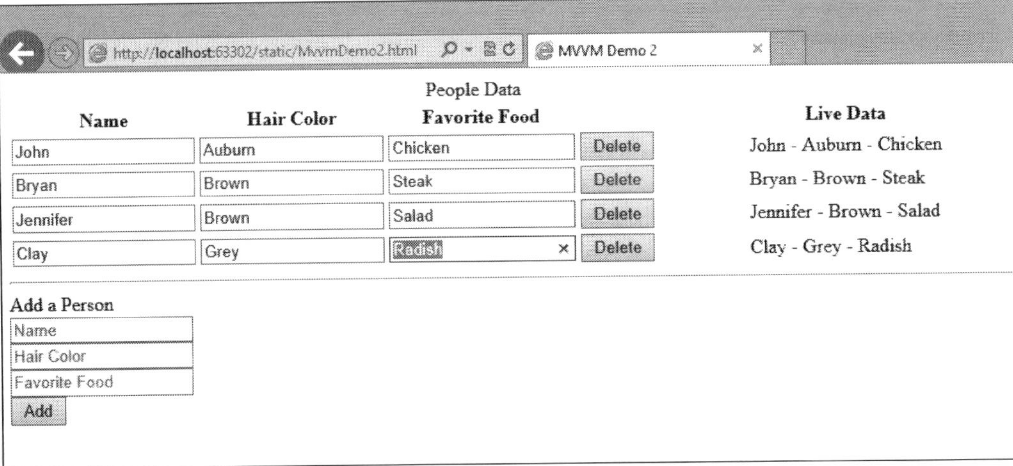

Click on the **Delete** button to see an entry disappear. You can also see that I have added a new person to the table and that I have made changes in the input boxes of the table and that those changes immediately show up on the right-hand side. This indicates that the View-Model is keeping track of the live data and updating its bindings accordingly.

Making better use of observable arrays

In the last several examples, we have been using an array called `people` to show a dynamic table with Kendo UI bindings. This has worked fine so far, but with more complicated Models and functionality we can run into a wall, so to speak. For example, there is no way to have the "live data" come from the Model objects themselves; we had to concatenate three `span` elements in the template to form the final output. This could cause problems for more complicated and full-featured pages, where you may have an array of Model objects that need to be able to handle events and calculate values on their own, instead of at the View-Model level.

Modify the row template like this:

```
<script id="row-template" type="text/x-kendo-template">
<tr>
<td><input type="text" data-bind="value: name.stuff" /></td>
<td><input type="text" data-bind="value: hairColor.stuff" /></td>
<td><input type="text" data-bind="value: favoriteFood.stuff" /></td>
<td><button type="button"
data-bind="click: deletePerson">Delete</button></td>
<td data-bind="text: dataString"></td>
```

```
</tr>
</script>
```

We have changed the property names in the `data-bind` declaration so that they point to an inner property that we created for them, called `stuff`. The important part of the example is that we also changed the final column to point to a calculated value function called `dataString`. The meaning of this will become clear as we continue. Next, update the JavaScript block for the View-Model so that it looks like this:

```
<script type="text/javascript">
var viewModel = kendo.observable({
people: [],
personName: "",
personHairColor: "",
personFavFood: "",
addPerson: function () {
this.get("people").push(new person({
name: this.get("personName"),
hairColor: this.get("personHairColor"),
favoriteFood: this.get("personFavFood")
            }));
this.set("personName", "");
this.set("personHairColor", "");
this.set("personFavFood", "");
        },
deletePerson: function (e) {
var person = e.data;
var people = this.get("people");
var index = people.indexOf(person);
people.splice(index, 1);
        }
    });

var person = function (data) {
var self = this;
this.name = kendo.observable({ stuff: data.name });
this.hairColor = kendo.observable({ stuff: data.hairColor });
this.favoriteFood = kendo.observable({ stuff: data.favoriteFood });
this.dataString = function () {
returnself.name.get("stuff") + " - " +
self.hairColor.get("stuff") + " - " +
self.favoriteFood.get("stuff");
        }
    };
```

```
viewModel.get("people").push(new person({ name: "John",
hairColor: "Blonde",
favoriteFood: "Burger" }));
viewModel.get("people").push(new person({ name: "Bryan",
hairColor: "Brown",
favoriteFood: "Steak" }));
viewModel.get("people").push(new person({ name: "Jennifer",
hairColor:"Brown",
favoriteFood: "Salad" }));

kendo.bind($("body"), viewModel);
</script>
```

We made several changes, so let's step through them carefully. The first important change is right at the top, where we have replaced the static array declaration with the `people` property as an empty array with the bracket notation `[]`. Secondly, we created a new type of object called `person` and gave it a constructor function with its own internal observable objects. Each of these observable objects needs an object to manage, simple values don't work quite as well, so we made an arbitrary property for them called `stuff`. The only thing going on here is that the properties of this new `person` object type are pointing to observable objects instead of simple data. Why? Because if the properties are not observable, then the View-Model will not be notified of the change and the user interface will not be updated through data-binding.

The purpose of this change is to enable calculated values local to the specific instance of the object, which we have done with the `dataString` function inside of the `person` constructor. As you can see, the `dataString` function extracts the values from the locally observable properties and returns them as a formatted string. This is significant because it means that every `person` object has its own copy of this function, and that the View-Model itself is not involved in this calculation. This means that each object inside of the View-Model's `people` array can observe changes specific to itself and calculate values based on those changes. This type of Model can become very useful for advanced scenarios.

After declaring the `person` constructor function, we manually added some new `person` objects to the `people` array and then called `kendo.bind()` as usual. When rendered, the page looks and behaves just as it did in the previous example, but now the Model objects are smarter. Here is the full source code of the updated View-Model:

```
<script id="row-template" type="text/x-kendo-template">
<tr>
<td><input type="text" data-bind="value: name.d" /></td>
<td><input type="text" data-bind="value: hairColor.d" /></td>
<td><input type="text" data-bind="value: favoriteFood.d" /></td>
<td><button type="button"
```

```
data-bind="click: deletePerson">Delete</button></td>
<td data-bind="text: dataString"></td>
</tr>
</script>
<script type="text/javascript">
var viewModel = kendo.observable({
people: [],
personName: "",
personHairColor: "",
personFavFood: "",
addPerson: function () {
this.get("people").push(new person({
name: this.get("personName"),
hairColor: this.get("personHairColor"),
favoriteFood: this.get("personFavFood")
                }));
this.set("personName", "");
this.set("personHairColor", "");
this.set("personFavFood", "");
            },
deletePerson: function (e) {
var person = e.data;
var people = this.get("people");
var index = people.indexOf(person);
people.splice(index, 1);
            }
        });

var person = function (data) {
var self = this;
            this.name = kendo.observable({ d: data.name });
this.hairColor = kendo.observable({ d: data.hairColor });
this.favoriteFood = kendo.observable({ d: data.favoriteFood });
this.dataString = function () {
returnself.name.get("d") + " - " +
self.hairColor.get("d") + " - " + self.favoriteFood.get("d");
            }
        };

viewModel.get("people").push(new person({
name: "John", hairColor: "Blonde",
favoriteFood: "Burger"
        }));
viewModel.get("people").push(new person({
```

```
    name: "Bryan", hairColor: "Brown",
    favoriteFood: "Steak"
            }));
    viewModel.get("people").push(new person({
    name: "Jennifer", hairColor: "Brown",
    favoriteFood: "Salad"
            }));

    kendo.bind($("body"), viewModel);
    </script>
    </body>
    </html>
```

And the output when the page is run:

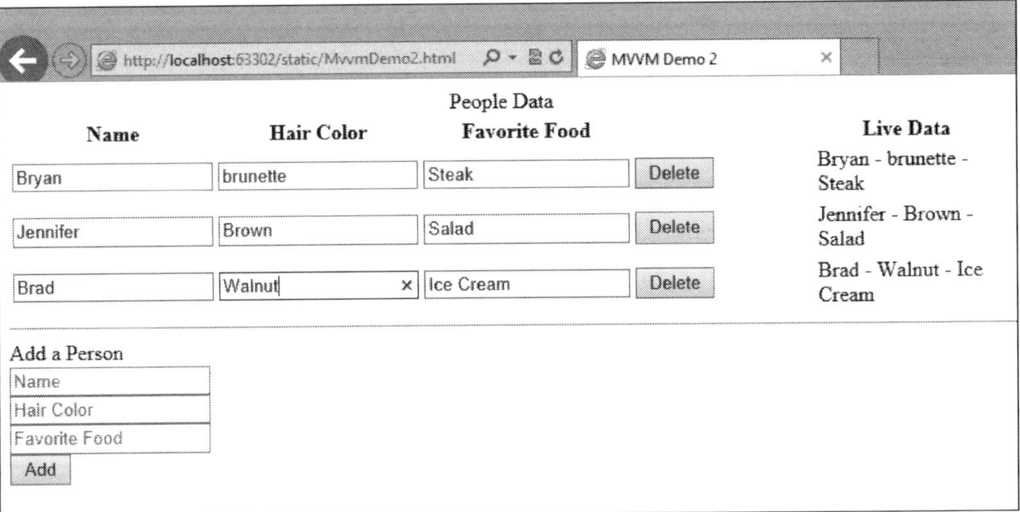

Data-bind properties for Kendo MVVM

There are thirteen different types of values that can be used inside of the `data-bind` Kendo UI attribute. Here is a summary of their definitions and uses.

The attr property

The `attr` property is used to bind the value of a View-Model to a specific HTML attribute of a page element. For example, this is very useful for setting attributes such as the `src` for an image or the `href` for an anchor tag.

```
... //View-Model definition
imageSource: 'http://www.images.com/randomImage.jpg',
...
<img data-bind="attr: {src: imageSource}" />
```

A binding like this would guarantee that the image would change along with the View-Model to allow for dynamically loading or changing images on a web page.

Note that the `attr` property can set multiple attributes at once when they are separated by commas like this:

```
data-bind="attr: {attribute1: value, attribute2: value, attribute3:
value, ...}"
```

This property can be used with any HTML element and with any valid HTML attribute (including custom HTML5 `data-*` attributes).

The checked property

The `checked` property is used to bind the checked status of an input element with type `checkbox` or `radio`. For checkboxes, the data-bound property can be either a Boolean (`true`/`false`) value or an array. For radio selections, the property needs to be a string. For example:

```
isChecked: true, ...

// Simple Boolean binding
// The data-bound property will be updated when the user clicks the
checkbox

<input type="checkbox" data-bind="checked: isChecked" />


animals: ["cow", "pig"], ...

// Array binding for checkboxes
// The array will change based on which checkboxes are checked by the
user
// The initial page will show both the "cow" and "pig" inputs as
checked

<input type="checkbox" value="horse" data-bind="checked: animals" />
<input type="checkbox" value="cow" data-bind="checked: animals" />
<input type="checkbox" value="pig" data-bind="checked: animals" />

tablet: "surface", ...
```

```
// String binding for radio buttons
// The string will change based on which radio option is selected by
the user
// The initial page will show the input with the value "surface" as
checked

<input type="radio" name="tablet" value="surface" data-bind="checked:
tablet" />
<input type="radio" name="tablet" value="ipad" data-bind="checked:
tablet" />
<input type="radio" name="tablet" value="android" data-bind="checked:
tablet" />
```

As you will see later, the `checked` binding can be very useful in conjunction with the `visible/invisible` bindings so that the checkboxes or radio buttons on the page will dynamically show or hide other portions of the page.

The click property

The `click` property binds the click event of a button to a function inside of the View-Model. It is a shortcut to the `events` binding that we will see later. Unlike a traditional click event wire-up, the Kendo UI framework will pass context data to the event handler to allow for a richer event-handling experience. For example, when a click event is bound within a row template, the event argument passed to the event handler will have access to the item from the source collection. This allows the event handler to operate against that Model data directly without any further DOM exploration and keeps all of the observable functionality in place.

Technically, Kendo UI supplies the DOM event wrapped in a jQuery event object to the event handler indicated in the binding, but it also manages the data property like we talked about in the previous paragraph. Since the event argument is still connected to the DOM event, you can call `stopPropogation()` and `preventDefault()` on that event argument to stop the DOM from performing any other actions in the page.

We already saw examples of the `click` binding in our code samples above so here are some of the snippets that we used there:

```
// Our example row template that included the click binding that will
// pass the data property to the event handler
<script id="row-template" type="text/x-kendo-template">
<tr>
<td><input type="text" data-bind="value: name.d" /></td>
<td><input type="text" data-bind="value: hairColor.d" /></td>
```

```
<td><input type="text" data-bind="value: favoriteFood.d" /></td>
<td><button type="button"
data-bind="click: deletePerson">Delete</button></td>
<td data-bind="text: dataString"></td>
</tr>
</script>

// Our example form that included the click binding that has no
// relevant data property to pass to the event handler
<form>
<header>Add a Person</header>
<input type="text" name="personName" placeholder="Name"
data-bind="value: personName" /><br />
<input type="text" name="personHairColor" placeholder="Hair Color"
data-bind="value: personHairColor" /><br />
<input type="text" name="personFavFood" placeholder="Favorite Food"
data-bind="value: personFavFood" /><br />
<button type="button" data-bind="click: addPerson">Add</button>
</form>

...

// This version of the click binding does not use the event argument
addPerson: function () {
this.get("people").push(new person({
name: this.get("personName"),
hairColor: this.get("personHairColor"),
favoriteFood: this.get("personFavFood")
    }));
this.set("personName", "");
this.set("personHairColor", "");
this.set("personFavFood", "");
},

// This version of the click binding uses the event argument to
// current data item from the source collection
deletePerson: function (e) {
var person = e.data;
var people = this.get("people");
var index = people.indexOf(person);
people.splice(index, 1);
}
```

The custom property

Kendo UI allows for custom bindings so that you can create custom behaviors related to the View-Model of your page. An example on the Kendo UI documentation site uses a jQuery UI `slideDown` and `slideUp` call based on a Boolean value in the View-Model as a short-cut to some UI transformations. Refer to the Kendo UI documentation for a more detailed API reference for custom bindings.

The disabled/enabled properties

The `disabled` and `enabled` bindings work on input, select, and text area HTML elements. Just as their names would indicate, they disable or enable the bound elements respectively. These bindings are designed for use with Boolean properties, but for the sake of JavaScript loose-typing they will consider the non-Boolean values `0`, `null`, `undefined`, and `""` (empty string) as `false` and all other non-Boolean values as `true`. An example code is as follows:

```
allowEdit: false, ...

// This input element will be initially disabled until the
View-Model's allowEdit
// View-Model's allowEdit property is changed to true
<input type="text" data-bind="enabled: allowEdit" />
```

The events property

The `events` binding is a convenient way to wire-up event handlers in your View-Model to events on HTML elements in your View. The click binding, as we saw above, is a specific example of this pattern and operates in exactly the same way. For example:

```
<button type="button" data-bind="events: {blur: blurHandler, click:
clickHandler,
mouseover: mouseHandler,...}">Interactive Button</button>
```

The html/text properties

The `html` binding sets the `innerHtml` content of an HTML element using the value of a property from the View-Model. This binding differs from the `text` binding in that it does not encode HTML tags before generating its output, which means that HTML tags in the View-Model property will be rendered as HTML instead of as text (which is probably what you want if you are using the `html` binding). An example:

```
spanContent: "<strong>Some Content</strong>",...
```

```
<span data-bind="html: spanContent"></span>
```

This would generate output like this in the source of the rendered page:

```
<span><strong>Some Content</strong></span>
```

The `text` binding works in exactly the same way as the `html` binding, except that it sets the simple text between element tags and it does encode HTML before output, so do not put HTML in the property containing the text to display unless you want the tags to show as part of the text output.

The invisible/visible properties

The `invisible` and `visible` bindings work on HTML elements that you want to either show or hide dynamically. Just as their names indicate, they make the given element invisible or visible respectively. These bindings are designed for use with Boolean properties, but for the sake of JavaScript loose-typing they will consider the non-Boolean values `0`, `null`, `undefined`, and `""` (empty string) as false and all other non-Boolean values as true. An example code is as follows:

```
showDetails: true, ...

// This element will be initially visible unless the View-Model's
// showDetails property is changed to false
<pdata-bind="visible: showDetails">All sorts of text here...</p>
```

As mentioned earlier, it can be very useful to connect the value of a checkbox or a radio button with the visible status of other elements on a page. This allows you to change what data is displayed on the page based on selections that the user makes. Here is a simple example:

```
showDetails: false, ...

<input type="checkbox" data-bind="checked: showDetails"
name="showDetails" />

<p data-bind="visible: showDetails">All sorts of text and details…</p>
```

This code will make the checkbox control the visibility of the paragraph element that would contain some text that you only want displayed if the checkbox is checked. This is probably simpler than code you would use in a normal web application, but it illustrates the basic point.

The source property

The source binding is designed to render a Kendo UI template using the value of a View-Model property. If the property is an array, then the Kendo UI framework will render the template for each element of the array. This template is specified by the data-template attribute attached to the HTML element in question, and should indicate the template by its `id` attribute. When the templates are rendered, they will be placed directly beneath the element with the source attribute in the DOM. This is why you would place the source attribute on the `tbody` element of a table so that the `tr` elements in the Kendo UI template will be rendered and placed directly beneath it in the DOM so that they will appear as rows in a `table`. This binding can work on any element where it makes sense to include a collection of lower level elements, a `table` is just a natural example; other good uses would be `ul`, `ol`, and `select` elements.

We saw the source binding with a table already in our code samples. I will paste a little of it here as a reminder:

```
// table with the source binding on the tbody element
<table>
<caption>People Data</caption>
<thead>
<tr>
<th>Name</th>
<th>Hair Color</th>
<th>Favorite Food</th>
<th></th>
<th>Live Data</th>
</tr>
</thead>
<tbody data-template="row-template" data-bind="source: people"></
tbody>
</table>
...
// the template that creates the rows
<script id="row-template" type="text/x-kendo-template">
<tr>
<td><input type="text" data-bind="value: name.d" /></td>
<td><input type="text" data-bind="value: hairColor.d" /></td>
<td><input type="text" data-bind="value: favoriteFood.d" /></td>
<td><button type="button"
data-bind="click: deletePerson">Delete</button></td>
<td data-bind="text: dataString"></td>
</tr>
</script>
```

This is a good example of using the `source` binding with an array of objects. The `source` binding can also be used with an array of simple values, in which case you would use the keyword `this` inside the template instead of a property name inside an object:

```
<script id="row-template" type="text/x-kendo/template">
<tr>
<td data-bind="text: this"></td>
</tr>
</script>
```

The `source` binding can also be used with a single object (as opposed to an array) in which case it behaves just like binding to an array with a single element. You can also bind to the View-Model itself if you want to access a single property within it as the `source`, in which case you reference the `source` as a property of the `this` keyword:

```
// table with the source binding on the tbody element
<table>
<caption>People Data</caption>
<thead>
<tr>
<th>Name</th>
<th>Hair Color</th>
<th>Favorite Food</th>
<th></th>
<th>Live Data</th>
</tr>
</thead>
<tbody data-template="row-template" data-bind="source: viewModel"></
tbody>
</table>
...
// the template that creates the rows
<script id="row-template" type="text/x-kendo-template">
<tr>
<td><input type="text" data-bind="value: this.name" /></td>
<td><input type="text" data-bind="value: this.hairColor" /></td>
<td><input type="text" data-bind="value: this.favoriteFood" /></td>
<td><button type="button"
data-bind="click: deletePerson">Delete</button></td>
<td data-bind="text: dataString"></td>
</tr>
</script>
...
<script type="text/javascript">
```

```
var viewModel = kendo.observable({
name: "john",
hairColor: "blonde",
favoriteFood: "burger"
    });
...
</script>
```

Notice how the structure is the same as if you were referencing a single object, but we are using the `this` keyword since we are referencing the View-Model directly.

When binding to a `select` element, note that you can use an array of simple values or an array of objects. If you just an array of objects, use the `data-text-field` to indicate which property contains the text to display within each `option`, and use the `data-value-field` to indicate which property contains the value within each `option` element.

The style property

The style binding is a great way to create a dynamic relationship between data in your View-Model and CSS styles on your page. It is a very simple binding that creates a direct relationship between the properties in your View-Model and the styles in your markup. An example:

```
<span data-bind="style: {color: myColor, fontWeight: myFontWeight}" />
<script type="text/javascript">
var viewModel = kendo.observable({
myColor: "orange",
myFontWeight: "bold"
    });
</script>
```

Obviously, this becomes a lot more useful if you tie some logic to the styles you are using in your page, such as changing the styles for alternating table rows or changing the color of text if it meets some special criteria (such as an overdrawn balance looking red).

Notice that we used the style property `fontWeight` which should look strange to you. If you need to reference styles that normally contain a hyphen (`font-weight`), you need to use a camel-cased version in the binding so that it works as a valid JavaScript property name. So `font-weight` becomes `fontWeight` in the actual binding statement.

Finally, if you set the style value to an empty string, it will reset the value back to its original setting.

The value property

The `value` binding works in a very similar way to the `text` binding, except that it sets the value of an input element instead of the text of a display element. The bound value in the View-Model is updated on blur by default, such as when you press *Tab* to leave the input element on the page. If you want the View-Model property to be updated based on a different DOM event, you can set that in the `data-value-update` property on the same element as the binding. We have already seen the use of the value binding in our code samples. Here is an example of using the data-value-update binding to customize some behavior:

```
// the row template
<script id="row-template" type="text/x-kendo-template">
<tr>
<td><input type="text" data-bind="value: name"
            data-value-update="keyup" /></td>
</tr>
</script>
```

Remember that this is a two-way binding and is most useful for retrieving data from the users as they fill out a form.

Much like the `checked` binding that we saw above, the `value` binding works with `select` elements in a similar way. By binding the `value` of a `select` element to a string property, it will be bound to the value of the selected `option` element inside of the `select` element if the options have values, or the `text` of the selected `option` element if no `value` is present. Here is how this would look in the markup:

```
// Binding using the value, the selectedCar property will be bound to
the numbers
<select data-bind="value: selectedCar">
<option value="1">Honda</option>
<option value="2">Toyota</option>
<option value="3">Ford</option>
</select>

// Binding using the text, the selectedCar property will be bound to
the text
// between the option tags
<select data-bind="value: selectedCar">
<option>Honda</option>
<option>Toyota</option>
<option>Ford</option>
</select>
```

Of course, you can also bind both the `source` and the `value` of a `select` element to the View-Model. You are not limited to a single binding in the `data-bind` property. Also, as you might expect, you can bind the value of a multiple-select element if you are binding it to an array (instead of a simple string) so that it can hold multiple values.

Declarative widgets through Data-Role MVVM attributes

Kendo's MVVM also allows declarative initialization of widgets through the `data-role` attribute. Declarative initialization is a different method of creating Kendo widgets by using the `data-role` attribute instead of setting up the widget through JavaScript. This is not as flexible as the JavaScript method, but it does allow for a lot of functionality with almost no code at all. Here is a section of code taken from the Kendo UI Web website that shows some basic set up as an introduction. The full details for these widgets can be found there.

```
<table>
<tr>
<th>Widget</th>
</tr>
<tr>
<td>
<h4>AutoComplete</h4>
<input data-role="autocomplete" data-text-field="name"
data-bind="source: colors, value: autoCompleteValue"/>
</td>
</tr>
<tr>
<td>
<h4>ComboBox</h4>
<select data-role="combobox"
data-text-field="name" data-value-field="value" data-bind="source:
colors, value: comboBoxValue"></select>
</td>
</tr>
<tr>
<td>
<h4>DatePicker</h4>
<input data-role="datepicker" data-bind="value: datePickerValue" />
</td>
</tr>
```

```
<tr>
<td>
<h4>DropDownList</h4>
<select data-role="dropdownlist"
data-text-field="name" data-value-field="value" data-bind="source:
colors, value: dropDownListValue"></select>
</td>
</tr>
<tr>
<td>
<h4>Grid</h4>
<div data-role="grid"
data-sortable="true" data-editable="true"
data-columns='["Name", "Price", "UnitsInStock",
{"command": "destroy"}]'
data-bind="source: gridSource"></div>
</td>
</tr>
<tr>
<td>
<h4>NumericTextBox</h4>
<input data-role="numerictextbox" data-format="c"
data-bind="value: numericTextBoxValue" />
</td>
</tr>
<tr>
<td>
<h4>Slider</h4>
<input data-role="slider" data-bind="value: sliderValue" />
</td>
</tr>
<tr>
<td>
<h4>TimePicker</h4>
<input data-role="timepicker" data-bind="value: timePickerValue" />
</td>
</tr>
<tr>
<td>
<h4>TabStrip</h4>
<div data-role="tabstrip" data-animation="false">
<ul>
<li class="k-state-active">First</li>
<li>Second</li>
</ul>
<div>
<h4>First page:</h4>
```

```
Pick a time: <input data-role="timepicker"
data-bind="value: timePickerValue"/>
</div>
<div>
<h4>Second page:</h4>
Time is: <span data-bind="text:
displayTimePickerValue"></span>
</div>
</div>
</td>
</tr>
<tr>
<td>
<h4>TreeView</h4>
<div data-role="treeview"
data-animation="false"
data-drag-and-drop="true"
data-bind="source: treeviewSource"></div>
</td>
</tr>
</table>
```

This is a great example of using multiple bindings together, and of which bindings rightly pertain to which widgets.

Summary

The Kendo MVVM framework brings complicated interactive JavaScript into the realm of simple HTML attributes, templates, and View-Model functions. It is a very powerful feature and is one that you are likely to become very accustomed to using in your web pages. Keep in mind as you develop code that Kendo is a system in which features can be built together very nicely; for example, you could use a Kendo data source object as the source binding for a `table` or `select` list.

When you have powerful tools like this within your reach, you will find that function-rich pages become normal instead of exceptionally difficult and that your programming experience will be better than ever. In the next chapter, we will learn about the Kendo UI HTML Editor widget. This widget adds a full-featured HTML editing box to your web pages so that users can create content in a friendly input area with formatting, images, and hyperlinks. It is especially useful if users can contribute content on your site, such as with a blog or a forum.

5 HTML Editor and Custom Tools

Interactive HTML editors are an important part of any website that encourages users to post their own written content. Forums and blogs frequently offer these controls so that users can create content with attractive styling just as if it was created in a word processor. It is especially useful for users who are unfamiliar with how to format text using HTML tags or CSS styles. For that matter, even users who are familiar with HTML and CSS can appreciate not having to type it all out. This chapter will introduce the following topics:

- Kendo Editor widget basics
- Configuring the Editor widget tools
- Using HTML snippets
- Customizing the Editor widget tools

Understanding the HTML Editor

The Kendo Editor widget creates an area on a web page where a user can create formatted text content. To see a basic example in action, copy this code into a new HTML page called `HtmlEditor.html`. This will allow you to see the widget in use on an actual page and will provide a starting point for the rest of the chapter.

```
<!DOCTYPE html>
<html>
<head>
<title></title>
<script src="/Scripts/kendo/jquery.js"></script>
<script src="/Scripts/kendo/kendo.all.js"></script>
<link href="/Content/kendo/kendo.common.css" rel="stylesheet" />
```

```
<link href="/Content/kendo/kendo.default.css" rel="stylesheet" />
<style type="text/css">
textarea {
width: 100%;
height: 300px;
        }
</style>
</head>
<body>
<textarea id="editor"></textarea>
<script type="text/javascript">
        $(document).ready(function () {
            $("#editor").kendoEditor();
        });
</script>
</body>
</html>
```

This is assuming all default settings since no settings or options are explicitly set.

Note that we have bound the `kendoEditor` function to a `textarea` element, this is important and you should always bind HTML Editor controls to a `textarea` element so that the functionality can degrade gracefully for browsers that may not support the required JavaScript features.

If we had implemented this using ASP.NET MVC, it would look like this in the view:

```
@using Kendo.Mvc.UI;

@{
ViewBag.Title = "Html Editor";
}
<style type="text/css">
textarea {
width: 100%;
height: 300px;
    }
</style>

<h2>Html Editor</h2>
@(Html.Kendo().Editor()
        .Name("htmlEditor"))
```

Note again that the Kendo MVC extensions will generate the HTML Editor within a `textarea` element, which is why the style declaration for `textarea` elements works in the page output.

Regardless of whether you use HTML or an MVC view, this is how the page output looks with all defaults assumed. I have added some text using the HTML Editor features to illustrate the purpose of the control:

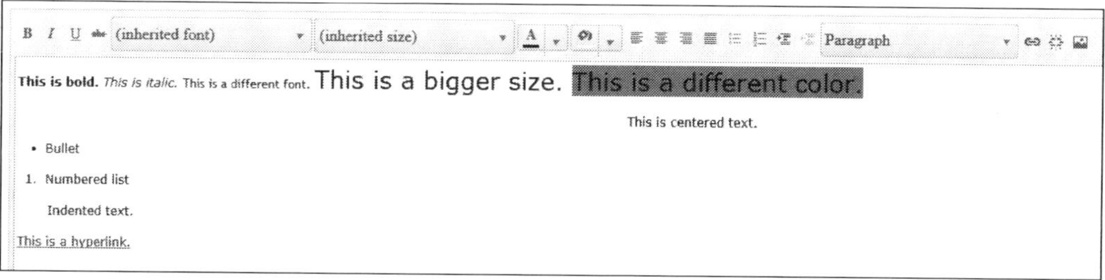

Take a look at all of the tool buttons across the top of the Editor widget. Click on them as you type text to observe what they do. Also, note that the different buttons generated by the Kendo HTML Editor all support the HTML `tabindex` so you can use the *Tab* key and the *Shift* + *Tab* key combination to move back and forth respectively between the commands in order if you want.

For many sites, this is probably sufficient functionality already. To use the formatted text that the user has created, simply retrieve the value of the `textarea` element and it will contain both the content and HTML markup.

Don't forget to check your input

Since you are openly allowing the user to post HTML markup within the content of his or her data, take extra care to sanitize the input before you place it into a database or load it into another page. Even though the HTML markup generated by the Kendo tool is safe, you can never trust the final markup that is transmitted to the server from the user's browser and must always treat it as if it may contain harmful code.

Before you use the formatted text, however, you also need to check whether the value you are processing has been HTML encoded or not. If you retrieve the raw value of the `textarea` element from the DOM, you will get HTML encoded data. This means that <strong>text</strong> becomes <strong>text</strong> which may or may not be what you actually want.

To get the non-HTML encoded data, you need to call the `value()` function on the `kendoEditor` object by using code like this:

```
var editor = $("#editor").data("kendoEditor");
var nonEncodedText = editor.value();
```

But again, you need to be careful with what you are doing. You cannot post non-HTML encoded data like this to most web servers without bypassing some important security measures. The safer option would be to post the data to the web server in an HTML encoded form, then decode it and sanitize on the server-side before using it. This way you can still rightly reject some potentially malicious code from the page outright before starting the process of interpreting the user input.

Here is an updated page with some buttons that show you the different outputs from the DOM `val()` function versus the `kendoEditor value()` function:

```
<!DOCTYPE html>
<html>
<head>
<title></title>
<scriptsrc="/Scripts/kendo/jquery.js"></script>
<scriptsrc="/Scripts/kendo/kendo.all.js"></script>
<link href="/Content/kendo/kendo.common.css" rel="stylesheet" />
<link href="/Content/kendo/kendo.default.css" rel="stylesheet" />
<style type="text/css">
textarea {
width: 100%;
height: 300px;
        }
</style>
</head>
<body>
<textarea id="editor"></textarea>
<button name="showKendoVal" id="showKendoVal" type="button">Show Kendo
Value</button><br />
<button name="showHtmlVal" id="showHtmlVal" type="button">Show HTML
Value</button>
<script type="text/javascript">
        $(document).ready(function () {
            $("#editor").kendoEditor();
            $("#showHtmlVal").click(function () {
alert($("#editor").val());
            });
var editor = $("#editor").data("kendoEditor");
            $("#showKendoVal").click(function () {
```

```
alert(editor.value());
            });
        });
</script>
</body>
</html>
```

This is the text retrieved from the Kendo `value()` function.

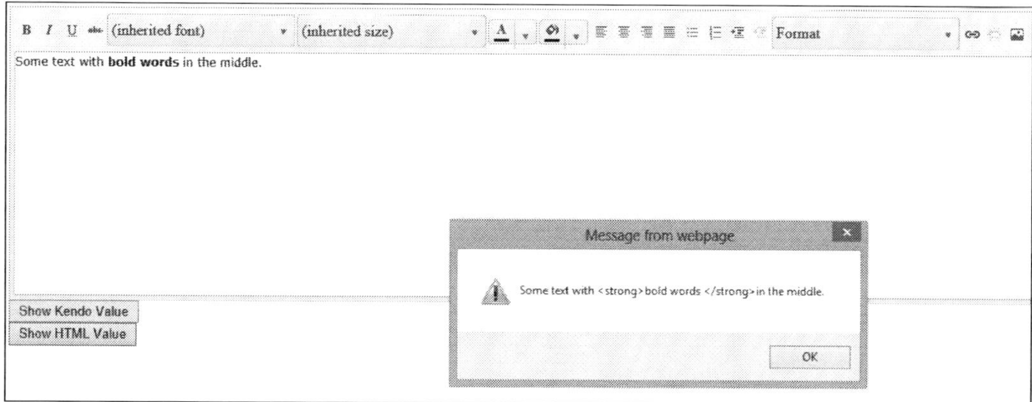

This is the text retrieved from the `innerHTML` of the Editor Widget.

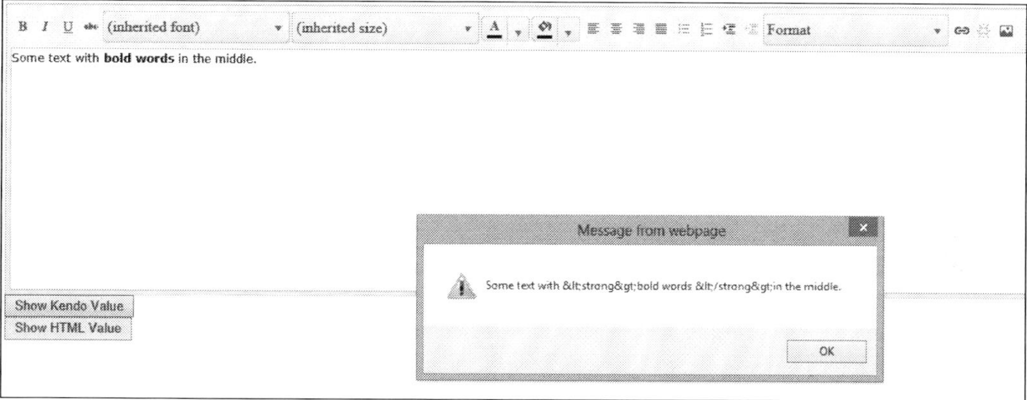

Adding and removing buttons from the toolbar

There are a few more standard tools that are available in the HTML Editor toolbar that are not included by default:

- Subscript
- Superscript
- View HTML

To include these tools, you need to specify the `tools` property when you create the `kendoEditor` object like this and list the specific tools that you want displayed:

```
$("#editor").kendoEditor({
tools: [
"bold",
"italic",
"underline",
"strikethrough",
"fontName",
"fontSize",
"foreColor",
"backColor",
"justifyLeft",
"justifyCenter",
"justifyRight",
"justifyFull",
"insertUnorderedList",
"insertOrderedList",
"indent",
"outdent",
"formatBlock",
"createLink",
"unlink",
"insertImage",
"subscript",
"superscript",
"viewHtml"
]
});
```

If you specify `tools` you need to name all the standard tools too, if you leave any out they will be removed from the toolbar on your page. Conversely, here is how you would add the subscript and superscript tools using ASP.NET MVC, curiously the `viewHtml` is not available in this method:

```
@(Html.Kendo().Editor()
.Name("htmlEditor")
.Tools(tools => tools
.SubScript()
.SuperScript()))
```

It could hardly be more concise, especially since with this method all of the default tools are assumed and you only have to add those that you want to include. If you wanted to clear out the default list of tools and then add only those that you want, you would first call `Clear()` within the `Tools` lambda expression and then add the specific tools that you wanted afterwards.

Here is the output with all of the standard tools included:

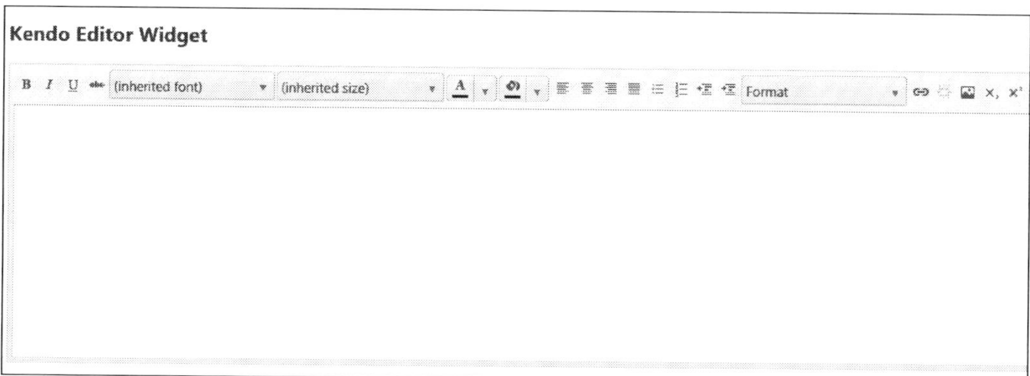

Adding the Styles tool

The Styles tool can be added to the HTML Editor toolbar to give the user access to some predefined styles that you have created. This could be useful if your users are using a special theme or if there are global styles that you want the users to have easy access to. To enable this, you configure the tools through the `kendoEditor` object and specify which options should appear in a drop-down list of styles. Here is an example:

```
$("#editor").kendoEditor({
tools: [
"bold",
"italic",
"underline",
```

```
"strikethrough",
"fontName",
"fontSize",
"foreColor",
"backColor",
"justifyLeft",
"justifyCenter",
"justifyRight",
"justifyFull",
"insertUnorderedList",
"insertOrderedList",
"indent",
"outdent",
"formatBlock",
"createLink",
"unlink",
"insertImage",
"subscript",
"superscript",
"viewHtml",
"style"
],
style:[
{text: "Big Blue", value:"bigBlue"},
{text: "Dark Grey", value:"darkGrey"}
],
stylesheets:[
"css/StyleTool.css"
]
});
```

Here are the contents of the `StyleTool.css` file:

```
.bigBlue {
font-size:large;
color:blue;
}
.darkGrey {
color:white;
background-color:#111111;
}
```

To make this work, I added the Style tool to the list of tools and then added the `style` configuration property and the optional `stylesheets` configuration property. The `style` configuration property defines the different options that appear in the Styles drop-down list, and which CSS classnames should be applied when these styles are selected for some text in the HTML editor `textarea`. The `stylesheets` configuration option allows you to import some additional stylesheets if they are necessary to display your custom styles.

Here is how you would implement these styles using ASP.NET MVC:

```
@(Html.Kendo().Editor()
.Name("htmlEditor")
.Tools(tools => tools
.SubScript()
.SuperScript()
.Styles(styles => styles
.Add("Big Blue", "bigBlue")
.Add("Dark Grey", "darkGrey"))
)
.StyleSheets(css =>css
.Add("/Content/StyleTool.css"))
)
```

Here is the output from this code:

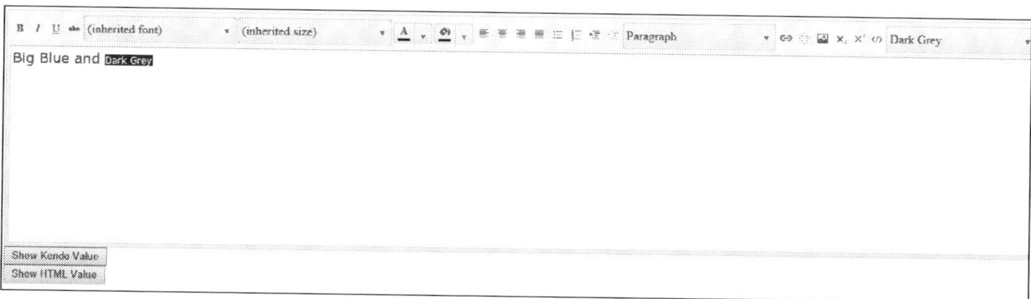

I included some styled text for the sake of demonstration and clicked on the **Styles** drop-down list to show how the options in that list are also styled to match their respective CSS classes.

Tool for inserting HTML snippets

The Snippets tool is a special toolbar option that is designed to insert predefined blocks of text into the editor window with a single click. It can be used for adding canned responses to common questions, signature blocks, time stamps, or any number of scenarios where pre-typed text would be useful. To enable this, just like the **Styles** option you configure the tools through the `kendoEditor` object and specify which options should appear in a drop-down list of styles. Here is an example:

```
$("#editor").kendoEditor({
tools: [
"bold",
"italic",
"underline",
"strikethrough",
"fontName",
"fontSize",
"foreColor",
"backColor",
"justifyLeft",
"justifyCenter",
"justifyRight",
"justifyFull",
"insertUnorderedList",
"insertOrderedList",
"indent",
"outdent",
"formatBlock",
"createLink",
"unlink",
"insertImage",
"subscript",
"superscript",
"viewHtml",
"style",
"insertHtml"
],
style:[
{text: "Big Blue", value:"bigBlue"},
{text: "Dark Grey", value:"darkGrey"}
],
stylesheets:[
"css/StyleTool.css"
],
```

```
insertHtml:[
{ text: "Today's date", value: "December 7, 2012" },
{ text: "Signature", value: "<p>Sincerely,<br/>John Adams</p>" }
]
});
```

Notice that this requires very little configuration to enable. We have included the `insertHtml` option in the `tools` configuration property and then added the `insertHtml` configuration property at the end of the `kendoEditor` definition. Inside the `insertHtml` configuration property, we have included an array of very simple objects. They define the title of each item that should appear in the drop-down list and the exact mark-up that should be pasted into the HTML Editor when the title is selected.

Here is how you would implement these Snippets using ASP.NET MVC:

```
@(Html.Kendo().Editor()
.Name("htmlEditor")
.Tools(tools => tools
.SubScript()
.SuperScript()
.Styles(styles => styles
.Add("Big Blue", "bigBlue")
.Add("Dark Grey", "darkGrey"))
.Snippets(snippets => snippets
.Add("Today's Date", DateTime.Today.Date.ToShortDateString())
.Add("Signature", "<p>Sincerely,<br/>John Adams</p>"))
)
.StyleSheets(css =>css
.Add("/Content/StyleTool.css"))
)
```

Here is the output from this code:

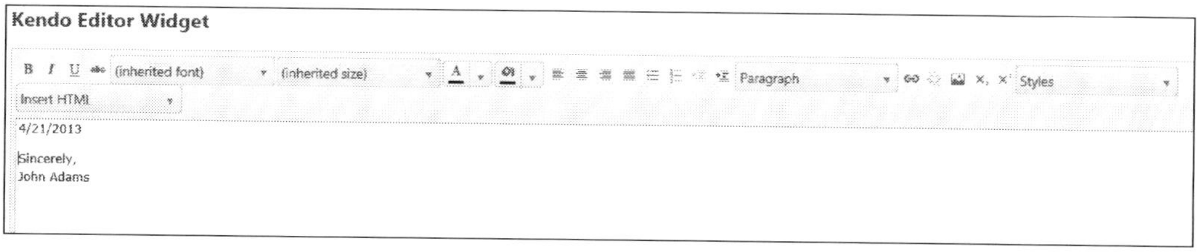

Customizing HTML Editor tools

The Kendo HTML Editor control allows you to add your own custom options to the toolbar. This is a remarkable touch of flexibility in the Kendo UI framework, and is something that you may find quite useful if the available built-in tools do not completely suit your needs. The HTML Editor can accept at least three types of custom tools. There could be more but these three appear in the published documentation on the Kendo UI website:

- Override Built-in Tools
- Custom Template Tools
- Custom In-line Tools

Drop-down list tools

If you would like to alter some of the built-in drop-down list tools, you can redefine which options appear inside them. This does not alter the nature of the tools or what the tools do. It only determines which options appear in the drop-down lists of the tools when you click on them. As an example, consider limiting which options appear in the font tool. By replacing the contents of the `items` array, you can customize exactly which options appear in the tool when it displays on the page:

```
$("#editor").kendoEditor({
tools: [
{
name: "fontName",
items:
[{text:"Garamond", value: "Garamond, serif"},
{text:"Calibri", value:"calibri, sans-serif"}]
}
]
});
```

This code sample demonstrates a customized `fontName` tool limited to two specific options. These two fonts are not included in the default `fontName` tool as we saw before, but you could also include default fonts in this custom list as well. Here is the output of the HTML Editor configured with this custom tool:

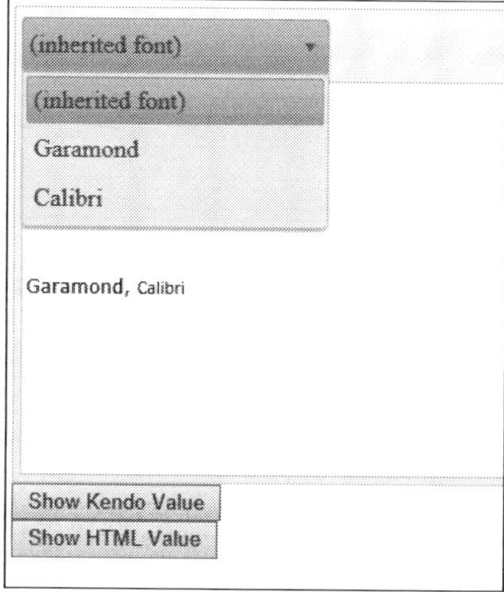

You will notice that the first two options in the list are not options that I defined in my source code—**inherited font** and **Verdana**. These appear because the HTML Editor is enabling the font on the page from the outer containing HTML markup and is calling it the **inherited font**. It then labels this same font by name in case that helps the user make a font selection, so **inherited font** and **Verdana** are actually both referring to the same font inherited from the outer HTML markup of the overall page.

This type of custom tool configuration should work with any of the custom tools that appear as a drop-down list such as the font name, font size, and format block tools.

Button tools

It seems unlikely that you will need to override many of these controls since it would probably be more effective to create your own tool instead. Just in case you wanted to see how it was done, however, here is a sample of code taken from the Kendo UI website that demonstrates how to replace the `viewHtml` tool with custom code that replaces its functionality:

```
<script type="text/x-kendo-template" id="viewHtml-template">
<div>
<textarea style="width: 400px; height: 300px;"></textarea>
<div class="viewHtml-actions">
<button class="k-button viewHtml-update">Update</button>
<button class="k-button viewHtml-cancel">Cancel</button>
</div>
</div>
</script>
<script>
```

```
$("#editor").kendoEditor({
tools:
[{
name: "viewHtml",
tooltip: "View HTML",
exec: function(e) {
var editor = $(this).data("kendoEditor");

var dialog = $($("#viewHtml-template").html())
.find("textarea").val(editor.value()).end()
.find(".viewHtml-update")
.click(function() {
editor.value(dialog.element
.find("textarea").val());
dialog.close();
})
.end()
.find(".viewHtml-cancel")
.click(function() {
dialog.close();
})
.end()
.kendoWindow({
modal: true,
title: "View HTML",
deactivate: function() {
dialog.destroy();
}
}).data("kendoWindow");

dialog.center().open();
}
}]
})
</script>
```

Here is the code as it appears on the page:

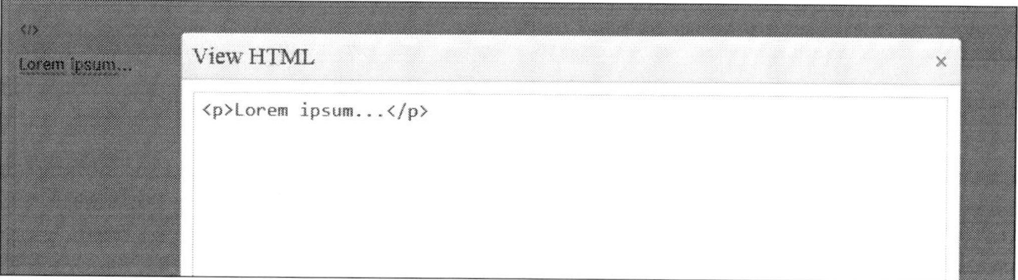

This source code includes both a template and the `kendoEditor` configuration. You can see that this code is basically opening a dialog, filling it with the content from the HTML Editor control, wiring up the events for the buttons inside the dialog, and then displaying it to the user. It gives an example, at least, of what overriding one of the built-in tools looks like. Note that the logic for the tool's execution is inside a property called `exec`; this is common for all custom button tools as well. The `tooltip` property is the text that is displayed when the mouse is hovered over the button in the toolbar.

Custom template tools

If you want to create your own custom tool that has a drop-down list of options, the custom template tool is the best choice. It allows you to use a Kendo UI template to markup how the tool should be displayed on the toolbar, and you can wire up its functionality separately so that your tool can do whatever it needs to do:

```
<textarea id="editor"></textarea>
<button name="showKendoVal" id="showKendoVal" type="button">Show Kendo
Value</button><br />
<button name="showHtmlVal" id="showHtmlVal" type="button">Show HTML
Value</button>
<script type="text/x-kendo-template" id="editorColor-template">
<label for="customTool">Editor BG:</label>
<select name="customTool" id="customTool"><option value=''>None</
option><option value="blue">Blue</option><option value="green">Green</
option></select>
</script>
<script type="text/javascript">
$(document).ready(function () {
$("#editor").kendoEditor({
tools: [
{
```

```
name: "editorBackground",
template: $("#editorColor-template").html()
}
]
});
$("#showHtmlVal").click(function () {
alert($("#editor").val());
});
var editor = $("#editor").data("kendoEditor");
$("#showKendoVal").click(function () {
alert(editor.value());
});
$("#customTool").change(function (e) {
$("#editor").data("kendoEditor").body.style.backgroundColor =
$("#customTool").val();
});
});
</script>
```

You can see the Kendo template where the `label` and `select` elements are declared. The behavior for the `select` element is defined in the jQuery code, but the custom drop-down list tool is added to the HTML Editor through the `tools` property.

Here is the output of the page with this custom tool:

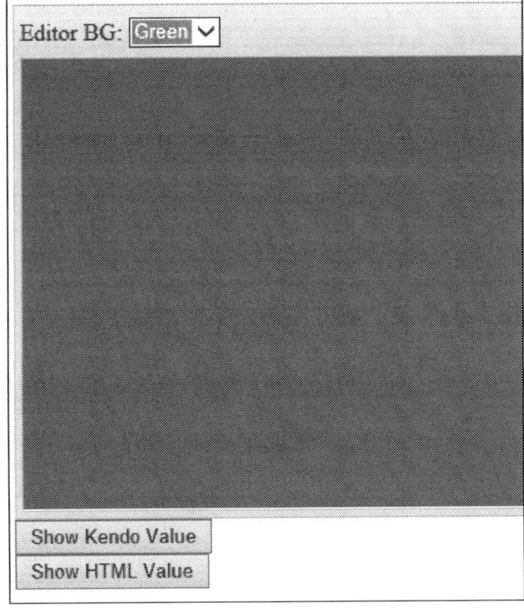

This is how you create custom tools that behave as a drop-down list. As you can see, the behavior is left completely up to you so you, can create whatever tool you need for your site's use case.

Custom in-line tools

If you want to create your own button tool on the toolbar, the in-line tool is the right choice. It allows you to define a tool name and the code to execute when that tool is selected from the toolbar.

```
$("#editor").kendoEditor({
tools: [
{
name: "addHr",
tooltip: "Insert Horizontal Rule",
exec: function (e) {
var editor = $(this).data("kendoEditor");
editor.exec("insertHtml", { value: "<hr/>" });
}
}
]
});
```

This code shows a custom tool called `addHr` that will add an `hr` element to the HTML Editor control when clicked. You can also see the use of the `exec` function on the `kendoEditor` where you can indicate one of the built-in functions/tools of the HTML Editor and then provide an object that supplies the parameters for it.

Here is the output from this code:

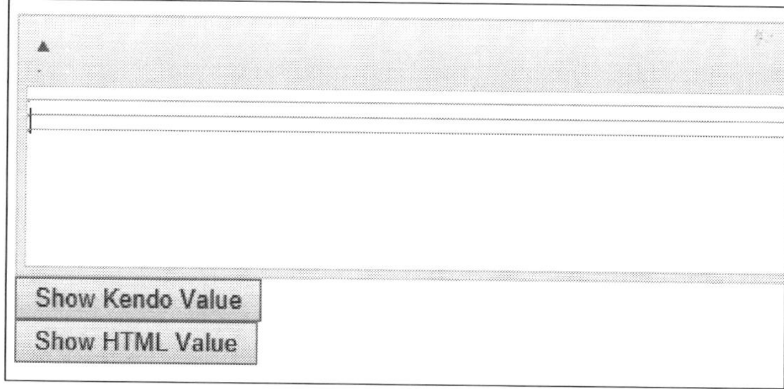

Using the HTML Editor API

The Kendo HTML Editor widget has a large set of API configuration options which allow you to fine-tune the widget to the specific needs and situation of your web page. It also exposes a set of methods and events that you can use to programmatically enable and react to functionality that the Edit widget exposes as it runs on the page. These options, taken together, are how you extend the Editor widget beyond its out of the box abilities.

Configuration options

We have already covered some of this in the material above, but here are the configuration options available for the HTML Editor control. As always, please check the Kendo UI Web documentation at `docs.kendoui.com/api/web/editor` for a more detailed list of configuration settings for these options, and to get the latest changes or additions to the API.

```
$("#editor").kendoEditor({
encoded: true,   // whether or not the editor should emit encoded html
                    tags
messages: {      // define custom labels for the built-in tools and
                    dialogs
bold: "Bold",
      …
   },
stylesheets: {…}, // see above, custom stylesheets to load for editor
tools: {…},    // see above, custom and built-in tools to display in the
                 editor
imageBrowser: {  // the imageBrowser tool can accept a custom
                    configuration
transport: {  // the endpoints to use for image operations
read: "imagebrowser/read",
destroy: "imagebrowser/destroy",
create: "imagebrowser/createDirectory",
uploadUrl: "imagebrowser/upload",
thumbnailUrl: "imagebrowser/thumbnail" // path for thumbnails of images
imageUrl: "/content/images/{0}",  // "{0}" is placeholder for virtual
                                        // path and image name
```

```
},
path: "/myInitialPath/",  // Initial path of images to display
fileTypes: ".png,.gif,.jpg,.jpeg",  // Allowed image file extensions
schema: {…}, // a schema can be defined to interpret data returned from
             // a remote endpoint when parsing data to display images
messages: {…} // custom messages for imageBrowser controls and dialogs
   }
});
```

Events

As with any HTML element or JavaScript object in a complex site, a web page fires events as the user performs certain actions within a page. By hooking into these events with your own JavaScript code, you can react to the page's changes and data in real time and organize the functionality of your page based on actions that the user performs. The HTML Editor control fires the following events in response to user actions:

- `change`: This event fires every time that the data inside of the Editor Widget changes.
- `execute`: This event fires fires when a tool is executed. It fires every time a tool bar button has been clicked and the code behind that button has been executed.
- `keydown`: The keydown event fires every time a user presses a key down while typing inside of the Editor Widget window. Hooking into this event allows you to respond to text as the user is typing it.
- `keyup`: The keydown event fires every time a user presses and releases a key while typing inside of the editor widget window. Hooking into this event allows you to respond to text as the user is typing it.
- `paste`: The paste event fires every time text is pasted into the Editor Widget area.
- `select`: The select event fires every time text inside of the Editor Widget has been selected by a user.

Summary

The HTML Editor gives you a lot of functionality for a very small amount of necessary coding. In most cases, the default control will meet all of your needs for HTML editing on a normal site. But, if you find yourself with a need for a highly customized tool, this HTML Editor supports a rich API, detailed configuration options, and easily accessible events for capturing and responding to use actions. This is a control that is not appropriate for every site, but when you need something like this, it is a tremendous boost to productivity to find it all in such a useful and usable package.

In the next chapter, we will cover two very important Kendo widgets—Menu and ListView. These widgets give you the ability to create responsive and feature-rich cascading page menus and organized data structures inside of your pages with the same Kendo approach that you have seen in all of the previous chapters. Building on what you already know, using these new widgets will be easy and you should be up and running before you know it.

6
Menu and ListView

The Kendo UI Menu widget is designed to give you an easy way to implement an interactive JavaScript menu that opens and closes as the user commands and providers a rich visual display on a web page. These types of menus are available through other tricks as well, such as CSS, but the Kendo UI widget gives you a much more configurable framework and access to a simplified JavaScript API.

The Kendo UI ListView widget is a control for visualizing a collection of data elements in a graphically pleasing way, especially if the data contains images or special styles. Like all Kendo UI options, the configuration is consistent and sensible and allows you to create great-looking content, and provides display options for editing and selection.

These controls are a good addition to your toolset for creating modern web pages.

Learning the Menu widget basics

The Menu widget creates a fantastic drop-down menu with fly-out sections for the menu's contents. It is functionally rich and requires very little code for most implementations. As an introduction, here is a code sample of a basic menu created from a static unordered HTML list:

```
<!DOCTYPE html>
<html>
<head>
    <title>Kendo UI Menu</title>
    <script src="/Scripts/kendo/jquery.js"></script>
    <script src="/Scripts/kendo/kendo.all.js"></script>
    <link href="/Content/kendo/kendo.common.css" rel="stylesheet" />
    <link href="/Content/kendo/kendo.default.css" rel="stylesheet" />
</head>
<body>
```

```
<div id="menuDemo">
    <ul id="menu">
        <li>
            Music
            <ul>
                <li>
                    Blues / Folk
                    <ul>
                        <li>Contemporary Blues</li>
                        <li>Contemporary Folk</li>
                        <li>Traditional American</li>
                        <li>World Folk</li>
                    </ul>
                </li>
                <li>
                    Christian / Gospel
                    <ul>
                        <li>Christian Rock / Hip Hop</li>
                        <li>Contemporary Christian</li>
                        <li>Traditional Gospel</li>
                    </ul>
                </li>
                ...
            </ul>
        </li>
        <li>
            Videos
            <ul>
                <li>Movies</li>
                <li>TV</li>
                <li>Trailers</li>
            </ul>
        </li>
        <li>
            Events
        </li>
        <li disabled="disabled">
            News
        </li>
    </ul>
</div>
<script>
    $(document).ready(function () {
        $("#menu").kendoMenu();
```

```
            });
        </script>
</body>
</html>
```

This is a menu showing different music styles, videos, and some other options just to demonstrate how the code looks. The top-level `<li>` elements in the unordered list all appear as actual menu headings in the output, in this example they are **Music**, **Videos**, **Events**, and **News**.

> Notice that each of these top-level elements contains its own name and then can optionally contain a nested unordered list (`<ul>`) within itself, which becomes the choices that appear when that top-level item is selected on the page.

Moving down the chain, each of the `<li>` elements in the nested list can also contain its own `<ul>` for a further nested menu of options. This creates a cascading effect where menu options can continue to expand as you move your mouse to different options. Also note that the final top-level `<li>` item, `News`, is marked with a disabled attribute which means that it will still display in the output but not be selectable.

Here is the output from this code as the page is first loaded:

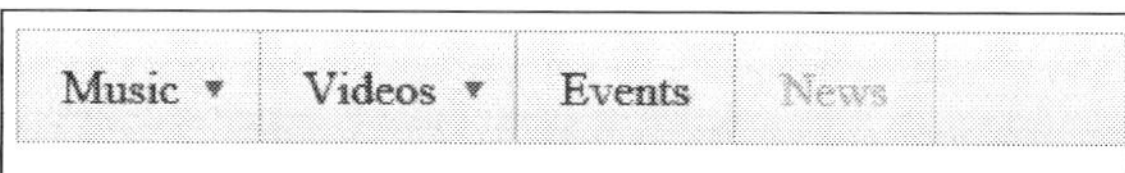

Here is the Menu widget once the mouse is hovered over some of the elements in the menu. Try this on your own and see how fast and fluid the menu reacts to these events; it is very impressive.

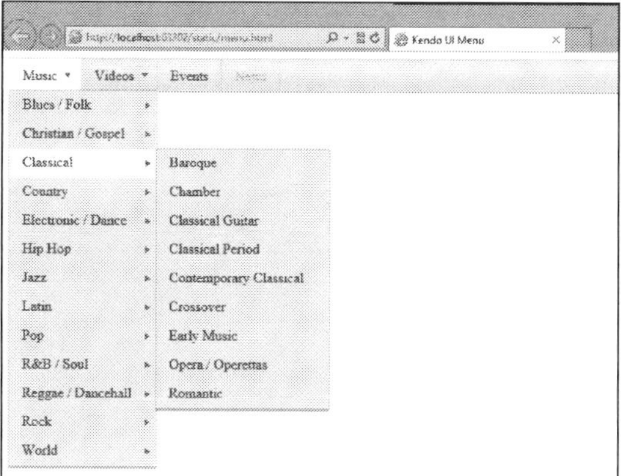

Like most of the widgets in the Kendo UI framework, the Menu widget does not have to run from static HTML, it can be fuelled by a `DataSource` object of either local or remote data. Here is the code adapted to use a local `DataSource` object instead of static HTML:

```
<!DOCTYPE html>
<html>
<head>
    <title>Kendo UI Menu</title>
    <script src="/Scripts/kendo/jquery.js"></script>
    <script src="/Scripts/kendo/kendo.all.js"></script>
    <link href="/Content/kendo/kendo.common.css" rel="stylesheet" />
    <link href="/Content/kendo/kendo.default.css" rel="stylesheet" />
</head>
<body>
    <div id="menuDemo">
    </div>
    <script type="text/javascript">
        var menuData = [
            {
                text: "Music",
                items: [
                    {
                        text: "Blues/Folk",
                        items: [
                            { text: "Contemporary Blues" },
                            { text: "Contemporary Folk" },
                            { text: "Traditional American" },
                            { text: "World Folk" }
                        ]
                    },
                    {
                        text: "Christian / Gospel",
                        items: [
                            { text: "Christian Rock / Hip Hop" },
                            { text: "Contemporary Christian" },
                            { text: "Traditional Gospel" }
                        ]
                    },

                    ...
                ]
            },
            {
                text: "Videos",
                items: [
                    { text: "Movies" },
                    { text: "TV" },
                    { text: "Trailers" }
```

```
                ]
            },
            {
                text: "Events"
            },
            {
                text: "News",
                enabled: false
            }
        ];
    </script>
    <script type="text/javascript">
        $(document).ready(function () {
            $("#menuDemo").kendoMenu(
                { dataSource: menuData });
        });
    </script>
</body>
</html>
```

Note that the `DataSource` object can be configured with all the options that you have seen in the earlier chapters, and could just as easily be configured with a transport property for remote data.

The output is identical to the static HTML we used the first time:

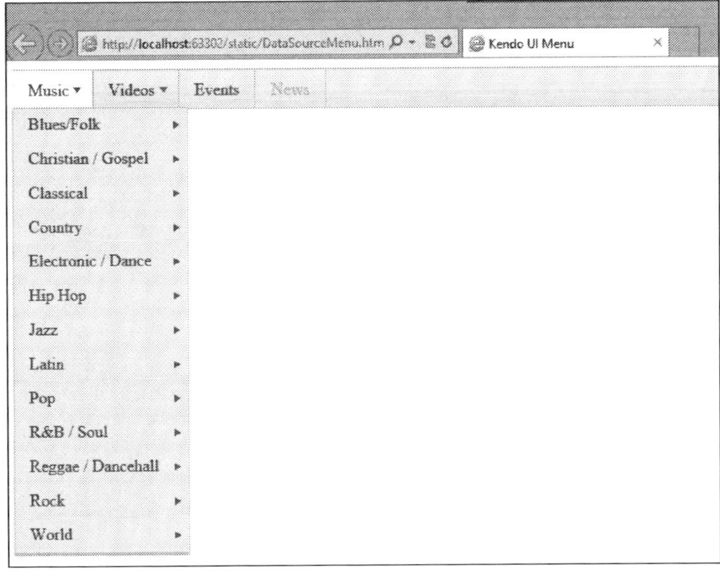

As is the case with most of the Kendo UI widgets, the interactive content on the page is identical whether the data comes from the page mark-up or from a JavaScript data source. To adapt this to use the MVC extension methods, we can create an MVC View with the following source code in the `cshtml` file:

```
@using Kendo.Mvc.UI;

@{
    ViewBag.Title = "Mvc Menu";
}

<h2>Mvc Menu</h2>
@(Html.Kendo().Menu()
    .Name("menuDemo")
    .Items(items =>
        {
            items.Add().Text("Music").Items(sub =>
            {
                sub.Add().Text("Blues / Folk").Items(subsub =>
                {
                    subsub.Add().Text("Contemporary Blues");
                    subsub.Add().Text("Contemporary Folk");
                    subsub.Add().Text("Traditional American");
                    subsub.Add().Text("World Folk");
                });
                sub.Add().Text("Christian / Gospel").Items(subsub =>
                {
                    subsub.Add().Text("Christian Rock / Hip Hop");
                    subsub.Add().Text("Contemporary Christian");
                    subsub.Add().Text("Traditional Gospel");
                });
                ...

            });
            items.Add().Text("Videos").Items(sub => {
                sub.Add().Text("Movies");
                sub.Add().Text("TV");
                sub.Add().Text("Trailers");
            });
            items.Add().Text("Events");
            items.Add().Text("News").Enabled(false);
        })
)
```

Note, how in this code sample, I have declared the data statically. It could just as easily be gathered from a different source using logic within C# code, or even left as part of the JavaScript and retrieved from a remote source across HTTP.

The output, as you can see from this screenshot, is identical to the other two code samples:

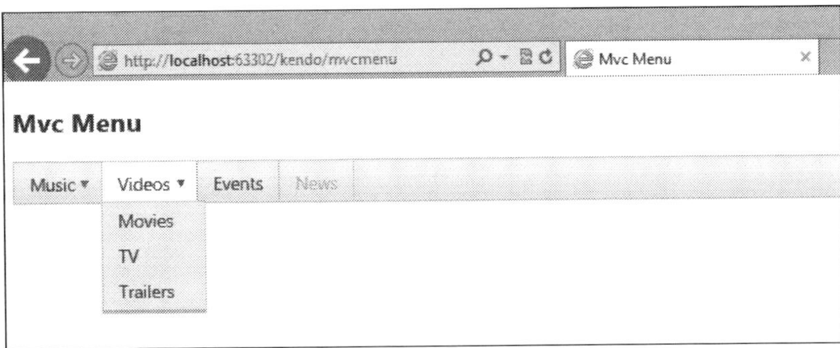

This illustrates three unique ways to create a Kendo UI Menu widget and the differences between them.

Menu items with images

Menu items so far have only included text. The Menu widget, however, can also contain an `imageUrl` property or a `spriteCssClass` property to display an image along with the text. The image or sprite will appear as an icon to the left of the menu item text.

Here is an example of using the `imageUrl` property to show an icon for the `Videos` menu item:

```
...
{
  text: "Videos",
  imageUrl: "images/reel.png",
  items: [
    { text: "Movies" },
    { text: "TV" },
    { text: "Trailers" }
  ]
},
...
```

By adding this property, the output now displays the image in the menu:

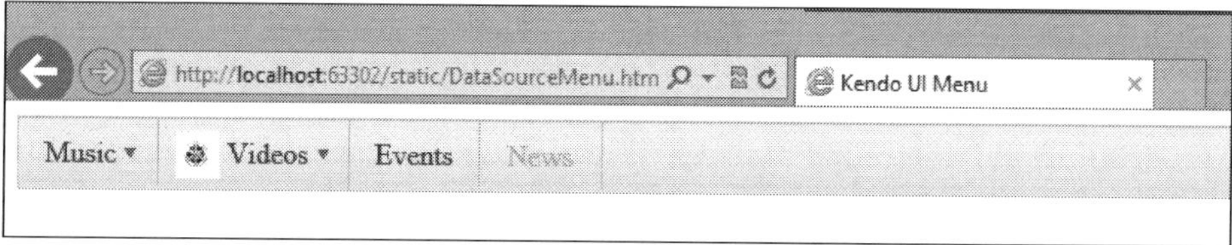

This is how the code sample would look in MVC:

```
items.Add().Text("Videos").ImageUrl("/static/images/reel.png").
Items(sub => {
  sub.Add().Text("Movies");
  sub.Add().Text("TV");
  sub.Add().Text("Trailers");
});
```

Notice the `ImageUrl` extension method that adds the image to the output.

To use a sprite, you would first set the background image of the menu items that should display the icons and then indicate a CSS class using the `spriteCssClass` property that will specify the pixel offset for each particular icon. Each menu item that has a `spriteCssClass` property specified will automatically be decorated with the `k-sprite` CSS class so that this is wired up properly. Here is a potential example:

```
<style>
#menuDemo .k-sprite {
  background-image: url("images/sprites.png");
}
.someIcon {
  background-position: 0 0;
}
.someOtherIcon {
  background-position: 0 -32px;
}
</style>
...
<script>
...
{
  text: "Videos",
  spriteCssClass: "someIcon",
  items: [
    { text: "Movies" },
    { text: "TV" },
```

```
        { text: "Trailers" }
      ]
    },
    ...
```

The CSS section of this sample shows assigning the `background-image` property for all of the `k-sprite` class-decorated elements and also designating two sprite pixel `background-position` styles. The script section shows the `spriteCssClass` property in use, which will assign that portion of the sprites image as the icon for that menu item.

Menu items with URLs

So far all of the examples I have shown are menu items that do not perform any actions when selected. All that you have to do is add the `url` property to the menu item in order to make it navigate when clicked on. So, for any menu item that you want to navigate the user to a different page, include a `url` property, as shown here, and it will do so:

```
...
{
  text: "Videos",
  spriteCssClass: "someIcon",
   url: "http://www.kendoui.com",
  items: [
    { text: "Movies" },
    { text: "TV" },
    { text: "Trailers" }
  ]
},
...
```

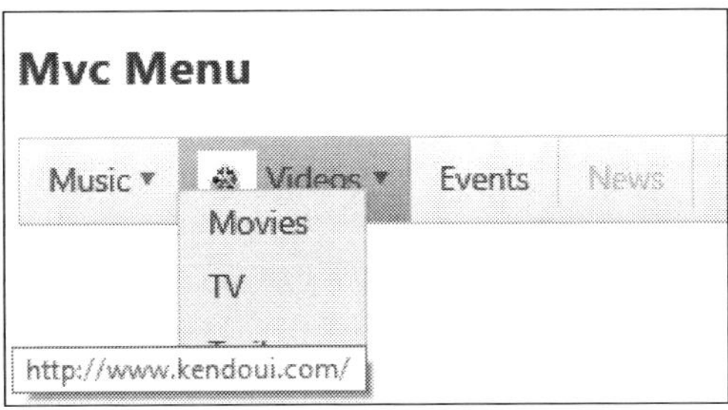

Notice how the web browser in this screenshot is showing the URL that the **Videos** menu item now navigates to.

Menu API configuration options

The Kendo UI Menu widget, as should be expected by now, is configurable through a full set of API properties and methods. These options are properties that can be configured, so that the Menu widget becomes suited to the needs of your web page and style. These configurations are specified at the point in code where you create the Menu widget. These sections will show you the options you can use.

The animation property

The animation action of the Kendo UI Menu can be configured for style, speed, and direction. When you configure the open action of the menu, Kendo will automatically assign the reverse behavior for the `close` action. If you want to configure the `close` action independently of the `open` action, then you should configure them both separately, as shown here:

```
...
$("menu").kendoMenu({
  animation: {
    close: {  // animation to use when closing a menu
      effects: "slideIn",  // 'slideIn' / 'fadeIn' / 'expand'
      duration: 10
    },
    open: {  // animation to use when opening a menu
      effects: "slideIn:Down", // You can assign a direction too
      duration: 10
    }
  }
});
...
// or you can disable animation entirely
$("menu").kendoMenu({
  animation: false
});
```

The direction property

The `direction` property determines which direction the menus will open when the user hovers over them. The available options here are `top`, `bottom`, `left`, and `right`.

```
$("menu").kendoMenu({
  direction: "bottom"
});
```

```
...
// or you can specify how each level of submenus open separately
$("menu").kendoMenu({
  direction: "bottom right" // "bottom" for menu, "right" for sub
menus
});
```

Some more options

There are a few additional options available for configuring menu behavior. You can configure how the menu behaves in relation to mouse movement and clicks with the `closeOnClick`, `openOnClick`, and `hoverDelay` properties. You can configure whether the overall menu is oriented horizontally or vertically with the `orientation` property, and you can instruct the Kendo UI framework on how you want menus to fit to a page with the `popupCollision` property. All of this is shown here:

```
$("menu").kendoMenu({
  closeOnClick: true,  // close menus when item is selected
  hoverDelay: 100,  // delay before menus open/close
  openOnClick: false,  // root submenus open with item is selected
  orientation: "vertical", // root menu orientation:
  popupCollision: "fit" // how to adjust menu to screen boundaries
                        // Use "fit flip" for vertical menus.
                        // Set to false to disable boundary detection
completely.
});
```

Configuring menu methods

Some of the methods for the Kendo UI Menu widget require that you get a reference to an existing menu item object (not just the HTML element) as a reference point for appending or inserting some additional menu items. In this case, you can access the menu item objects through a reference to the Kendo Menu like this:

```
var menu= $("#menuDemo").kendoMenu().data("kendoMenu");
```

In this code, you can get a reference to the Kendo Menu object from the same line of code where you instantiate it. This way, you can reference this object in other parts of your page and JavaScript logic. You can also get a reference to the Kendo Menu object by calling `.data(...)` on the HTML element that contains it at any point in your code, but doing it in one step is nice.

Once you have this reference, you can access the children inside of the Kendo Menu through the `element` property:

```
menu.element.children("li").eq(3);
```

In this code sample, we are accessing the fourth `li` element in the children of this particular menu object. The return value here will be a JavaScript object that can be used as the reference point for the `append`, `insertAfter`, and `insertBefore` methods.

The append(), insertAfter(), and insertBefore() methods

The `append` method takes two arguments: the JSON notation of the new menu item(s) to be appended as children, and a reference to the menu item that will be the parent of the newly appended items:

```
var menu = $("menu").data("kendoMenu");
var referenceItem = menu.element.children("li").eq(1);

menu.append(
  [{
    text: "new menu item",
    url: "http://www.music.com",
    items: [...]
  }],
  referenceItem
);
```

This code would append this menu item as a child to the second menu item on the page. The `insertAfter` and `insertBefore` methods work exactly the same way, except that they insert the new menu items at the same menu level and either after or before the reference item respectively.

All of these methods return the Menu object to support method chaining.

The close(), enable(), open(), and remove() methods

These methods for the Kendo UI Menu do not require a JavaScript object reference; they operate directly on the HTML elements within the menu on the page. Because of this, you can use a jQuery selector type syntax to choose which item(s) to act upon in a familiar syntax.

The `enable` method takes two parameters: the selector for the HTML element(s) and then a `true` or `false` value to indicate whether the item should be enabled (true) or disabled (false):

```
var menu = $("menu").data("kendoMenu");
menu.enable("#secondItem", false);
```

This particular code sample will disable the element with an HTML `id` value of `secondItem`.

The other methods here, that is, `close`, `open`, and `remove`, only take a single parameter which is the selector of the HTML element(s). Please note that the element's ID values or class names are not assigned by the framework for you, you have to assign these values to your elements yourself in order to select them:

```
var menu = $("menu").data("kendoMenu");
menu.close(".green");

menu.open("#item3");

menu.remove("#lastItem");
```

> All of these methods return the Menu object to support method chaining.

Menu events

There are three events fired by the Kendo UI Menu: `close`, `open`, and `select`. Each of these is given an event argument with an `item` property that contains the HTML `<li>` element that was closed, opened, or selected, as shown here:

```
<script>
  $(document).ready(function () {
    function onSelected(e) {
      var menu = $("#menu").data("kendoMenu");
      menu.enable(".green", false);
      alert("disabling green menu");
    }
```

```
        $("#menu").kendoMenu({ select: onSelected });

    });
</script>
```

This code sample shows a method wired up to handle the select event, which will then disable all menu items with a class name of `green`. Since this code is not considering which specific element was selected, it will fire the same code regardless of which element was selected. Here is a different example:

```
<script type="text/javascript">
  $(document).ready(function () {
    function onSelected(e){
      alert(e.item.innerHTML);
    };
    var menu= $("#menuDemo").kendoMenu(
      { dataSource: menuData, select: onSelected }).data("kendoMenu");
  });
</script>
```

This code examines the specific element that was selected and alerts its `innerHTML` property back to the user.

The Kendo UI ListView

The Kendo UI ListView widget is designed to present a collection of data on a web page with a richer set of functionality than a standard HTML list. The ListView widget retrieves its data through a Kendo `DataSource` object, it presents its data through one or more Kendo Template blocks, and it allows interaction with its data by giving the user the ability to both select and edit the data on the page.

ListView basics

Basically, the ListView widget displays a collection of data by using a template and a `DataSource` object:

```
<!DOCTYPE html>
<html xmlns="http://www.w3.org/1999/xhtml">
<head>
    <title>ListView</title>
    <script src="/Scripts/kendo/jquery.js"></script>
    <script src="/Scripts/kendo/kendo.all.js"></script>
    <link href="/Content/kendo/kendo.common.css" rel="stylesheet" />
    <link href="/Content/kendo/kendo.default.css" rel="stylesheet" />
```

```
    <style type="text/css">
        .animal {
            width:250px;
            height:200px;
            position:relative;
            float:left;
        }
        .animal-label {
            font-size:large;
        }
        .animal-image {
            max-height:100px;
            max-width: 150px;
            margin: 5px;
        }
        #listView {
            width:750px;
            height:100%;
        }
    </style>
</head>
<body>
    <div id="listView"></div>

    <script type="text/x-kendo-tmpl" id="template">
        <div class="animal">
            <img src="../images/#= imageName #" alt="#= animalName #
              image" class="animal-image" />
            <div class="animal-label">#= animalName #</div>
        </div>
    </script>
    <script type="text/javascript">
        var animals = [
            { animalName: "African Elephant",
              imageName: "african-elephant.jpg" },
            { animalName: "African Lion", imageName: "african-lion.
jpg" },
            { animalName: "Alpaca", imageName: "alpacas.jpg" },
            { animalName: "Badger", imageName: "badger.jpg" },
            { animalName: "Black Bear", imageName: "bear-black.jpg" },
            { animalName: "Bison", imageName: "bison.jpg" },
            { animalName: "Jack-Rabbit",
              imageName: "black-tailed-jackrabbit.jpg" },
            { animalName: "Caribou", imageName: "caribou.jpg" },
```

```
                { animalName: "Giraffe", imageName: "giraffe.jpg" },
                { animalName: "Hummingbird", imageName: "humming-bird.jpg" 
},
                { animalName: "Jaguar", imageName: "jaguar.jpg" },
                { animalName: "Lemur", imageName: "lemur.jpg" },
                { animalName: "Red Fox", imageName: "red-fox.jpg" },
                { animalName: "Striped Skunk", imageName: "striped-skunk.
jpg" }
            ];

            $(document).ready(function () {
                $("#listView").kendoListView({
                    dataSource: animals,
                    template: kendo.template($("#template").html())
                });
            });
        </script>
</body>
</html>
```

The following code sample, from the top down, shows some styles for the elements that will appear inside the ListView widget. These style declarations are important in order to properly lay out the images inside the ListView widget on the web page:

```
<style type="text/css">
  .animal {
    width:250px;
    height:200px;
    position:relative;
    float:left;
  }
  .animal-label {
    font-size:large;
  }
  .animal-image {
    max-height:100px;
    max-width: 150px;
    margin: 5px;
  }
  #listView {
    width:750px;
    height:100%;
  }
</style>
```

We then create the `div` element that will contain the ListView widget and the Kendo UI Template that structures the individual ListView elements. This template determines how each item in the ListView will be rendered inside the web page. Any changes to the ListView items must occur here:

```
<div id="listView"></div>
<script type="text/x-kendo-tmpl" id="template">
  <div class="animal">
    <img src="../images/#= ${imageName #}" alt="#= ${animalName #}
      image" class="animal-image" />
    <div class="animal-label">#= ${animalName #}</div>
  </div>
</script>
```

We then have the JavaScript object literal that contains some data and the instantiation of the ListView where the `dataSource` and `template` properties are set:

```
<script type="text/javascript">
        var animals = [
            { animalName: "African Elephant",
              imageName: "african-elephant.jpg" },
            { animalName: "African Lion", imageName: "african-lion.
jpg" },
            { animalName: "Alpaca", imageName: "alpacas.jpg" },
            { animalName: "Badger", imageName: "badger.jpg" },
            { animalName: "Black Bear", imageName: "bear-black.jpg" },
            { animalName: "Bison", imageName: "bison.jpg" },
            { animalName: "Jack-Rabbit",
              imageName: "black-tailed-jackrabbit.jpg" },
            { animalName: "Caribou", imageName: "caribou.jpg" },
            { animalName: "Giraffe", imageName: "giraffe.jpg" },
            { animalName: "Hummingbird", imageName: "humming-bird.jpg"
},
            { animalName: "Jaguar", imageName: "jaguar.jpg" },
            { animalName: "Lemur", imageName: "lemur.jpg" },
            { animalName: "Red Fox", imageName: "red-fox.jpg" },
            { animalName: "Striped Skunk", imageName: "striped-skunk.
jpg" }
        ];

        $(document).ready(function () {
            $("#listView").kendoListView({
                dataSource: animals,
                template: kendo.template($("#template").html())
            });
```

```
        });
    </script>
```

As always, remember that the `DataSource` object can be fully configured to point to remote data sources, can be structured using a schema, or can use any of the other options that you might want to take advantage of in a production scenario.

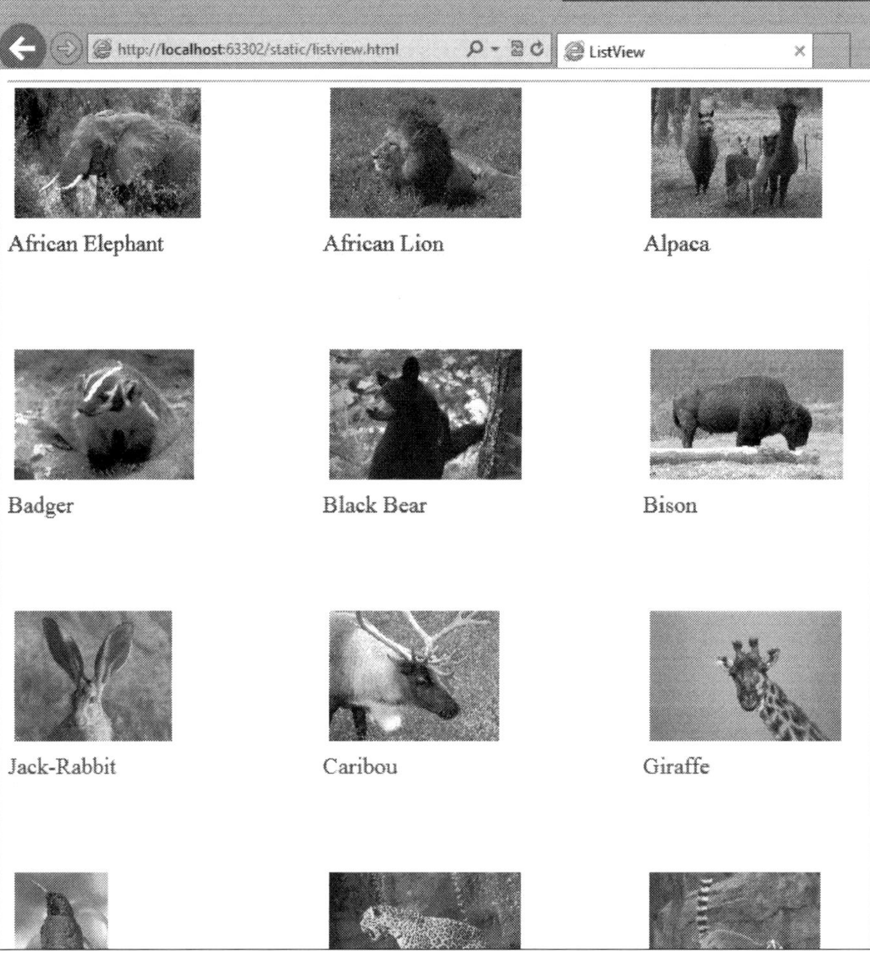

You can see how each element from the `DataSource` object has been rendered with the template, styled, and presented on the page as you would expect.

Selecting elements with ListView

The ListView widget has a richer set of behaviors to offer than simply displaying data, however, and to start let's look at how it allows "selection" of elements. In this code sample, I have added some more properties and an event handler to the ListView instantiation logic to demonstrate this:

```
        $(document).ready(function () {
            $("#listView").kendoListView({
                dataSource: animals,
                template: kendo.template($("#template").html()),
                selectable: "multiple",
                change: notifyUser
            });

            function notifyUser(e) {
                var selected = $.map(this.select(), function (item) {
                    return animals[$(item).index()].animalName;
                });
                alert(selected.join(", "));
            }
        });
    </script>
```

The `selectable` property has been set with `multiple` to allow for multiple selection of items (you can select multiple items on the page by holding the *Ctrl* button on the keyboard while clicking with a mouse). We also added an event handler for the `change` event so that we can see an alert box that displays which elements have been selected.

In the `notifyUser` event handler function, I want to explain what is happening because it looks a bit confusing at first glance. The variable selected is given an array value of all of the selected elements' `animalName` property values. It does this by using `$.map` on the results of `this.select()`. What is `this.select()`? Well, when Kendo fires an event from a widget, it sets the context of that event handler so that this refers to the Kendo widget that fired the event. So, in this case, this is a reference to the ListView itself. This means that calling `this.select()` in this event handler will return a collection of all of the selected elements within the ListView. The function as the second parameter of `$.map` then grabs the `animalName` property from each of these elements by using its index from the `animals` array. The result of this code is an array of strings containing all of the `animalName` values of the selected elements from the ListView. This is then displayed to the user using `[array].join()`.

Here is the output with some items selected and the alert box showing from the event handler:

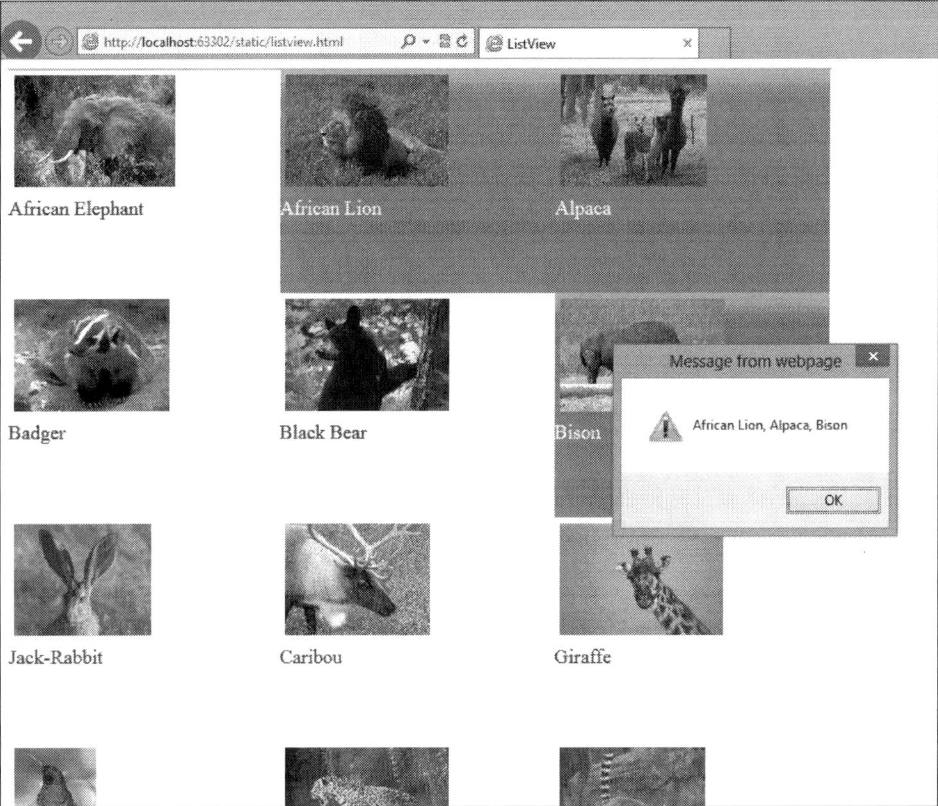

Notice how the names of the animals are all showing up in the alert box that has popped up on the page. This is great because it means that you can accurately track selections that the user makes within your ListView and respond to those actions however you need to.

Editing elements with ListView

The ListView widget also provides a good syntax for allowing edits to the data within the `DataSource` object. You need to create a separate template to display that allows the user to make edits and then make sure that you assign some of the Kendo-specific class names, so that it displays and understand the commands correctly. Here is the code of the new template. Place it right beneath the template we created in the last example.

```
    <script type="text/x-kendo-tmpl" id="edit-template">
        <div class="animal">
            <img src="images/#= imageName #" alt="#= animalName #
image"
                class="animal-image" />
            <div class="animal-label">
                <input type="text" data-bind="value:animalName"
name="animalName"
                    required="required" /></div>
            <div>
                <a class="k-button k-button-icontext k-update-button"
                    href="\\#"><span class="k-icon k-update"></
span>Save</a>
                <a class="k-button k-button-icontext k-cancel-button"
                    href="\\#"><span class="k-icon k-cancel"></
span>Cancel</a>
            </div>
        </div>
    </script>
```

> Did you notice the unusual characters in the `href` attribute of the two buttons in the template? The double-backslash characters, `\\#`, prevent the hash mark from being rendered as part of the Kendo template. If this hash mark was not escaped with these backslashes, the template would not render at all.

Next, we have added some more configurations to the JavaScript block that creates our ListView widget. Specifically, we now have an `editTemplate` property that points to the template that we just created:

```
<script type="text/javascript">
        var animals = [
            { animalName: "African Elephant",
              imageName: "african-elephant.jpg" },
            ...

        ];

        $(document).ready(function () {
            $("#listView").kendoListView({
                dataSource: animals,
                template: kendo.template($("#template").html()),
                editTemplate: kendo.template($("#edit-template").
html())
            });
```

```
        });
    </script>
</body>
</html>
```

Here is a screenshot where the name of the Caribou has been edited to Reindeer:

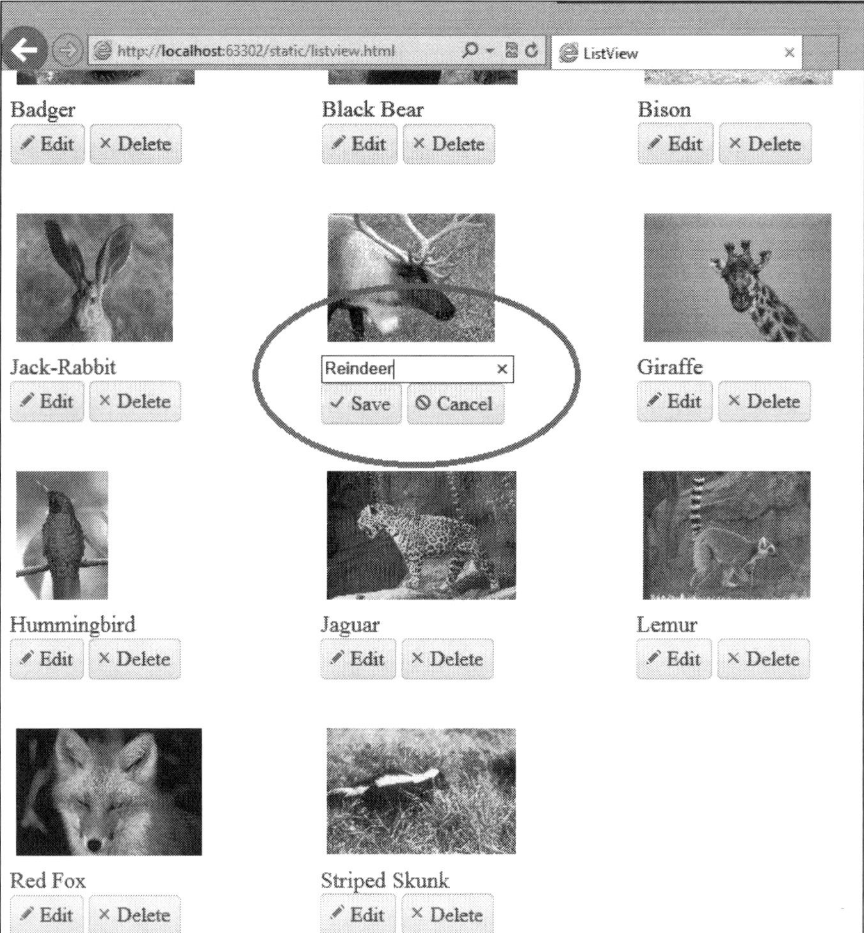

ListView API and configuration

We have already covered several of the aspects of the ListView in our preceding examples; here are the remaining configuration properties from the documentation:

```
$("#listView").kendoListView({
  autoBind: true, // if false, you must call read() manually
```

```
  dataSource: ..., // demonstrated above
  editTemplate: ..., // demonstrated above
  navigatable: false, // whether or not keyboard navigation is enabled
  selectable: false, // true/false or "single"/"multiple" are valid
options
  template: ..., // demonstrated above
  altTemplate: ... // template used for alternating styles if desired
});
```

ListView methods

The ListView widget has several methods available. Most of them are designed to manipulate the items within the ListView, so that you can control the behavior through code. Like with any widget, you need a reference to the listView JavaScript object before you can call these methods, like this:

```
var listView = $("#listView").data("kendoListView");
...
listView.add(...)
```

Get the reference through the `.data(...)` method and then you can call the ListView-specific methods. Here is a brief overview of the methods that take no parameters:

- `add`: Inserts an empty item into the ListView and prepares it for editing
- `cancel`: Cancels changes in currently edited items
- `clearSelection`: Clears ListView's selected items and triggers the `change` event
- `refresh`: Reloads the data and reprints the ListView
- `save`: Saves the edited ListView item. If validation succeeds, it will call the datasource's `sync` method.

There are a few additional methods that do take parameters.

The edit method

This method edits the specified ListView item and triggers the `edit` event. This method takes a single parameter which is the ListView item that needs to be edited. Here is a sample:

```
var listView = $("#listView").data("kendoListView");
...
listView.edit(listView.element.children().first());
```

The remove method

This method removes the specified ListView item and triggers the `remove` event. It also triggers the datasource's `sync` method.

```
var listView = $("#listView").data("kendoListView");
...
listView.remove(listView.element.children().first());
```

The select method

This method selects the specified ListView item. If this method is called without any arguments, it will return a collection of all of the selected items in the ListView. This is what we did in the code sample for selecting items. Here is a code sample for using the method with a parameter:

```
var listView = $("#listView").data("kendoListView");
...
listView.select(listView.element.children().first());
```

ListView events

The ListView widget exposes several events for hooking into its lifecycle and behavior. We have already seen some of these in our examples. These events can all be assigned to handlers during the ListView instantiation as we save earlier in the chapter. Here is a list:

- `change`: Fires when the ListView selection is changed
- `dataBound`: Fires when the ListView has received data from the `DataSource` object and is about to render it
- `dataBinding`: Fires when the data is about to be rendered on the page
- `edit`: Fires when the ListView enters edit mode
- `remove`: Fires before the ListView item is removed

Summary

The Menu and ListView widgets are great tools for structuring data on your web pages. The Menu widget makes it simple to create interactive JavaScript menus for navigation and even for displaying data with graphics. The ListView widget should become a standard option for you when you want a standard way of rendering collections of data elements on a web page. It gives you the ability to hook up functionality that would otherwise require a lot of code and debugging.

In the next chapter, we will take a look at the Kendo UI PanelBar widget. Its API is very similar to the Kendo UI Menu widget, as you will see, and it is a powerful way to render accordion controls in a web page. Much like the Kendo UI Menu widget, its primary responsibility is to organize hierarchical content in a way that saves screen space, but still provides a sensible structure for users to understand.

7
Implementing PanelBar and TabStrip

The PanelBar and TabStrip widgets are special Kendo UI controls for organization data, which make it possible for a web page to contain a large amount of content but display only one piece of that content at a time. These content sections are broken up into panels with the PanelBar widget, or into tabs with the TabStrip widget. In both cases, the effect is very similar and is a very useful way of keeping a web page from becoming too cluttered. This chapter will explain the basics of implementing the PanelBar and TabStrip controls with both HTML and ASP.NET MVC, and then illustrate the following features:

- Adding images to PanelBar and TabStrip items
- Adding URLs to PanelBar and TabStrip items
- Loading AJAX content with PanelBar and TabStrip
- Controlling PanelBar and TabStrip animation effects

PanelBar basics

The PanelBar widget is the Kendo UI way of implementing an interactive JavaScript "accordion" on a web page. This type of control is very useful for displaying lists of data that could potentially take up a large amount of screen space, but compressing it into a format that still makes sense to users. As an introduction, here is a code sample of a basic PanelBar created from a static unordered HTML list. This HTML list will be reformatted into an accordion control that displays a single area of the list at a time. As you will see, when you run the code sample, this allows a large amount of data to be visually compressed into a smaller space. It also allows the user to select which area of the list he or she is interested in viewing and hides the details of the other sections. This gives a powerful demonstration of some of the commonality between Kendo widget implementations:

Note that I have used the same data as in the last chapter for the Menu control.

```
<!DOCTYPE html>
<html>
<head>
    <title>Kendo UI PanelBar</title>
    <script src="/Scripts/kendo/jquery.js"></script>
    <script src="/Scripts/kendo/kendo.all.js"></script>
    <link href="/Content/kendo/kendo.common.css" rel="stylesheet" />
    <link href="/Content/kendo/kendo.default.css" rel="stylesheet" />
</head>
<body>
        <div id="panelBarDemo">
            <ul id="panelBar">
                <li>
                    Music
                    <ul>
                        <li>
                            Blues / Folk
                            <ul>
                                <li>Contemporary Blues</li>
                                <li>Contemporary Folk</li>
                                <li>Traditional American</li>
                                <li>World Folk</li>
                            </ul>
                        </li>
                        <li>
                            Christian / Gospel
                            <ul>
                                <li>Christian Rock / Hip Hop</li>
                                <li>Contemporary Christian</li>
                                <li>Traditional Gospel</li>
                            </ul>
                        </li>
                    ...
                    </ul>
                </li>
                <li>
                    Videos
                    <ul>
                        <li>Movies</li>
                        <li>TV</li>
```

```
                    <li>Trailers</li>
                </ul>
            </li>
            <li>
                Events
            </li>
            <li disabled="disabled">
                News
            </li>
        </ul>
    </div>
    <script>
        $(document).ready(function () {
            $("#panelBar").kendoPanelBar();
        });
    </script>
</body>
</html>
```

This source code creates a PanelBar with the same data from the Menu in the last chapter. The top-level `<li>` elements in the unordered list all appear as actual accordion headings in the output. In this example, just as in the menu example, they are **Music**, **Videos**, **Events**, and **News**. Notice that each of these top-level elements contains its own name and then can optionally contain a nested unordered list (`<ul>`) within itself which becomes the choices that appear when that top-level item is selected on the page. Moving down the chain, each of the `<li>` elements in the nested list can also contain its own `<ul>` list for a further nested menu of options, which is impressive as not all accordion implementations can handle this level of nested data. This creates a cascading effect where menu options can continue to expand as you move your mouse to different options. Also note that the final top-level `<li>` item, `News`, is marked with a `disabled` attribute which means that it will still display in the output but not be selectable.

Here is the output from this code:

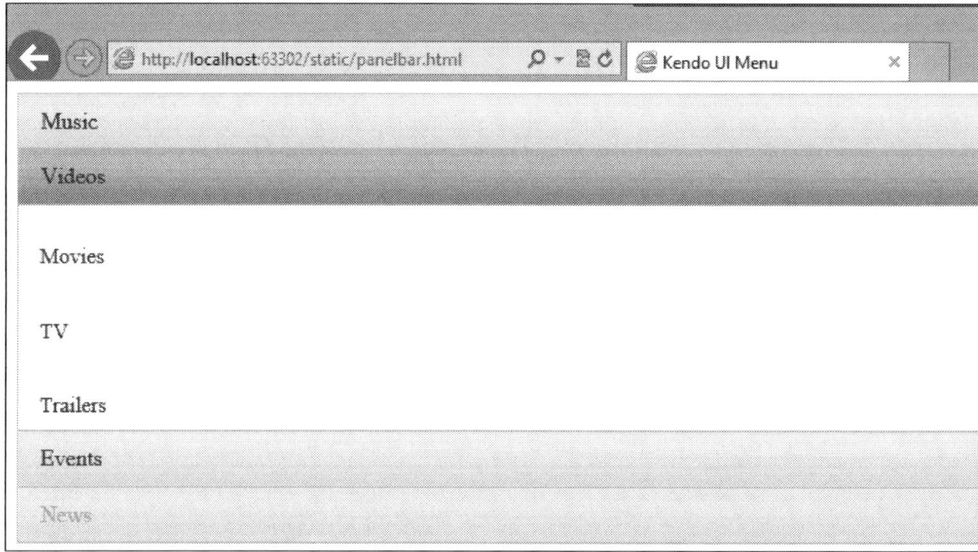

The **Videos** panel was clicked before this screenshot was taken so that you can see some of the data opened, it normally starts with all of the panels closed.

Just as before with the Menu widget, the PanelBar widget does not have to run from static HTML, it can be fuelled by a `DataSource` object of either local or remote data. Here is the code adapted to use a datasource instead of static HTML:

```
<body>
    <div id="panelBarDemo">
    </div>
    <style type="text/css">
      #panelBarDemo img{
        max-height: 30px;
        max-width: 30px;
      }
    </style>
    <script type="text/javascript">

        var panelBarData = [
            {
                text: "Music",
                items: [
                    {
                        text: "Blues/Folk",
                        items: [
```

```
                            { text: "Contemporary Blues" },
                            { text: "Contemporary Folk" },
                            { text: "Traditional American" },
                            { text: "World Folk" }
                        ]
                    },
                    {
                        text: "Christian / Gospel",
                        items: [
                            { text: "Christian Rock / Hip Hop" },
                            { text: "Contemporary Christian" },
                            { text: "Traditional Gospel" }
                        ]
                    },
                    ...
                ]
            },
            {
                text: "Videos",
                imageUrl: "/Images/reel.png",
                items: [
                    { text: "Movies" },
                    { text: "TV" },
                    { text: "Trailers" }
                ]
            },
            {
                text: "Events"
            },
            {
                text: "News",
                enabled: false
            }
        ];
    </script>
    <script type="text/javascript">
        $(document).ready(function () {
            $("#panelBarDemo").kendoPanelBar({ dataSource:
panelBarData} );
        });
    </script>
</body>
</html>
```

Note that the DataSource object can be configured with all the options that you have seen in earlier chapters and could just as easily be configured with a transport property for remote data.

In this code sample, we have also implemented a new feature, the imageUrl property for the **Videos** tab. By specifying the URL of an image in the project, the output will show this image next to the tab's title on the screen, which you can see in the following screenshot:

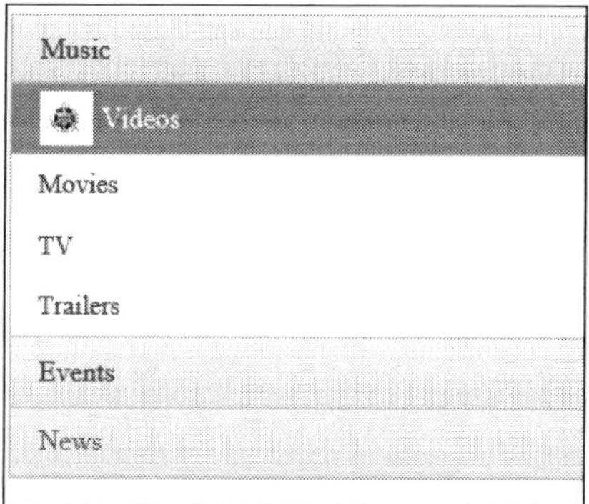

To adapt this to use the MVC extension methods, you would create an MVC View with this source code in the cshtml file:

```
@using Kendo.Mvc.UI;

@{
    ViewBag.Title = "Mvc PanelBar";
}

<style type="text/css">
    li img {
        max-height: 25px;
        max-width: 25px;
    }
</style>
```

```
<h2>Mvc Menu</h2>
@(Html.Kendo().PanelBar()
    .Name("panelBarDemo")
    .Items(items =>
        {
            items.Add().Text("Music").Items(sub =>
            {
                sub.Add().Text("Blues / Folk").Items(subsub =>
                {
                    subsub.Add().Text("Contemporary Blues");
                    subsub.Add().Text("Contemporary Folk");
                    subsub.Add().Text("Traditional American");
                    subsub.Add().Text("World Folk");
                });
                sub.Add().Text("Christian / Gospel").Items(subsub =>
                {
                    subsub.Add().Text("Christian Rock / Hip Hop");
                    subsub.Add().Text("Contemporary Christian");
                    subsub.Add().Text("Traditional Gospel");
                });
                ...
            });
            items.Add().Text("Videos").ImageUrl("/static/images/reel.
png").Items(sub => {
                sub.Add().Text("Movies");
                sub.Add().Text("TV");
                sub.Add().Text("Trailers");
            });
            items.Add().Text("Events");
            items.Add().Text("News").Enabled(false);
        })
)
```

Note, how in this code sample, we have declared the data statically. It could just as easily be gathered from a different source using logic within C# code, or even left as part of the JavaScript and retrieved from a remote source across HTTP. We can also see here how the image is supplied through ASP.NET MVC syntax instead of through the JavaScript in the last example.

The output, as you can see from this screenshot, is identical to the other two code samples:

This illustrates three unique ways to create a Kendo UI PanelBar widget, just like the Menu widget from before, and the differences between them.

Adding sprite images to PanelBar items

We have already seen some examples of how the PanelBar widget can contain an `imageUrl` property to display an image next to a section title. It can also use a more advanced image option by specifying a sprite image through the `spriteCssClass` property. In either case, the image or sprite will appear as an icon to the left of the menu item text.

As we have already partially seen, here is an example of using the `imageUrl` property to show an icon for the `Videos` menu item:

```
...
{
  text: "Videos",
  imageUrl: "/images/reel.png",
  items: [
    { text: "Movies" },
    { text: "TV" },
    { text: "Trailers" }
  ]
},
...
```

By adding this property, the output now displays the image in the menu:

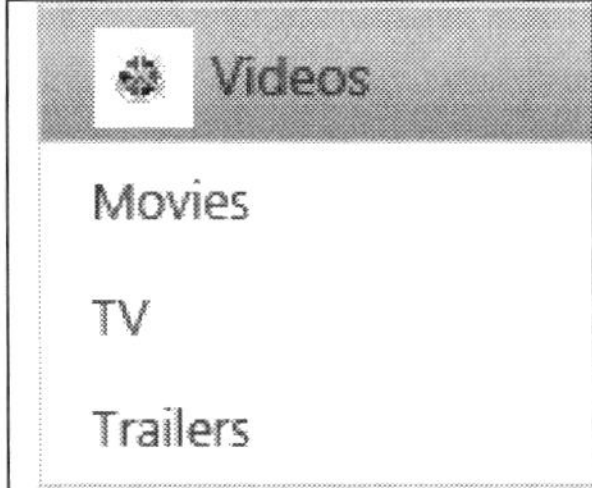

This is how the code sample looks when using MVC syntax:

```
items.Add().Text("Videos").ImageUrl("/images/reel.png").Items(sub => {
  sub.Add().Text("Movies");
  sub.Add().Text("TV");
  sub.Add().Text("Trailers");
});
```

Notice the `ImageUrl` extension method that adds the image to the output.

To use a sprite, you would first set the background image of the menu items that should display the icons and then indicate a CSS class using the `spriteCssClass` property that will specify the pixel offset for each particular icon. Each menu item that has a `spriteCssClass` property specified will automatically be decorated with the `k-sprite` CSS class so that this is wired up properly. Here is a potential example:

```
<style>
#panelBarDemo .k-sprite {
  background-image: url("images/sprites.png");
}
.someIcon {
  background-position: 0 0;
}
.someOtherIcon {
  background-position: 0 -32px;
}
</style>
...
<script>
...
{
  text: "Videos",
  spriteCssClass: "someIcon",
  items: [
```

```
        { text: "Movies" },
        { text: "TV" },
        { text: "Trailers" }
      ]
    },
    ...
```

The CSS section of this sample shows assigning the `background-image` property for all of the `k-sprite` class-decorated elements and also designating two sprite pixel `background-position` styles. The script section shows the `spriteCssClass` property in use which will assign that portion of the sprite's image as the icon for that menu item.

Adding URLs to PanelBar items

So far all of the examples we have seen are PanelBar items that do not perform any actions when selected. All that we have to do is add the `url` property to the PanelBar item in order to make it navigate when clicked on. So, for any PanelBar item where we want to navigate the user to a different page, include a `url` property and it will do so:

```
    ...
    {
      text: "Videos",
      spriteCssClass: "someIcon",
       url: "http://www.microsoft.com",
      items: [
        { text: "Movies" },
        { text: "TV" },
        { text: "Trailers" }
      ]
    },
    ...
```

Loading AJAX content with PanelBar

Instead of embedding all of the content into one page, a PanelBar widget can be used to load content from other URLs dynamically using AJAX. This will reduce the overall size of the page since only one section of the PanelBar will be loaded at a time. It can also allow you to load content from other locations in your site that may change independently of the site that contains your PanelBar, which can reduce duplicate text or markup. To enable this functionality, use the `contentUrls` property of the PanelBar to indicate which sites contain the markup that should be placed inside the accordion:

```
$("#panelId").kendoPanelBar({
  ...
  contentUrls: [
    "content1.html",
    "content2.html"  ]
});
```

Secondly, we have to create placeholders in the HTML markup to indicate where this AJAX content will appear once it has loaded. All this requires is a structure like the following code with `<li>` elements that contain empty `<div>` elements which will receive the AJAX content at the appropriate time:

```
<ul id="panelBarDemo">
    <li>
      Remote content
      <div></div>
    </li>
    <li>
      More content
      <div></div>
    </li>
</ul>
```

With this combination of markup and JavaScript code, the PanelBar will load `content1` for the first tab, `content2` for the second tab, and so on. It is a good idea to keep the content on these pages very simple so that it can fit into the PanelBar areas without being distorted.

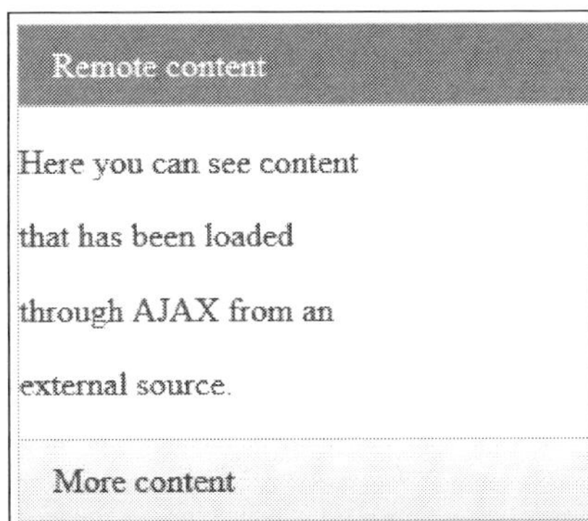

Controlling PanelBar animation effects

The animation features of the PanelBar can be controlled through the animation property when configuring the PanelBar object in JavaScript. The `animation` property can be set to `false` to completely disable all animation effects, or it can be configured like the following code sample for specific behaviors:

```
$("#panelId").kendoPanelBar({
  ...
  expandMode: "single",  // "multiple" for multiple open tabs at once
  animation: {
    collapse: {
      duration: 1000,  // milliseconds for animation effect
      effects: "fadeOut"  //"fadeout" is the only option for collapse
    },
    expand: {
      duration: 500,
      effects: "expandVertical fadeIn" // choose either or both of
these
    }
});
```

The only available animation effect for the collapse action is `fadeOut`. For the `expand` action, you can choose `expandVertical`, which is the normal action for expanding a PanelBar, and `fadeIn` which changes the opacity as it expands.

Introducing the TabStrip widget

The TabStrip widget is very similar to the PanelBar widget. In fact, they perform nearly the same function except that the PanelBar Widget organizes content into panels that are stacked vertically while the TabStrip widget organizes content into panels that are stacked horizontally. They are so similar, in fact, that we will use nearly the same code to demonstrate both of them. You have already seen the PanelBar widget in the preceding sections. Now we will take a look at the TabStrip widget and see how it functions within web pages.

TabStrip basics

The TabStrip widget creates a series of tabs that are used to show only one specific section of content at a time. The content within a tab can be almost anything, ranging from simple text and markup all the way up to large `<div>` sections with enough content to fill an entire web page. You have surely seen web pages that have tabs across the top of the screen to organize different types of material onto a single web page. The Kendo TabStrip widget is one way to create this effect on your own pages.

To start, copy the following code into a new HTML page and run it in a web browser:

```
<!DOCTYPE html>
<html>
<head>
    <title>Kendo UI TabStrip</title>
    <script src="/Scripts/kendo/jquery.js"></script>
    <script src="/Scripts/kendo/kendo.all.js"></script>
    <link href="/Content/kendo/kendo.common.css" rel="stylesheet" />
    <link href="/Content/kendo/kendo.default.css" rel="stylesheet" />
</head>
<body>
        <div id="panelBar">
            <ul>
                <li>
                    Music
                </li>
                <li>
                    Videos
                </li>
                <li>
                    Events
                </li>
                <li disabled="disabled">
                    News
                </li>
            </ul>
            <div>Next concert in May of 2013!</div>
            <div>Next music video in July of 2013!</div>
            <div>Memorabilia signing on April 15th</div>
            <div></div>
        </div>
        <script>
            $(document).ready(function () {
                $("#panelBar").kendoTabStrip();
            });
        </script>
</body>
</html>
```

For this widget, the markup is required to follow a specific pattern. The TabStrip itself must be declared on a `<div>` element that contains an unordered list (`<li>`) and a collection of `<div>` elements right after the unordered list. This is all evident in the preceding code sample. The unordered list contains all of the tab titles. The collection of `<div>` elements contains all of the content that appears within each of the tabs in the same order they appear in the markup. This is how this particular example appears when run inside of a web browser:

Using TabStrip with a datasource

Much like the PanelBar, the TabStrip can be configured to use a datasource instead of being created on top of existing HTML markup already on a web page. To adapt the code sample from the last section into this pattern, replace the body of the page with this code:

```
<body>
  <div id="panelBar">
  </div>
  <script>
    $(document).ready(function () {
      $("#panelBar").kendoTabStrip({
        dataTextField: 'text',
        dataContentField: 'content',
        dataSource: [
        {
          text: 'Music',
          content: 'Next concert in May of 2013!'
        },
        {
          text: 'Videos',
          content: 'Next music video in July of 2013!'
        },
        {
          text: 'Events',
          content: 'Memorabilia signing on April 15th'
        },
        {
          text: 'News',
          content: ''
```

```
          }
        ]
      });
    });
  </script>
</body>
```

The output from this code is exactly the same as before, except that the **News** tab is not disabled since there is not a property to define a disabled element using a datasource:

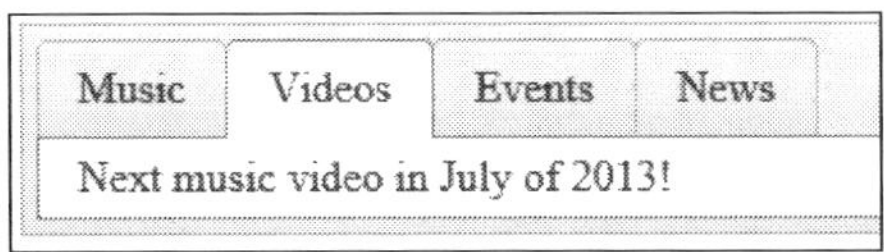

Adding images to the TabStrip widget

All of the TabStrip tabs so far have only included text. The TabStrip widget, however (just like the PanelBar widget), can also contain an `imageUrl` property to display an image next to a tab's title. It can also use a more advanced image option by specifying a sprite image through the `spriteCssClass` property. In either case, the image or sprite will appear as an icon to the left of the tab's title text. Here is an example of using the `imageUrl` property to show an icon for the `Videos` menu item:

```
...
{
  text: "Videos",
  imageUrl: "/images/reel.png",
  content: "Next music video in July of 2013!"
}
...
```

By adding this property, the output now displays the image in the menu:

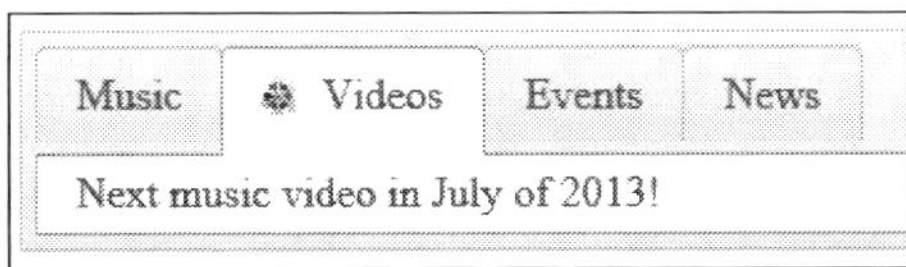

This is how the same code sample looks when using MVC syntax:

```
@using Kendo.Mvc.UI;

@{
    ViewBag.Title = "Mvc TabStrip";
}

<style type="text/css">
    li img {
        max-height: 25px;
        max-width: 25px;
    }
</style>

<h2>Mvc TabStrip</h2>
@(Html.Kendo().TabStrip()
    .Name("tabStripDemo")
    .Items(items =>
        {
            items.Add().Text("Music")
                .Content("Next concert in May of 2013!");
            items.Add().Text("Videos")
                .Content("Next music video in July of 2013!")
                .ImageUrl("/images/reel.png");
            items.Add().Text("Events")
                .Content("Memorabilia signing on April 15th");
            items.Add().Text("News").Enabled(false);
        })
)
```

You should be able to notice quite a few similarities to the code we used earlier for the PanelBar widget. To use a sprite with the TabStrip, you can follow the same procedures as we discussed for the PanelBar.

Adding URLs to TabStrip tabs

To use a TabStrip tab as a hyperlink to another page, you can configure the `url` property for that tab and it will take on this role. By doing this, we are no longer using the tab to show any content on the page, it simply navigates directly to another web page when it is clicked.

```
...
{
  text: 'News',
```

```
    content: '',
    url: 'http://www.kendoui.com'
  }
  ...
```

After altering the code in this way, the `News` tab will become a hyperlink instead of an actual tab to display content.

Loading AJAX content with TabStrip

To load AJAX content into a tab, we need to indicate the URL for each tab's content in the configuration. This follows the same pattern as the other options within the TabStrip, so this should look very familiar to you by now:

```
<script>
  $(document).ready(function () {
    $("#panelBar").kendoTabStrip({
      dataTextField: 'text',
      dataContentField: 'content',
      dataImageUrlField: 'dataImageUrl',
      dataUrlField: 'url',
      dataContentUrlField: 'contentUrl',
      dataSource: [
        {
            text: 'Remote Content',
            contentUrl: 'content1.html'
        },
          {
            text: 'More Content',
            contentUrl: 'content2.html'
          }
        ]
    });
  });
</script>
```

When we run the web page in a browser, it appears like this with the remote content loaded dynamically as we click on the tab's titles:

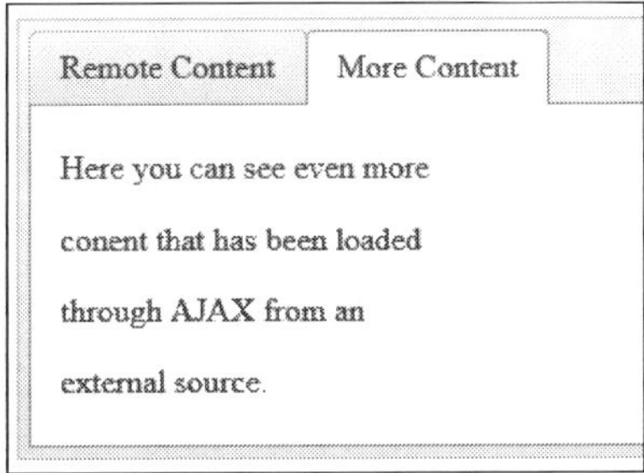

Controlling the TabSrip widget's animation effects

The animation effects for the TabStrip widget are exactly the same as for the PanelBar widget. They are controlled through the `animation` property when configuring the TabStrip object in JavaScript. The `animation` property can be set to `false` to completely disable all animation effects, or it can be configured like the following code sample for specific behaviors:

```
$("#tabSripId").kendoTabStrip({
  ...
  animation: {
    collapse: {
      duration: 1000,  // milliseconds for animation effect
      effects: "fadeOut"  //"fadeout" is the only option for collapse
    },
    expand: {
      duration: 500,
      effects: "expand:vertical fadeIn" // choose either or both of
these
    }
});
```

The only available animation effect for the collapse action is `fadeOut`. For the `expand` action, you can choose `expand:vertical`, which is the normal action for expanding a TabStrip, and `fadeIn` which changes the opacity as it expands.

Summary

The PanelBar widget is a highly configurable JavaScript accordion widget that gives you considerable "bang for your buck". For a categorized list of data elements that you need to compress into a smaller amount of screen space, the PanelBar widget is the perfect choice for your web page. The TabStrip widget is an easy JavaScript tab framework that allows you to organize your page content with tabs and even load remote content dynamically onto your page when a tab is clicked. Both of these great widgets should add useful features to your website.

In the next chapter, you will learn about the Kendo UI Slider widgets and how to use them to collect input from users in a graphically interesting way. The slider widgets present an HTML input as a visual bar where the user can drag a handle to the desired option instead of typing a number into a field in a form.

8
Slider Essentials

The Kendo UI framework includes special widgets called sliders that show a slider bar on a web page, so that a user can drag a handle to increase and decrease the slider in order to choose a value. These sliders normally have tick marks and labels that indicate the highest and lowest numbers available as well as range between them. These widgets are great visual tools to help users select numbers on a fixed scale, instead of just typing in a value that may or may not be appropriate. This could be useful in a rating system, for example, or on any input control where only a certain set of numbers are allowed. As you will see, Kendo UI allows for a good level of configurability, so you can customize the appearance and functionality of the UI to suit your needs.

Introducing Slider and RangeSlider

The first thing we should cover is the two different types of slider widgets that Kendo UI makes available. There is the standard Kendo **UI Slider** widget and there is a Kendo **UI RangeSlider** widget. The Kendo UI RangeSlider widget is designed for more advanced scenarios where your page needs to capture a range (a bottom and a top number) of numbers from a user in a single page element instead of just a single value.

It is important to understand that these slider widgets are special visual aids for use in supplying a number into an input HTML element. The final output of a slider widget is the number that the user has selected and this number is set as the value of the input HTML element underneath. This is important so that the input element can then be posted inside of an HTML form and used by a web server on the other end when the form is posted.

Along these lines, be sure to follow this pattern when creating a Kendo UI Slider widget on your page:

```
<!— value is optional, but will set the initial value of the slider if
present -->
<input id="sliderId" value="2" />
...
<script>
  $(function(){
    $("#sliderId").kendoSlider({...});
  });
</script>
```

The `kendoSlider` method needs to be bound to an actual input HTML element. So what about the Kendo UI RangeSlider widget? It uses two numbers but an input control contains only one value. How does it maintain these two separate values? The answer is that it uses two input elements inside of a container `div` tag:

```
<div id="rangeSliderId">
  <input />
  <input />
</div>
...
<script>
  $(function(){
    $("#rangeSliderId").kendoRangeSlider({...});
  });
</script>
```

This way, the Kendo UI RangeSlider widget is created on a `div` element and it builds its range values into the two input elements inside of that container `div` to properly render it on the page.

Using Slider and RangeSlider with the MVC extension methods

The following code sample illustrates the basics of instantiating slider widgets by using ASP.NET MVC extension methods. The `Name` method must be called for all the Kendo widgets to work properly.

```
@(Html.Kendo().Slider().Name("horizontalSlider"))
...
@(Html.Kendo().RangeSlider().Name("horizontalRangeSlider"))
```

Implementing the basics

As an introduction, I have created a sample page that shows sliders and range sliders in a variety of configurations. We will use this same code sample in the following sections where we discuss the features and options. In this sample, we have fixed the positions of the elements using CSS absolute positioning. This is not necessarily best practice for web page design, but it works to show these controls in isolation. In this first code block, we are creating the HTML markup necessary to contain the Slider widgets. Each Slider is created on top of a `div` element with input elements inside. This will be explained more after the following code sample:

```
<!DOCTYPE html>
...
<body>

  <!-- Two slider widgets -->
    <div id="sliders">
        <h2 style="position:absolute;top:5px;left:40px">Slider
Widgets</h2>

       <!-- vertical slider widget -->
        <div style="position:absolute;top:65px;left:100px;">
            <input id="verticalSlider" value="2" /></div>

        <!-- horizontal slider widget -->
        <div style="position:absolute;top:285px;left:15px;">
            <input id="horizontalSlider" value="7" /></div>
    </div>

  <!-- Two rangeslider widgets -->
    <div id="rangeSliders">
        <h2 style="position:absolute;top:5px;left:300px">
            RangeSlider Widgets</h2>

        <!-- vertical rangeslider widget -->
        <div style="position:absolute;top:65px;left:388px"
            id="verticalRangeSlider">
            <!-- these inputs are required for containing the two
                 Values in the range -->

            <input /><input />
        </div>

        <!-- horizontal rangeslider widget -->
        <div id="horizontalRangeSlider"
```

```
            style="position:absolute;top:285px;left:300px;">
            <!-- these inputs are required for containing the two
                 Values in the range -->
            <input /><input />
        </div>
    </div>
```

You will see that we have created four separate slider widgets on the page, two of them are normal slider widgets and two of them are range slider widgets. The following JavaScript code section is what transforms the HTML markup into Kendo widgets for the web page. You can also see some of the configuration options in these samples, which we will discuss in detail in just a few paragraphs.

```
    <script>
        $(document).ready(function () {
       // create the vertical slider widget
            $("#verticalSlider").kendoSlider({
                min: -10,
                max: 20,
                orientation: "vertical",
                smallStep: 2,
                largeStep: 10,
                tickPlacement: "both"
            });

            // create the horizontal slider widget
            $("#horizontalSlider").kendoSlider({
                min: 0,
                max: 20,
                smallStep: 1,
                largeStep: 5
            });

            // create the vertical rangeslider widget
            $("#verticalRangeSlider").kendoRangeSlider({
                min: 0,
                max: 20,
                orientation: "vertical",
                selectionStart: 2,
                selectionEnd: 6,
                smallStep: 1
            });

            // create the horizontal rangeslider widget
            $("#horizontalRangeSlider").kendoRangeSlider({
```

```
                min: 0,
                max: 30,
                selectionStart: 5,
                selectionEnd: 15,
                smallStep: 1,
                largeStep: 5,
                tickPlacement: "none"
            });
        });
    </script>
</body>
</html>
```

Here is the output from executing the preceding code block:

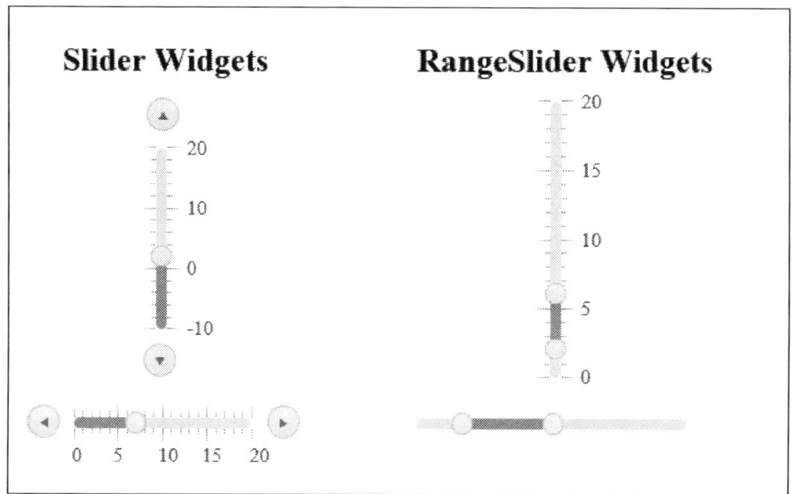

We organized the content on the page so that you could see the different slider widgets and their output. The two sliders on the left, one vertical and one horizontal, are both normal slider widgets. The two sliders on the right side, one vertical and one horizontal, are both range slider widgets. I also adjusted properties on each of them so that they are showing unique options for the sake of demonstration. We will cover these options as we go through the rest of this chapter.

Basic implementation using MVC extension methods

The following code sample illustrates how to instantiate these same sliders by using the ASP.NET MVC extension methods. I have only included the actual slider widgets, not the full HTML page.

```
<div id="sliders">
    <h2 id="slidersLabel">Slider Widgets</h2>
    @(Html.Kendo().Slider().Name("verticalSlider")
        .HtmlAttributes(new { id = "verticalSlider" })
        .Min(-10)
        .Max(20)
        .Orientation(SliderOrientation.Vertical)
        .Value(5)
        .SmallStep(2)
        .LargeStep(10)
        .TickPlacement(SliderTickPlacement.None)
        .Tooltip(tt =>
            tt.Format("{0}")))
    @(Html.Kendo().Slider().Name("horizontalSlider")
        .HtmlAttributes(new { id = "horizontalSlider" })
        .Min(0)
        .Max(20)
        .Orientation(SliderOrientation.Horizontal)
        .Value(7)
        .SmallStep(1)
        .LargeStep(5)
        .TickPlacement(SliderTickPlacement.Both))
</div>
<div id="rangeSliders">
    <h2 id="rangeSlidersLabel">RangeSlider Widgets</h2>
    @(Html.Kendo().RangeSlider().Name("verticalRangeSlider")
        .HtmlAttributes(new { id = "verticalRangeSlider" })
        .Min(0)
        .Max(20)
        .Orientation(SliderOrientation.Vertical)
        .Values(new double[] { 2, 6 })
        .SmallStep(1))
    @(Html.Kendo().RangeSlider().Name("horizontalRangeSlider")
        .HtmlAttributes(new { id = "horizontalRangeSlider" })
        .Min(0)
        .Max(30)
```

```
            .Orientation(SliderOrientation.Horizontal)
            .Values(new double[] { 5, 15 })
            .SmallStep(1)
            .LargeStep(5)
            .TickPlacement(SliderTickPlacement.Both))
    </div>
```

Just as in the normal JavaScript and HTML example above, the output from these MVC extensions creates the same output. All four of the sliders appear with the same options and configuration and also have the same behavior.

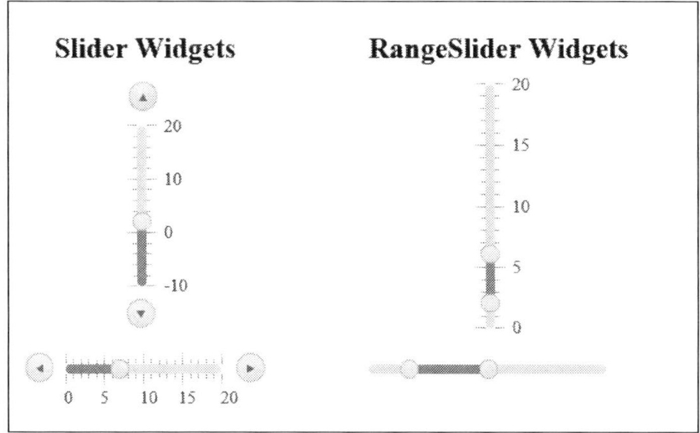

Using tooltips and pop-up texts

The slider widgets give several visual cues to the user to indicate their value and their control functions. There are tooltips, or hover effects, which indicate what the buttons at the end of the sliders will do. These tooltips are always present, they do not require any additional configuration or code, although they can be customized using the API. The following screenshot shows the tooltip text that appears over the **Increase** button:

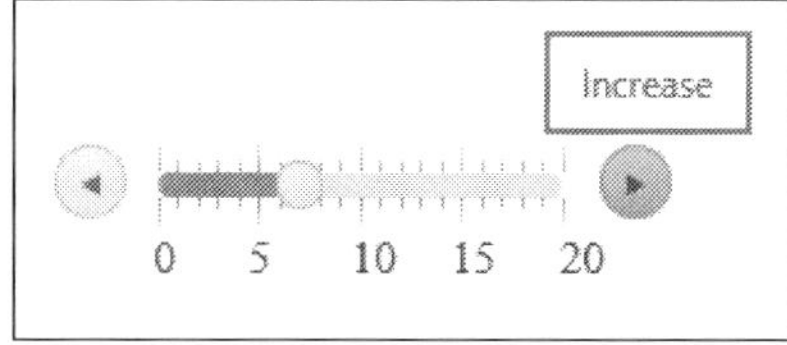

The following screenshot shows the tooltip text that appears over the **Decrease** button:

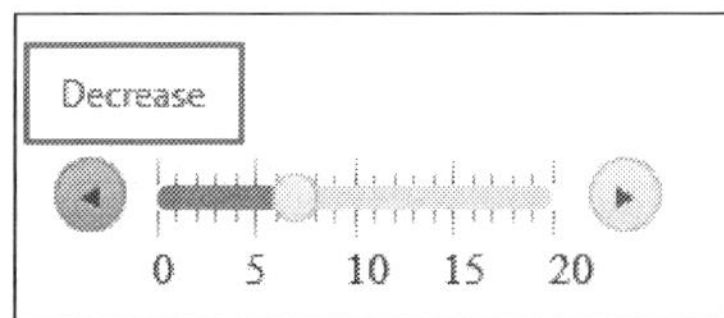

There are also tooltip labels that indicate the value of the tick marks, if present, and that indicate how to interact with the slider control by dragging with the mouse. The following screenshot shows the tooltip text over the tick mark that represents the number **18**:

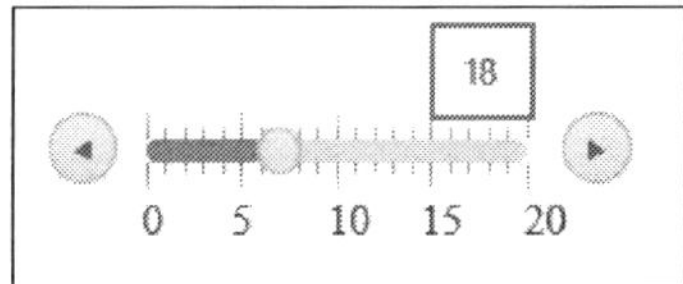

The following screenshot shows the tooltip text over the **drag** handle:

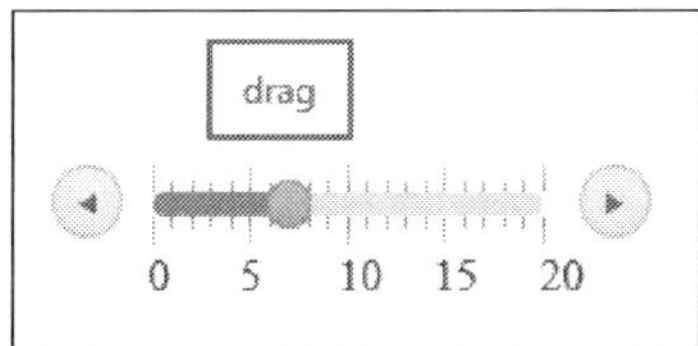

Lastly, when a user drags the controls of a range slider widget, the page will show a label that indicates the currently selected range. The following screenshot shows the tooltip text over the selected range, in this case, showing that the handles are positioned at **4** and **15**:

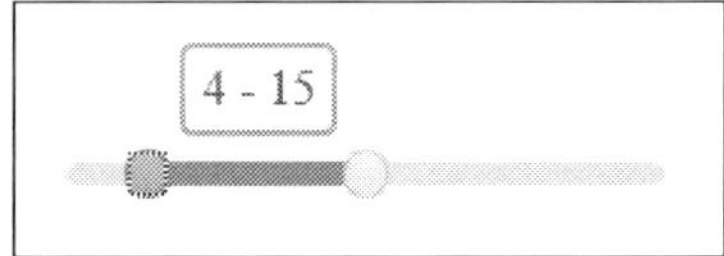

Learning keyboard controls

It is also important to note that the slider controls can also be manipulated using the keyboard arrow buttons and the *Page Up* and *Page Down* buttons when the slider widget has the focus on the page. Pressing the arrow button either up or down will increase or decrease the value of the slider by the number contained in the `smallStep` property. Pressing *Page Up* or *Page Down* will increase or decrease the value of the slider by the number contained in the `largeStep` property.

These properties, `smallStep` and `largeStep`, can be set when the slider widget is instantiated in JavaScript as we saw in our earlier sample code:

```
$("#verticalSlider").kendoSlider({
  min: -10,
  max: 20,
  orientation: "vertical",
  smallStep: 2,
  largeStep: 10,
  tickPlacement: "both"
});
```

The numbers do not have to be even, they can be any whole number increment that makes sense for your application.

Customizing the user interface of the slider widgets

Many of the properties of the slider widgets can be used to customize how the user can interact with them on the web page. The text that shows up in the tooltips and tick mark labels can be customized to show different text that may be more specific to your page. You can also customize the orientation of the sliders and their default values.

Tooltip customization

The `tooltip` property of the slider widgets can be customized with a custom format or a custom template and can also be disabled completely, if unwanted. For example, imagine that your slider widget is intended for the user to select degrees (such as on a thermometer). You could customize the format of the tooltip to reflect that unique format. You will also see that when changing the format of the tooltip, the format of the data labels will automatically change to match it:

```
$("#verticalSlider").kendoSlider({
  min: -10,
  max: 20,
  orientation: "vertical",
  smallStep: 2,
  largeStep: 10,
```

```
    tickPlacement: "both",
    tooltip: {
      format: "{0}"
    }
  });
```

The default format is "{0}", so by adding the degree symbol after this, it will appear properly on the page:

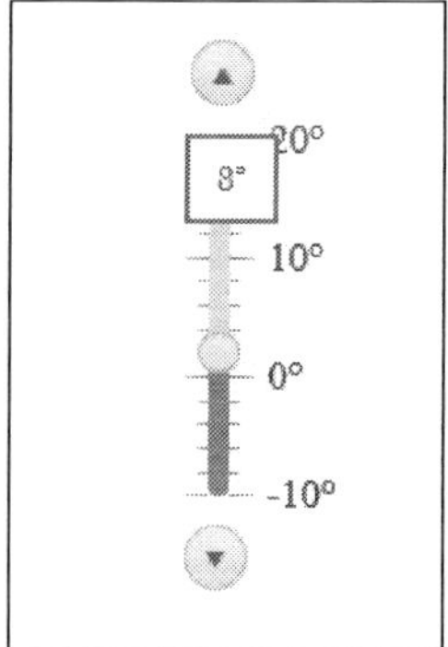

Notice how the labels and the tooltip both changed to match the new format. Also note that I added the format using a degree symbol that was not HTML encoded, the Kendo UI system handled the appropriate encoding for me.

The full options for configuring the `tooltip` property are displayed here:

```
// options for a kendoSlider
tooltip: {
  enabled: true,  // enable tooltips or not
  format: "{0}",  // format string for tooltips
  template:{
    value: "..."  // template value for tooltips
    }
  }
}
...
// options for a kendoRangeSlider
tooltip: {
  enabled: true,  // enabled or not
  format: "{0}",  // format string for tooltips
  template:{
    selectionStart: "...",  // template value for start range
          selectionEnd: "..."  // template value for end range
    }
  }
}
```

You should not use both a format and a template, since both of those properties are designed to customize the display of the tooltips. The template, as you have seen in previous chapters, would need to follow the normal Kendo template syntax and could be used to create a highly customized tooltip for your slider control.

Customizing tooltip options using MVC extension methods

This is how a configured tooltip looks when using ASP.NET MVC extension methods.

```
...
.Tooltip(tt =>
  tt.Enabled(true)
  .Format("{0}")
  .Tempalte("template would go here")) @* misspelled in the Kendo code
*@
```

Remember that, just as in JavaScript, you would not set both the format and the template at the same time. Also note that the Kendo library has misspelled a word, it has "tempalte" instead of "template". Be sure to check your code here in case Telerik has fixed the spelling.

Customizing the default values

A slider widget can be configured to start with a specific default value. For a normal Kendo slider widget, this comes in the form of the `value` property either of the input HTML element or in the initialization of the Kendo slider widget in JavaScript, as shown here:

```
<input id="sliderId" value="4" />

... // or

$("#sliderId").kendoSlider({
  value: 4,
  ...
}
```

Either of these methods will set the initial, or default value of the slider widget to the number `4`.

For the Kendo range slider, you need to set both of the numbers for the range, so you need to use different properties called `selectionStart` and `selectionEnd` or set the value properties of both of the inputs in the HTML:

```
<div id="rangeSliderId">
  <input value="2" />
  <input value="8" />
</div>

... // or

$("#rangeSliderId").kendoRangeSlider({
  selectionStart: 2,
  selectionEnd: 8
  ...
}
```

Both of these methods will set the start of the selected range to `2` and the end of the selected range to `8`.

Customizing tick placement

The tick marks and data labels on the slider widgets can also be customized by choosing one of four supported options for their display: `topLeft`, `bottomRight`, `both`, and `none`. These are set through the configuration property called `tickPlacement`.

```
$("#sliderId").kendoSlider({
  tickPlacement: "topLeft"
  ...
});
```

Placing the tick at the top left

The `topLeft` tick placement option will place the tick marks on the left side of a vertical slider or on the top side of a horizontal slider.

```
$("#sliderId").kendoSlider({
  tickPlacement: "topLeft"
  ...
});
```

Here is the output:

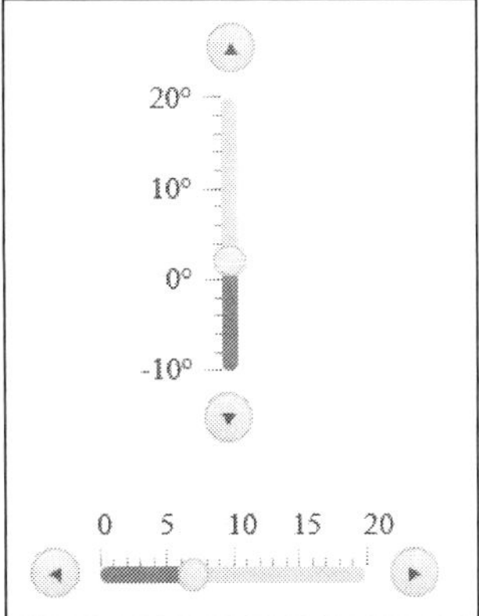

Placing the tick at the bottom right

The `bottomRight` tick placement option will place the tick marks on the right side of a vertical slider or on the bottom side of a horizontal slider:

```
$("#sliderId").kendoSlider({
  tickPlacement: "bottomRight"
  ...
});
```

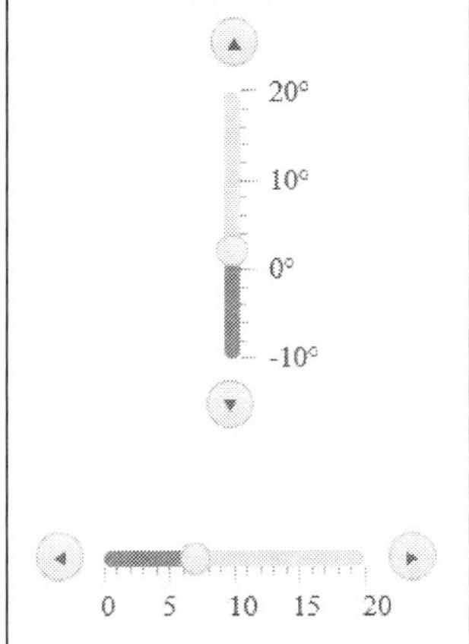

Placing ticks on both sides

The both tick placement option will place the tick marks on both sides of a slider:

```
$("#sliderId").kendoSlider({
  tickPlacement: "both"
  ...
});
```

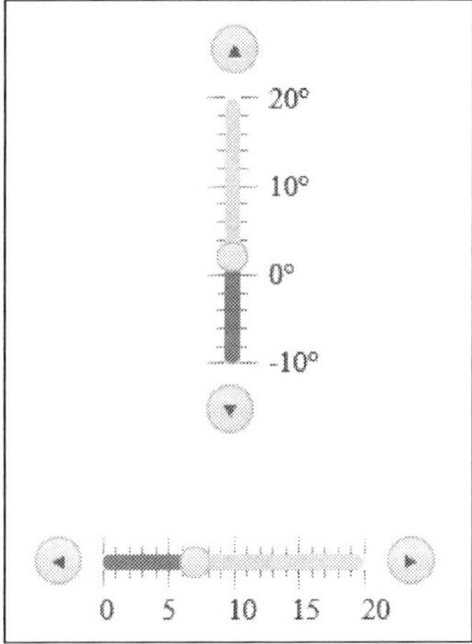

Removing the ticks entirely

The none tick placement option will remove all tick marks from a slider:

```
$("#sliderId").kendoSlider({
  tickPlacement: "none"
  ...
});
```

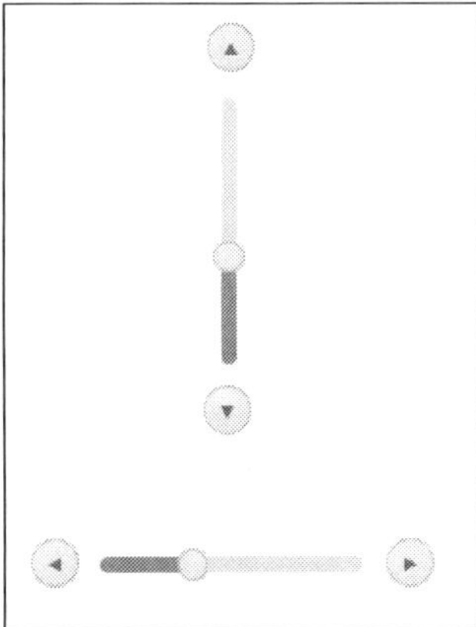

Customizing slider orientation

You have already seen the two orientations of the slider widgets—horizontal and vertical, but here is a brief look at the code necessary to enable these two options:

```
$(function(){
  orientation: "vertical"  // "horizontal" or "vertical"
  ...
}
```

[If you do not set the orientation, the default orientation will be horizontal.]

Learning API methods

When interacting with the slider widgets, you must reference the JavaScript object through the `data()` method as usual:

```
// Kendo Slider Widget
var slider = $("#sliderId").data("kendoSlider");

// Kendo RangeSlider Widget
var rangeSlider = $("#rangeSliderId").data("kendoRangeSlider");
```

The enable and disable Methods

The slider widgets support methods for enabling and disabling the controls in the web page through the `enable()` and `disable()` methods. The syntax is the same for both slider widgets and range slider widgets, assuming you have the correct reference to the object through JavaScript.

```
// get a reference to the slider
var slider = $("sliderId").data("kendoSlider");

// disable a slider
slider.disable();

// enable a slider
slider.enable();
```

A disabled slider widget appears as partially transparent, or grayed out, on the web page. In the following screenshot, the slider on the left is disabled and the slider on the right is enabled:

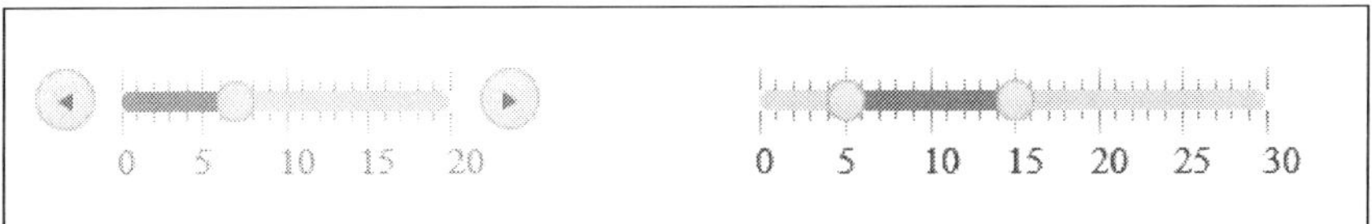

Using the values

The value of a slider widget can be both set and retrieved from the JavaScript API. The syntax is different between the slider and the range slider since they each use a different number of values internally.

Using values from a Kendo slider

Setting and retrieving values for a Kendo slider is straightforward since it contains only a single value, as shown here:

```
// get a reference to the slider
var slider = $("#sliderId").data("kendoSlider");

// set the value of the slider to 7
slider.value(7);

// get the value of the slider
var sliderValue = slider.value(); // returns a number
```

Using values from a Kendo range slider

When setting or retrieving values from a range slider, you must communicate using JavaScript arrays so that you can hold both values from the slider object.

```
// get a reference to the slider
var rangeSlider = $("#rangeSliderId").data("kendoRangeSlider");

// set the values for the range slider to 2 and 8
rangeSlider.value([2,8]);

// get the values from the range slider
var sliderValues = rangeSlider.value(); // returns an object array
```

Hooking into events

Just as with the other Kendo UI widgets, event handlers can be bound during object instantiation, or later through a JavaScript `bind()` method call. These examples will only show the instantiation code.

Using the change event

The slider widgets will fire a `change` event when the user changes the value of a slider either through clicking one of the arrows, moving the slider with the mouse, or using the keyboard controls.

The change event for a Kendo slider widget

The `change` event for a Kendo slider widget can be bound and used like the following:

```
$("#sliderId").kendoSlider({
  change: changeHandler,
  ...
});

...

function changeHandler (e){
  alert(e.value);  // e.value contains the new value of the slider
}
```

The `e.value` property will contain the new value of the slider widget so that you can respond to the event properly in your JavaScript code.

The change event for a Kendo range slider widget

The `change` event for a Kendo range slider widget can be bound as shown in the following code snippet this. It differs from the `change` event for the slider widget in that it passes an array to the event handler instead of a single value.

```
$("#rangeSliderId").kendoRangeSlider({
  change: changeHandler,
  ...
});

...

fuction changeHandler (e){
```

```
    alert(e.value.toString());  // e.value is an array of the new range
values
}
```

The slide event

The `slide` event is identical in syntax to the `change` event, but it only fires when the user moves the slider by using the mouse, it will not fire for keyboard events or button clicks. The preceding examples for the `change` event are valid for the `slide` event as well.

```
$("#sliderId").kendoSlider({
  slide: changeHandler,
  ...
});
```

The change and slide events with MVC extension methods

This is how event handlers can be wired up by using ASP.NET MVC extension methods. Please note that the output is identical to the one outlined before; this is simply the syntax necessary for executing the following code using MVC. See the previous sections for more information.

```
.Events(events => events
  .Slide("slideHandler")
  .Change("changeHandler"))
```

Summary

The Kendo UI Slider and Kendo UI RangeSlider widgets are very handy tools for collecting numbers for an input element in a web page. When collecting numbers that must fall within a specified range, these widgets are much friendlier than returning error messages to the user about a number being invalid. I would suggest using them where appropriate to make your site much more interesting for your users.

In the next chapter, you will learn about the Splitter and the TreeView widgets that allow you to load resizable dynamic content into your pages and to organize hierarchical content in a tree-like display. These widgets will help you build powerful pages that can handle and load content on the fly and display content in organized patterns.

9
Implementing the Splitter and TreeView Widgets

In this chapter, you will learn about two different widgets from the Kendo UI Web framework, the Splitter widget and the TreeView widget. The Splitter widget is a tool used for organizing content inside of a web page. It creates block-like regions within the web page that can contain normal page elements or even additional Splitter widget controls to further subdivide the content area. The TreeView widget is a tool used for displaying data that is organized hierarchically, such as in tree. A good example of data organized this way is a folder structure on a hard drive. Folders can contain files or additional folders. When diagrammed, this creates a nested structure such as a tree and is well suited for the TreeView widget.

The Splitter widget

The Kendo UI Splitter widget is a powerful tool for creating a dynamic page layout. It generates bordered sections within a web page that can be resized, scrolled, collapsed, and nested. These sections are built on top of `div` elements and extend these underlying `div` elements with impressive functionality. As you see how to use this widget throughout this section, I am sure you can imagine many ways of putting it to use.

Learning the Splitter widget

The Kendo UI Splitter widget is designed to extend `div` HTML elements into flexible content areas that can split up elements of your web pages, hence the name "splitter". These content areas become resizable blocks that allow the user to choose which portions of a page should occupy more of the visible screen. Each of these blocks can be configured with specific behaviors and options, such as scroll bars and the ability to collapse page elements with a single click.

Here is a sample of some HTML markup that can be used with the Kendo UI Splitter widget. Take special note of how the `div` elements are organized and nested; it will become important when you see the JavaScript code that instantiates the Kendo objects:

```
<div id="outerSections" style="height: 600px">
  <div id="outerTopSection" style="height: 200px">
    <div id="topSubSections" class="k-pane" style="height: 200px">
      <div style="height: 200px" class="k-pane"></div>
      <div style="height: 200px" class="k-pane"></div>
    </div>
  </div>
  <div id="outerMidSection" style="height: 200px" class="k-pane">
    <div class="k-pane"></div>
  </div>
  <div id="outerBottomSection" style="height: 200px" class="k-pane">
    <div id="bottomSubSections" class="k-pane" style="height: 200px">
      <div style="height: 200px" class="k-pane"></div>
      <div style="height: 200px" class="k-pane"></div>
      <div style="height: 200px" class="k-pane"></div>
    </div>
  </div>
</div>
```

The outer-most `div`, the one with the `id` value of `outerSections`, contains three `div` elements between its tags. You can also see that each of these `div` elements beneath the `outerSections` `div` contain child `div` elements of their own. These child elements will become Kendo UI Splitter widget sections within the larger `outerSections` area. Two of these child `div` elements, `topSubSections` and `bottomSubSections`, also contain a further nested hierarchy that will become nested Kendo UI Splitter widget sections within the `outerTopSection` and `outerBottomSection` areas respectively.

In this JavaScript code block, you can see that there are three `kendoSplitter` widgets created independently. The first Splitter widget is organized in a vertical sequence; it is the outer-most area and will contain the following two Splitter widget objects within itself. The second and third Splitter widget areas are organized horizontally and are nested within other Splitter widget objects, as you will see in the following screenshot:

```
<script type="text/javascript">
  $(function () {
    $("#outerSections").kendoSplitter({
      orientation: "vertical",
      panes: [
```

```
          { collapsible: false, size: "200px", scrollable: false },
          { collapsible: false, size: "200px", scrollable: false },
          { collapsible: false, size: "200px", scrollable: false }
        ]
      });
      $("#topSubSections").kendoSplitter({
        orientation: "horizontal",
        panes: [
          { collapsible: true, scrollable: false },
          { collapsible: true, scrollable: false }
        ]
      });
      $("#bottomSubSections").kendoSplitter({
        orientation: "horizontal",
        panes: [
          { collapsible: true, scrollable: false },
          { collapsible: true, scrollable: false },
          { collapsible: true, scrollable: false }
        ]
      });
    });
  </script>
```

You can see the three Splitter widget areas that are stacked vertically down the page. The top-most area contains two horizontally stacked areas inside of it. The bottom-most area contains three horizontally stacked areas. These all match to the HTML and JavaScript code that you just saw.

Loading content

The contents of the Splitter widget areas you just saw were all empty for the sake of demonstration. This is not necessary, however. The content areas can contain all of the normal HTML content that a `div` element would normally contain. For example, you could fill some of the areas up with text, as done in the following code snippet:

```
<div id="topSubSections" class="k-pane" style="height: 200px">
  <div style="height:200px" class="k-pane">
    Lorem ipsum dolor sit amet, consectetur adipisicing elit...
  </div>
  <div style="height:200px" class="k-pane">
    Lorem ipsum dolor sit amet, consectetur adipisicing elit...
  </div>
</div>
```

This text will now appear within the Splitter widget box and be resized or collapsed as necessary:

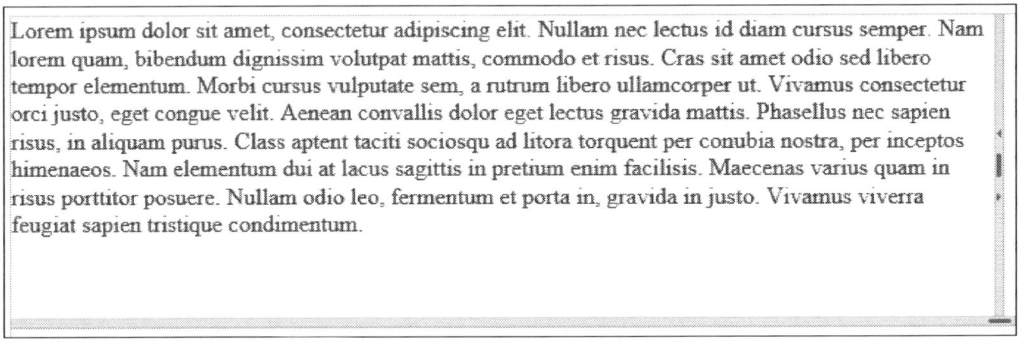

Lorem ipsum dolor sit amet, consectetur adipiscing elit. Nullam nec lectus id diam cursus semper. Nam lorem quam, bibendum dignissim volutpat mattis, commodo et risus. Cras sit amet odio sed libero tempor elementum. Morbi cursus vulputate sem, a rutrum libero ullamcorper ut. Vivamus consectetur orci justo, eget congue velit. Aenean convallis dolor eget lectus gravida mattis. Phasellus nec sapien risus, in aliquam purus. Class aptent taciti sociosqu ad litora torquent per conubia nostra, per inceptos himenaeos. Nam elementum dui at lacus sagittis in pretium enim facilisis. Maecenas varius quam in risus porttitor posuere. Nullam odio leo, fermentum et porta in, gravida in justo. Vivamus viverra feugiat sapien tristique condimentum.

Loading content with AJAX

A more configurable method of populating the contents of these Splitter widget areas is to load it via AJAX calls. To enable this functionality, simply use the `contentUrl` property of the JavaScript object literal that defines a Splitter widget content area and indicate the page that you want to load via AJAX. The Kendo UI Framework will take care of the rest for you.

```
$("#bottomSubSections").kendoSplitter({
  orientation: "horizontal",
  panes: [
    { collapsible: true, scrollable: false },
    { collapsible: true, scrollable: false },
    { collapsible: true, scrollable: false,
```

```
        contentUrl: "LoremIpsum.html" }
    ]
});
```

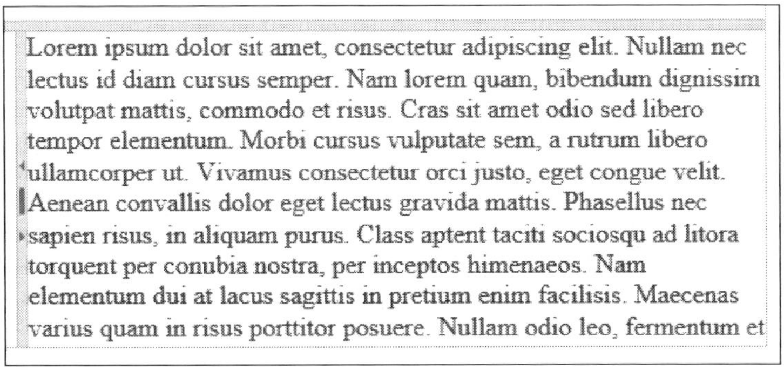

Lorem ipsum dolor sit amet, consectetur adipiscing elit. Nullam nec lectus id diam cursus semper. Nam lorem quam, bibendum dignissim volutpat mattis, commodo et risus. Cras sit amet odio sed libero tempor elementum. Morbi cursus vulputate sem, a rutrum libero ullamcorper ut. Vivamus consectetur orci justo, eget congue velit. Aenean convallis dolor eget lectus gravida mattis. Phasellus nec sapien risus, in aliquam purus. Class aptent taciti sociosqu ad litora torquent per conubia nostra, per inceptos himenaeos. Nam elementum dui at lacus sagittis in pretium enim facilisis. Maecenas varius quam in risus porttitor posuere. Nullam odio leo, fermentum et

Hooking into Splitter events

The Kendo UI Splitter widget is equipped with a range of rich behaviors. Most of these behaviors, whether enacted through a user action or through a method call, trigger an event. Like any event in JavaScript, you can attach your own event handler functions to these events and respond to the actions with your own custom code. This section will show the different events available on the Kendo UI Splitter widget and demonstrate how to hook into them.

The collapse event

The `collapse` event fires when a user collapses a Kendo UI Splitter widget section by clicking on the collapse icon between two of the panes. This icon appears as a small triangle that is pointing in the direction that the `collapse` action will move it. The following is the code that is used to wire up the `collapse` event with an event handler:

```
// Binding during Splitter Widget creation
$("#splitterElement").kendoSplitter({
  ...
  collapse: collapseEventHandler
  ...
});


// Dynamic binding and unbinding
var splitter = $("#splitterElement").data("kendoSplitter");
splitter.bind("collapse", collapseEventHandler);
spliter.unbind("collapse", collapseEventHandler);
```

The contentLoad event

The `contentLoad` event fires when content is loaded into a Kendo UI Splitter widget pane. The normal use of this event is to react to the point when AJAX content has finished loading from the remote source. The following is the code that is used to wire up the `contentLoad` event with an event handler:

```
// Binding during Splitter Widget creation
$("#splitterElement").kendoSplitter({
  ...
  contentLoad: contentLoadEventHandler
  ...
});

// Dynamic binding and unbinding
var splitter = $("#splitterElement").data("kendoSplitter");
splitter.bind("contentLoad", contentLoadEventHandler);
spliter.unbind("contentLoad", contentLoadEventHandler);
```

The expand event

The `expand` event fires when a Kendo UI Splitter widget pane is expanded by a user clicking on the expand icon after a pane has been collapsed. This icon appears as small triangle pointing in the direction that the pane will expand when clicked, as shown here:

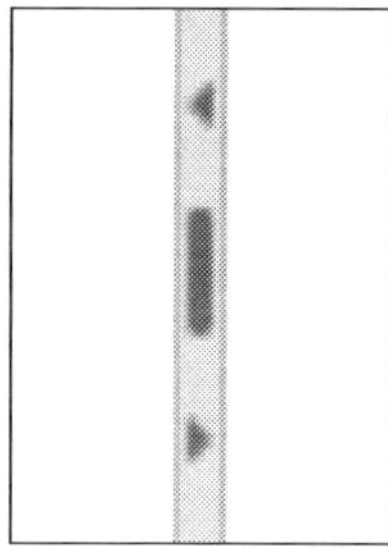

The following is the code that is used to wire up the `expand` event with an event handler:

```
// Binding during Splitter Widget creation
$("#splitterElement").kendoSplitter({
  ...
  expand: expandEventHandler
  ...
});
```

```
// Dynamic binding and unbinding
var splitter = $("#splitterElement").data("kendoSplitter");
splitter.bind("expand", expandEventHandler);
spliter.unbind("expand", expandEventHandler);
```

The layoutChange event

The `layoutChange` event fires when the layout of a Kendo UI Splitter widget has changed. This event is more generic than `expand`, `collapse`, and `resize`, so it will often appear in conjunction with those events since all of them also indicate that the layout has changed. The following is the code that is used to wire up the `layoutChange` event with an event handler:

```
// Binding during Splitter Widget creation
$("#splitterElement").kendoSplitter({
  ...
  layoutChange: layoutChangeEventHandler
  ...
});

// Dynamic binding and unbinding
var splitter = $("#splitterElement").data("kendoSplitter");
splitter.bind("layoutChange", layoutChangeEventHandler);
spliter.unbind("layoutChange", layoutChangeEventHandler);
```

The resize event

The `resize` event is fired when a user drags the handle between two Kendo UI Splitter widget panes in order to resize them. This event is also triggered during `collapse` and `expand`. The following is the code that is used to wire up the `resize` event with an event handler:

```
// Binding during Splitter Widget creation
$("#splitterElement").kendoSplitter({
  ...
  resize: resizeEventHandler
  ...
});

// Dynamic binding and unbinding
var splitter = $("#splitterElement").data("kendoSplitter");
splitter.bind("resize", resizeEventHandler);
spliter.unbind("resize", resizeEventHandler);
```

Making calls to Splitter API methods

The Kendo UI Splitter widget is equipped with a range of methods that enable its rich behaviors. Most of these methods, when fired, trigger an event. Like any event in JavaScript, you can attach your own event handler functions to these events and respond to the actions with your own custom code. This section will show the different methods available on the Kendo UI Splitter widget.

Getting a reference to the splitter object

The first thing to remember when working with methods on all Kendo UI widgets is that you must get a reference to the JavaScript object before these methods are available. To do this, you must use the JavaScript method `.data()`. Here is an example:

```
var splitter = $("#splitterElement").data("kendoSplitter");
```

Notice how jQuery is used to select the **Document Object Model** (**DOM**) element where the Kendo UI Splitter widget has been created and then the `.data()` function has been called with the parameter text `kendoSplitter` indicating the type of object that we are trying to get. Now that the Kendo UI Splitter widget instance has been retrieved, methods can be called from the `splitter` variable directly.

```
splitter.collapse("#outerPane");
```

Using the ajaxRequest method

The `ajaxRequest` method is used to load AJAX content into a specific Kendo UI Splitter widget pane. This method takes three parameters. The first parameter is a string used to select the specific pane into which the AJAX content should be loaded. It uses jQuery syntax to select the element, so to select an element with an `id` value of `pane1`, you would use `#pane1` to select it. The second parameter is the URL of the remote endpoint that contains the content to load into the pane. The third parameter is optional and is used to send data to the remote endpoint if it takes parameters in order to send the data back. Here is a code sample showing the method in action:

```
// Get a reference to the Kendo UI Splitter Widget
var splitter = $("#splitterElement").data("kendoSplitter");

// Call the ajaxRequest method
splitter.ajaxRequest("#pane1", "someContent.html");
```

Note that this method will cause the `contentLoad` event to fire.

Using the collapse method

The `collapse` method is used to collapse a specific Kendo UI Splitter widget pane. This method takes one parameter. The parameter is a string used to select the specific pane which should be collapsed. It uses jQuery syntax to select the element, so to select an element with an `id` value of `pane2`, you would use `#pane2` to select it. Here is a code sample of the method in action:

```
// Get a reference to the Kendo UI Splitter Widget
var splitter = $("#splitterElement").data("kendoSplitter");

// Call the collapse method
splitter.collapse("#pane2");
```

Note that this method will cause the `layoutChange` and `resize` events to fire, but it will not cause the `collapse` event to fire since the user did not initiate the action with the mouse.

Using the expand method

The `expand` method is used to expand a specific Kendo UI Splitter widget pane. This method takes one parameter. The parameter is a string used to select the specific pane which should be expanded. It uses jQuery syntax to select the element, so to select an element with an `id` value of `pane2`, you would use `#pane2` to select it. Here is a code sample of the method in action:

```
// Get a reference to the Kendo UI Splitter Widget
var splitter = $("#splitterElement").data("kendoSplitter");

// Call the expand method
splitter.expand("#pane2");
```

Note that this method will cause the `layoutChange` and `resize` events to fire, but it will not cause the `expand` event to fire since the user did not initiate the action with the mouse.

Using the max and min methods

The `max` and `min` methods are used to set the maximum or minimum size of a specific Kendo UI Splitter widget pane. These methods take two parameters. The first parameter is a string used to select the specific pane that will be configured. It uses jQuery syntax to select the element, so to select an element with an `id` value of `pane3`, you would use `#pane3` to select it. The second parameter is a string value representing the new maximum or minimum size. This value is represented either as a number of pixels or as a percentage. Here is a code sample of the method in action:

```
// Get a reference to the Kendo UI Splitter Widget
var splitter = $("#splitterElement").data("kendoSplitter");

// Call the max method
splitter.max("#pane3", "300px");

// Call the min method
splitter.min("#pane3", "25%");
```

Note that this method will not cause any events to fire.

Using the size method

The `size` method is used to set the size of a specific Kendo UI Splitter widget pane. This method takes two parameters. The first parameter is a string used to select the specific pane that will be configured. It uses jQuery syntax to select the element, so to select an element with an `id` value of `pane4`, you would use `#pane4` to select it. The second parameter is a string value representing the new size. This value is represented either as pixels or as a percentage. It must fall within the range of the max and min size values. Here is a code sample of the method in action:

```
// Get a reference to the Kendo UI Splitter Widget
var splitter = $("#splitterElement").data("kendoSplitter");

// Call the size method
splitter.size("#pane4", "300px");
```

Note that this method will cause the `layoutChange` and `resize` events to fire.

Using the toggle method

The `toggle` method is used to switch the state of a specific Kendo UI Splitter widget pane between collapsed and expanded. If the pane is currently expanded, the toggle method will collapse it. If the pane is currently collapsed, the toggle method will expand it. This method takes two parameters. The first parameter is a string used to select the specific pane that will be toggled. It uses jQuery syntax to select the element, so to select an element with an `id` value of `pane5`, you would use `#pane5` to select it. The second parameter is an optional Boolean value (`true` or `false`) that indicates a specific state that the pane should be set to irrespective of its current state. A value of `true` sets the pane to an expanded state. A value of `false` sets the pane to a collapsed state. Here is a code sample of the method in action:

```
// Get a reference to the Kendo UI Splitter Widget
var splitter = $("#splitterElement").data("kendoSplitter");

// Call the toggle method
splitter.toggle("#pane5");

// Force the pane to expand
splitter.toggle("#pane5", true);

// Force the pane to collapse
splitter.toggle("#pane5", false);
```

Note that this method will cause the `layoutChange` and `resize` events to fire, but it will not trigger the `collapse` or `expand` events.

TreeView

The Kendo UI TreeView widget is a useful widget when you need to display data that is organized hierarchically. Files on a hard disk and business organizational structures are good examples of data that is organized in this way. The data has a top-level element (such as root folder or a CEO) and then has several individual elements (such as files or employees) and groups (such as folders or departments) beneath that top-level element. Each group can have further levels of groups such that the final diagram can be imagined as a tree with a root and many branches (groups of elements) that divide many times and ultimately end with leaves (individual elements). As you can imagine, data like this is not always very easy to visualize and lay out on a web page. Fortunately, the Kendo UI TreeView widget comes to our rescue as an easy way to display this data complete with rich interaction and configuration options.

Learning TreeView

The Kendo UI TreeView widget is designed to work with data that is nested in HTML unordered lists. These are a natural fit for a TreeView to work since they can be nested hierarchically just as Kendo UI intends to display and organize them. Much like the other Kendo UI widgets that organize data, the TreeView widget can be instantiated on top of HTML that has already been rendered on a web page or it can build the HTML itself when fed data through a data source object. Here is a simple example of instantiating a Kendo UI TreeView widget on top of pre-rendered HTML:

```
<div class="demo-section">
  <ul id="treeview">
  <li data-expanded="true">
    Organization Chart
    <ul>
  <li data-expanded="true">
    Administration
    <ul>
    <li>Office Manager</li>
    <li>Resource Manager</li>
    <li>Administrative Assistant</li>
    </ul>
  </li>
  <li data-expanded="true">
    Consulting
    <ul>
    <li data-expanded="true">
      Software Development
      <ul>
    <li>Desktop Applications</li>
    <li>Web Applications</li>
      </ul>
    </li>
    <li>Business Intelligence</li>
    </ul>
  </li>
  <li>Special Projects</li>
  <li>Portals and Collaboration</li>
    </ul>
  </li>
  </ul>
</div>
<script>
  $(document).ready(function () {
```

```
    $("#treeview").kendoTreeView();
    });
  </script>
```

This page shows an organization chart categorized by department and job function. As you can see in the following screenshot, the Kendo UI TreeView widget does a nice job of displaying this. The HTML is capable of rendering hierarchical data without any assistance from the Kendo UI Framework, but ordinary HTML does not offer collapsible sections or any of the other special behaviors that you will see as you read on in this section.

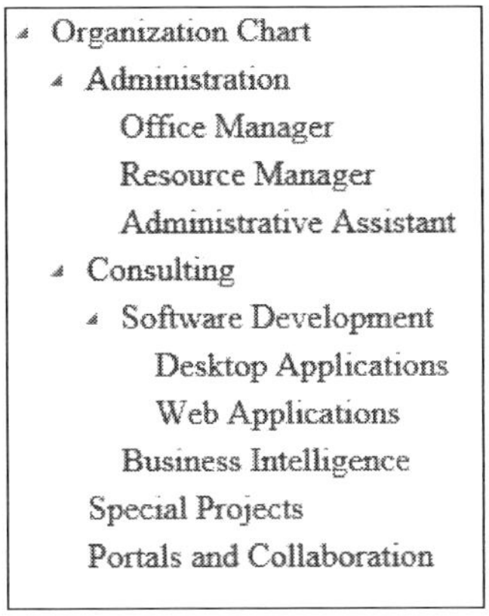

- Organization Chart
  - Administration
    - Office Manager
    - Resource Manager
    - Administrative Assistant
  - Consulting
    - Software Development
      - Desktop Applications
      - Web Applications
    - Business Intelligence
  - Special Projects
  - Portals and Collaboration

Binding to a data source

As you just saw, the Kendo UI TreeView widget is designed to work either on top of existing HTML markup or it can bind to a JavaScript data source. Much like the other Kendo UI widgets that are designed to display and organize data, this data is best contained within a Kendo `DataSource` object that supports the many functions inherent within the Kendo Framework. To display the page that you saw earlier in this fashion, you can use the following code:

```
<script>
  $(document).ready(function () {
  var orgChart = [{
    text: 'Organization Chart', expanded: true, items: [
    { text: 'Administration', expanded: true, items: [
      { text: 'Office Manager' },
      { text: 'Resource Manager' },
      { text: 'Administrative Assistant' }
      ]
    },
    { text: 'Consulting', expanded: true, items: [
```

```
        {
        text: 'Software Development', expanded: true, items: [
          { text: 'Desktop Applications' },
          {text: 'Web Applications'}
        ]
        },
        {text: 'Business Intelligence'}
        ]
      },
      { text: 'Special Projects' },
      { text: 'Portals and Collaboration' }
      ]
    }];
    $("#treeview").kendoTreeView({
      dataSource: orgChart
    });
    });
  </script>
```

Notice how each element can contain its own list of child elements through the items property, such as how the `Software Development` group contains two child elements: `Desktop Applications` and `Web Applications`. These child elements can also contain their own list of child elements, and so on. This is how a tree of data is formed and this is how the Kendo UI TreeView widget processes the data into a graphical tree on the web page. As with any Kendo `DataSource` connection, the data can be bound to a remote source and does not have to be hardcoded into the page.

Using drag and drop

Since the Kendo UI TreeView widget is enabled with special functionality through the Kendo Framework, it can do much more than standard HTML unordered lists. One of these special functions is `dragAndDrop`. When this feature is enabled on a Kendo UI TreeView widget, the user can click on an element in a TreeView and drag it around to anywhere else on that TreeView. Not only this, but if there are multiple TreeView widgets on the same page with drag and drop enabled, the user can drag elements from one TreeView widget to another! To enable this functionality, all you have to do is set the `dragAndDrop` property of the Kendo UI TreeView widget to `true`.

```
$(document).ready(function() {
  $("#treeview").kendoTreeView({
    dataSource: files,
    dragAndDrop: true
  });
});
```

When this has been enabled, the elements of the TreeView widget show a darkened background as a mouse hovers over them to help instruct the user that they are interactive. When an element in the TreeView is dragged, an icon appears next to it to help indicate what action will happen when the mouse button is released. The + sign indicates that an item will be added to a hierarchical section, as shown in the following screenshot:

However, if the mouse is hovering in a position that will leave the item within a list, the icon changes to a picture that looks like a short list of items. At the same time, a small line will appear within the list that will receive the item to indicate where it will be placed, as shown here:

Configuring animation effects

You may have already noticed that the Kendo UI TreeView widget places small triangular icons next to each section of the tree layout where items exist underneath another item. If you click on one of these triangular icons with your mouse, the section will either collapse into a hidden state or will expand into a visible state. When this transition between hidden and visible occurs, the Kendo UI Framework will animate it with some effects that make it visually appealing. These effects can be configured to suit your own personal preference:

```
$("#treeview").kendoTreeView({
  ...
  animation: {
    expand: {         // configure the expand animation
      duration: 200, // milliseconds of animation
      hide: false,    // ?
      show: true,     // ?
      effects: "expandVertical fadeIn" // one or both of these
    },
    collapse: {       // configure the collapse animation
      duration: 200, // milliseconds of animation
      hide: false,    // ?
      show: true,     // ?
      effects: "fadeOut" // "fadeOut" is the only option here
    }
  }
  ...
});
```

Displaying images

The Kendo UI TreeView widget is designed to enable an attractive layout for your content. To this end, the Kendo UI Framework has built-in support for displaying small images inside of the TreeView widget next to the items that you are displaying. This can be done in one of two ways. The first way is to use individual image files for each image that you want to display. The second way is to use a CSS sprite image that contains many images together that are offset by a certain number of pixels.

To use individual image files in a Kendo UI TreeView widget, you can use the `imageUrl` property of the TreeView items. The following is how this appears in code:

```
var orgChart = [{
  text: 'Organization Chart', expanded: true, items: [
  {
    text: 'Administration', expanded: true,
    imageUrl: '/Images/icon-organizational-chart.gif',
    items: [
    { text: 'Office Manager' },
    { text: 'Resource Manager' },
    { text: 'Administrative Assistant' }
    ]
  },
  {
    text: 'Consulting', expanded: true,
    imageUrl: '/Images/icon-organizational-chart.gif',
    items: [
    {
    text: 'Software Development', expanded: true, items: [
      { text: 'Desktop Applications' },
      {text: 'Web Applications'}
    ]
    },
    {text: 'Business Intelligence'}
    ]
  },
  {
    text: 'Special Projects',
    imageUrl: '/Images/icon-organizational-chart.gif',
  },
  {
    text: 'Portals and Collaboration',
    imageUrl: '/Images/icon-organizational-chart.gif',
  }
  ]
}];
```

Using images like this renders the graphics against the left side of the TreeView widget directly in-line with the text of each TreeView item that is decorated with an `imageUrl` property, as shown in the following screenshot:

The other way to use images with your TreeView widget is to reference them from a CSS sprite image file. By using sprite images, you can decrease the number of times your web page has to call the server for separate image files and this can increase the performance of your site. If you have a sprite image that contains your images, you can reference it as follows in code:

```
<style type="text/css">
.org{
  background-image: url('/Images/icon-organizational-chart.gif');
  max-height: 25px;
  max-width: 25px;
  }
</style>
<script>
  $(document).ready(function () {
  var orgChart = [{
    text: 'Organization Chart', expanded: true, items: [
    {
      text: 'Administration', expanded: true,
      spriteCssClass: 'org',
      items: [
      { text: 'Office Manager' },
      { text: 'Resource Manager' },
      { text: 'Administrative Assistant' }
      ]
    },
    ...
```

Using sprites like this renders the graphics against the left side of the TreeView widget directly in-line with the text of each TreeView item that is decorated with an `imageUrl` property, similar to how the images were rendered previously.

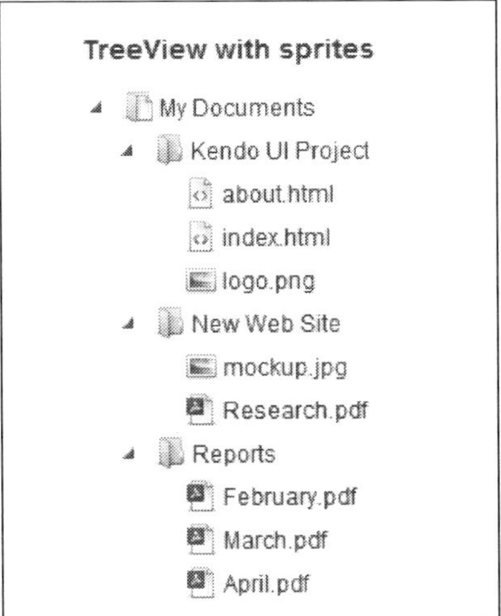

Using templates

The Kendo UI TreeView widget is highly configurable. Along with the ability to add images and sprites, as you just saw in the previous section, it can also be customized through the use of Kendo templates. These templates can be used to create a display that is customizable into any display that you want. As an example, consider the following code sample that is used to create a special TreeView display with icons to the right of each item that can be clicked to remove the item from the Tree View display:

```
<script id="treeview-template" type="text/kendo-ui-template">
  #: item.text #
  # if (!item.items) { #
    <a class='delete-link' href='\#'>[x]</a>
  # } #
</script>

<script>
$("#treeview").kendoTreeView({
  template: kendo.template($("#treeview-template").html()),
  ...
});

// Delete button behavior
```

```
$(document).on("click", ".delete-link", function(e) {
  e.preventDefault();
  var treeview = $("#treeview").data("kendoTreeView");
  treeview.remove($(this).closest(".k-item"));
});
</script>
```

First, notice the template block at the top of the code sample. The template is specifying that the item text is displayed. Then, only if the item does not have a collection beneath it, the anchor link is displayed that can be clicked to delete the item from the TreeView widget. Second, notice that the template is set in the TreeView setup code using the `template` property. Finally, notice that the anchor link's behavior has been wired up using an event handler. The function to delete an item from a TreeView relies on the TreeView API and must be wired up using JavaScript. Here is a screenshot of the way this looks on a web page:

Hooking into TreeView events

The Kendo UI TreeView widget fires several different types of events during the course of its operation. These events provide you, the developer, with the opportunity to run your own code in response to actions that the TreeView runs as it operates. Some of these actions are directly related to user involvement, such as when a user clicks on something. Some of them are more indirect and fire as the TreeView widget changes its state such as when it loads content. Since there are a large number of events associated with the TreeView widget, we will examine them here with brief descriptions for each one:

- `collapse`: The `collapse` event fires when the user clicks on an arrow icon that causes a section of the TreeView widget to collapse.

- `dataBound`: The `dataBound` event is triggered after the data source change event has been processed, such as when items are added or removed from the data source or when the data source is initially populated.
- `drag`: The `drag` event is triggered when an item is dragged from or within a TreeView widget. The `drag` event supplies a lot of very specific details about its location to the event handler which can be used in your custom code.
- `dragEnd`: The `dragEnd` event is triggered when an item has been released at the end of the drag action and it is inserted back into a TreeView widget in a new location.
- `dragStart`: The `dragStart` event is triggered at the start of a drag action as the user begins to drag an item from a TreeView widget.
- `drop`: The `drop` event is triggered when an item is dropped after a drag action. The `drop` event supplies a lot of very specific details about its location to the event handler which can be used in your custom code.
- `expand`: The `expand` event fires when the user clicks on an arrow icon that causes a section of the TreeView widget to expand.
- `select`: The `select` event is triggered when a node is selected by a user clicking on it with the mouse.
- `navigate`: The `navigate` event is triggered when the focus changes from one TreeView node to something else on the page.

Making calls to the TreeView API methods

The Kendo UI TreeView widget is equipped with a wide range of methods that enable its rich behaviors. These methods allow you to manipulate the TreeView widget manually in all of the ways that it supports. By using these API methods, you can configure and engage the TreeView widget however your application needs. Like the events section just discussed, there are many methods that the TreeView widget supports. I will list them all here with brief descriptions:

- `append`: The `append` method appends an element to the end of an existing TreeView widget section.
- `collapse`: The `collapse` method collapses an expanded TreeView widget section.
- `dataItem`: The `dataItem` method retrieves a model data item that is bound to a TreeView widget element.
- `enable`: The `enable` method enables or disables a TreeView widget element.
- `expand`: The `expand` method expands a collapsed TreeView widget section.

- `findByText`: The `findByText` method finds a TreeView element by its text value.
- `findByUID`: The `findByUID` method finds a TreeView element by its `UID` value.
- `insertAfter`: The `insertAfter` method inserts a new element after the specified element in a TreeView widget.
- `insertBefore`: The `insertBefore` method inserts a new element before the specified element in a TreeView widget.
- `parent`: The `parent` method retrieves the parent of an element in a TreeView widget.
- `remove`: The `remove` method removes an element from a TreeView widget.
- `select`: The `select` method marks an element in a TreeView widget as selected.
- `setDataSource`: The `setDataSource` method sets the data source of a TreeView widget.
- `text`: The `text` method can get or set the text value of an element in a TreeView widget.
- `toggle`: The `toggle` method collapses an expanded TreeView section or expands a collapsed TreeView section.

Summary

The Kendo UI Splitter and the Kendo UI TreeView widgets offer a lot of functionality as you develop your web pages. The Splitter widget is an impressive tool in organizing content sections that are collapsible, expandable, and resizable. This type of functionality is not normally so easy. The TreeView widget offers a feature-rich version of a hierarchical unordered HTML list with some very useful features for graphics, collapsible tree sections, and a large number of methods and events. Both of these widgets should add a lot of value to your web site.

In the next chapter, you will learn about two final widgets from the Kendo UI Web Framework, the Window and the Upload widgets. The Window widget allows you create and manage modal pop-up pages with specialized content. The Upload widget gives you a richer set of features around the traditional HTML upload element for a great file-upload experience for the users of your website.

10
The Upload and Window Widgets

Modern web applications have advanced to the point that file uploads and dialog boxes have matured from simple, unattractive HTML elements into interactive and customizable controls. This powerful functionality does not come for free, however; it requires well written JavaScript and CSS styling. The Kendo UI Framework for the Web provides prebuilt controls that give you this functionality for very little effort. This chapter will explore these controls and illustrate their use.

Uploading files

File uploads have traditionally been a clumsy element within web pages. Uploading multiple files was an even worse experience, often requiring multiple HTML upload elements which forced users to click on a separate button for every file. The Kendo UI Framework provides a specialized Upload widget that helps both users and developers in this process. Instead of clicking on buttons for every file, users can simply drag and drop as many files as necessary onto a web page and have them upload automatically, and asynchronously, in the background. Developers, likewise, can program to receive multiple files simultaneously and receive file uploads through JavaScript without causing web pages to become slow and unresponsive.

Learning the Upload widget

Since the Upload widget is designed to upload the contents of one or more files to a server, even the most basic implementation of this widget requires a server that can accept file uploads. You can accomplish this by using your ASP.NET MVC project. To receive the file uploads, you need to create an action method that accepts `IEnumerable<HttpPostedFileBase>` as an input parameter. The following is how the server will receive the files from the Kendo UI Upload widget:

```
// Action method to receive uploaded files
[HttpPost]  // This attribute guarantees that only
            // Form POST requests can call this action method
public ActionResult Submit(IEnumerable<HttpPostedFileBase> files)
{
  if (files != null)
  {
    // ...
    // Process the files and save them
    // ...
  }

  return View();
}
```

With this server code in place to receive the uploaded files, you can now build the page that will host the Kendo UI Upload widget from where the user will choose the files to upload. The following code sample shows an HTML form that has been configured for use as a Kendo UI Upload widget. Take special note that the form has two required input elements: a file input and a submit input. These are the normal input elements that you should expect for any form that uploads files, but in this case, there is also a `script` element that creates a special Kendo UI Upload widget on the file upload element.

Here is the HTML for the index view:

```
<form method="post" action="submit" style="width:45%">
  <div>
    <input name="files" id="files" type="file" />  // HTML file upload
    <p>
      <input type="submit" value="Submit" class="k-button" /> //
Submit button
    </p>
  </div>
</form>
<script>
```

```
    $(document).ready(function() {
      $("#files").kendoUpload();  // Create the Kendo Upload Widget
    });
  </script>
```

The following is how this markup will appear on an actual web page. Take special note that the file input element is displayed as a button instead of the normal style that you see with default HTML.

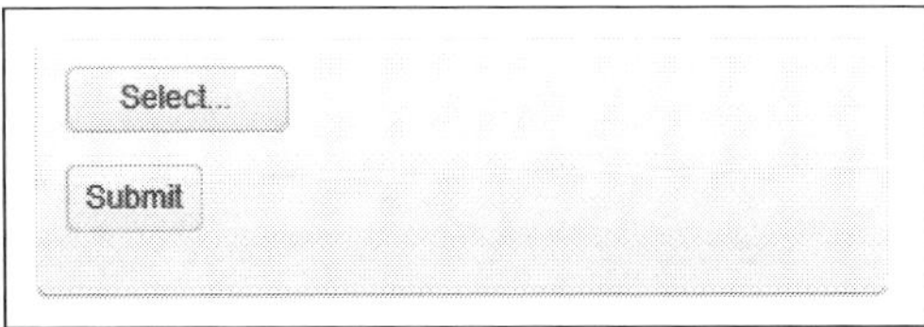

With all of this in place, you can click on the **Select** button to choose a file to upload to the server. Once you have selected that file and clicked **OK**, the server will receive the file and will run any processing instructions that you have set in the server-side code.

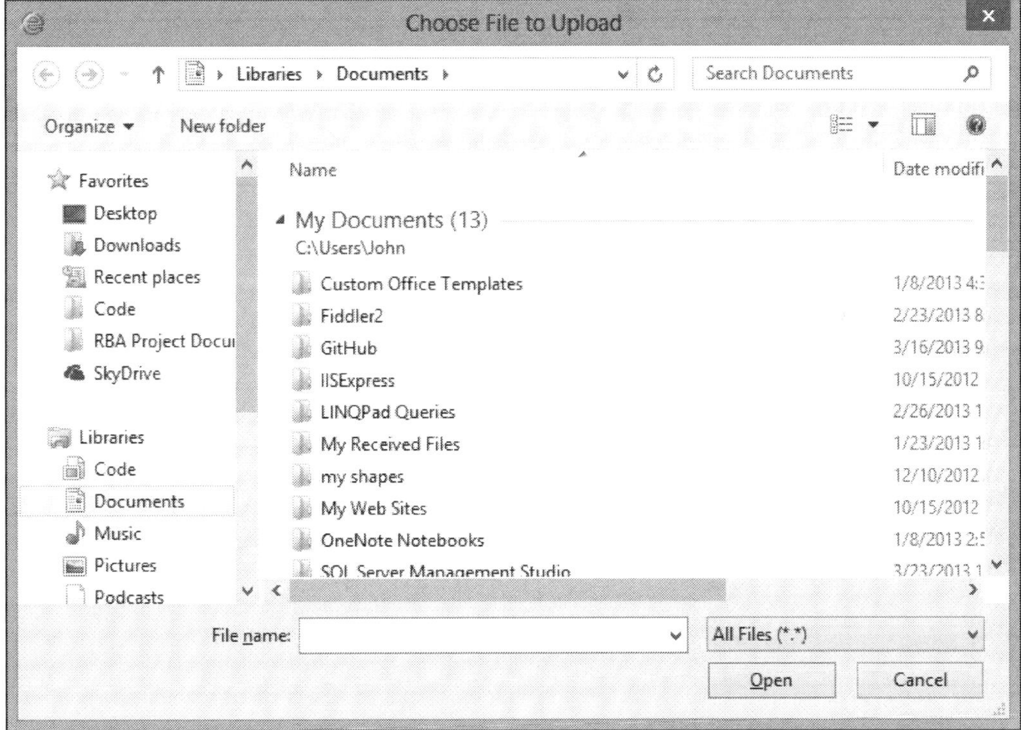

The preceding screenshot shows the file selection dialog that will appear on the user's computer, so that he or she can choose the files to upload.

By adding a breakpoint within the action method code that receives the uploaded files, you can see how ASP.NET MVC interprets the posted data using Visual Studio 2012. The following is a screenshot of an uploaded file and the objects that display information about that uploaded file. In this case, I uploaded a small text file called Reflection.linq. You can see that the web server has received the file successfully and is able to process it as you see fit. This screenshot is showing Visual Studio in debug mode, which allows us to see the internal state of objects. Also, in this screenshot, we can see that the first object in the IEnumerable<HttoPostedFileBase> is a file with the FileName property value of Reflection.linq:

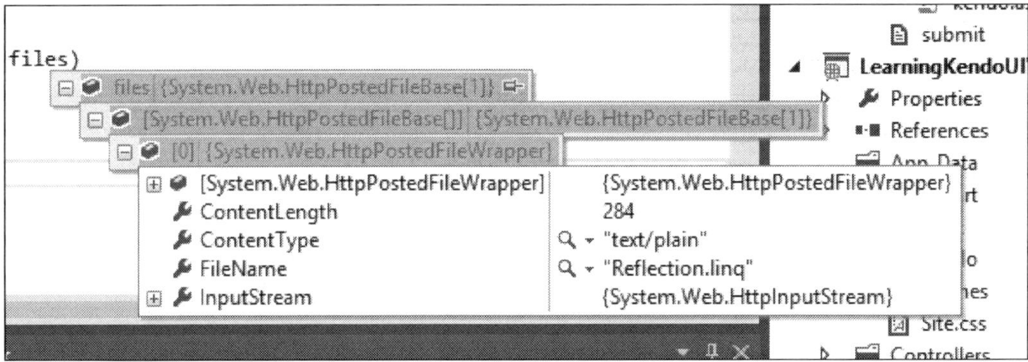

Enabling asynchronous uploads

While the upload experience that we just saw is already a superior experience to a traditional HTML upload element, the experience can get much better. JavaScript is now capable of sending file uploads asynchronously, or in the background, which means that the user does not have to submit a form that causes the page to reload. In other words, the process can run faster and smoother and requires less involvement. To enable this functionality, all you have to do is add the async configuration property to the Kendo Upload widget instantiation block. The following code sample shows how to do it:

```
<form method="post" action="submit" style="width:45%">
  <div>
    <input name="files" id="files" type="file" />
    <p>
      <input type="submit" value="Submit" class="k-button" />
    </p>
  </div>
</form>
```

```
<script>
  $(document).ready(function() {
    $("#files").kendoUpload(
    {
      async: {        // async configuration
        saveUrl: "save",    // the url to save a file is '/save'
        removeUrl: "remove", // the url to remove a file is '/remove'
        autoUpload: true    // automatically upload files once selected
      }
    }
    );
  });
</script>
```

This functionality also requires some changes to the server. Although the majority of this code is the same as in the earlier example, this action method returns `ContentResult` instead of an `ActionResult`, because this action method is not sending a new web page back to the browser. Instead, it sends back a string result that notifies the JavaScript in the web page that the file upload(s) completed successfully. If something goes wrong with the file upload(s), the server will send an error code, such as a code `500` internal server error.

```
public ContentResult Save(IEnumerable<HttpPostedFileBase> files)
{
  // The Name of the Upload component is "files"
  if (files != null)
  {
    foreach (var file in files)
    {
      // ...
      // Process the files and save them...
      // ...
  }

  // Return an empty string to signify success
  return Content("");
}
```

Uploading multiple files simultaneously

By default, the Kendo UI Upload widget enables uploading multiple files at the same time, but you can specify this setting explicitly, as in the following code sample:

```
<script>
  $(document).ready(function() {
    $("#files").kendoUpload(
      {
        multiple: true
      }
    );
  });
</script>
```

To upload multiple files, use the *Ctrl* key while you click on the files in the upload window. See the following screenshot for a display of multiple files selected at once. When you click the **OK** button, all of the files will be uploaded together to the server and will be processed in a single transaction. No more multiple buttons and dialogs required!

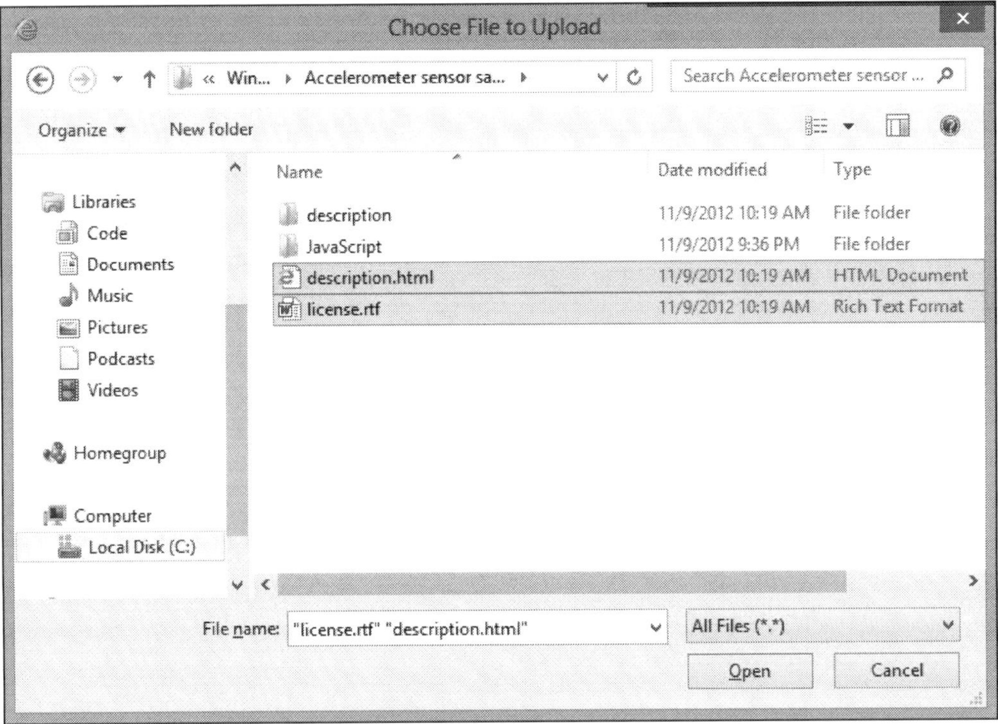

Removing uploaded files

As files are uploaded with the Kendo UI Upload widget, you will see a list of the filenames appear on the page in the file upload area. If you are using the standard upload behavior, not the `async` configuration, the files listed on the page have not yet been uploaded to the server. Rather, their filenames have been stored in preparation for when you click the **Submit** button on the page to submit the HTML with the files attached. You can see a list of files in the following screenshot that have been marked for upload; they have not yet been sent to the server:

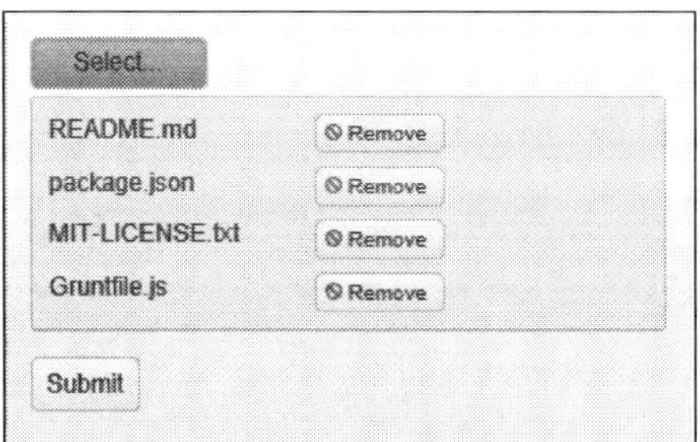

Since these files have not yet been uploaded, you can click the **Remove** button beside any of these files to remove them from the list without any side effects. If you are using the asynchronous file upload functionality, however, the files are uploaded instantly to the server and there is no way to remove them until they have already been fully uploaded. As you can see in this next screenshot, this file has already been loaded asynchronously to the server and has already been saved somewhere by that sever code:

There is still a way to remove the file, but it requires some extra code on the server to make this work. Specifically, for removing asynchronous automatic uploads, another controller action method is required. This action method receives a list of one or more file names and deletes them from the server since they have already been uploaded and saved. The Kendo UI Upload widget calls this method automatically when the **Remove** button is clicked on the page.

```
public ContentResult Remove(string[] fileNames)
{
  // The parameter of the Remove action must be called "fileNames"
```

```
    if (fileNames != null)
    {
      foreach (var fullName in fileNames)
      {
        // ...
        // delete the files
        // ...
      }
    }

    // Return an empty string to signify success
    return Content("");
  }
```

Tracking upload progress

While a file is being uploaded asynchronously, you can see the progress of the upload with a progress bar displayed beneath the filename and a swirling circle of dots to indicate that the action is still occurring. The following screenshot shows a file upload in progress:

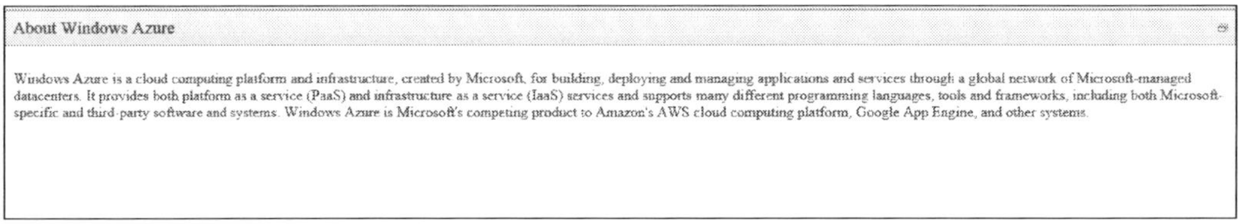

Cancelling an update in progress

While a file upload is taking place asynchronously, a button will appear beside the progress bar for cancelling the upload. If you click this button, it will attempt to cancel the asynchronous upload that is in progress. You should note that cancelling asynchronous uploads is never a guaranteed success. Most file uploads occur very quickly and it is unlikely that you will be able to cancel it in time. Also, even if you are able to click the **Cancel** button in time, the process will still continue for a short period of time before the background threads respond to the cancellation. This is just to say that cancelling a file upload may work, but it also may not and it is hard to predict either way.

Using file drag and drop

If you are using the asynchronous file upload functionality, there is another special feature that you can take advantage of. Since the asynchronous file upload processes the files immediately through JavaScript, the web page can enable some special behavior, such as dragging and dropping files onto the page using your mouse. This functionality is also enabled by default, so you can take advantage of it without any further configuration. All you have to do is drag a file from your computer and drop it on the screen where the Kendo UI Upload widget is present. As you drag the file onto the page, you will see the page react by showing some text instructing the user where to drop the file. When the file is dropped, the upload starts immediately.

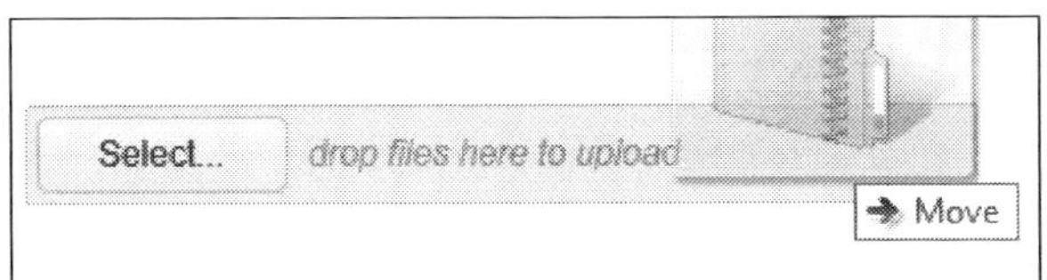

The Kendo UI Window widget

JavaScript has long supported pop-up windows that can send messages to a user in a web browser. These messages can be simple text for the user to see, they can be confirmation boxes to ask permission, or they can even sometimes prompt the user to enter some information. Of course, these pop-up messages have two big problems. First, they are unattractive and have the appearance of a system message instead of a coherent portion of a website. Second, they have been so overused and abused in the past that many users disable them entirely or make it a habit to avoid sites that use them because they are annoying at best and a potential security risk at worst.

Modern web programmers have found a solution to this problem. JavaScript frameworks have been created that can create a different kind of pop-up message. Instead of using the actual system prompts that JavaScript did in the past, they have found a way to display hovering HTML `div` elements that are not actual pop-up messages at all, they are a true portion of the page that can be hidden or displayed on demand. The Kendo UI Window widget is a tool to build these nice hovering page elements.

Since the underlying concept to this technology is hiding and displaying specific HTML `div` elements, the basic use of this widget is simply to create a Kendo UI Window widget directly on a `div` tag. This will hide it until you are ready to show it and, once you are ready to show it, it will animate it onto the screen as a hovering element above the rest of your page. See the following code sample for a basic example:

```
<div id="window">
  <p>Windows Azure is a cloud computing platform
  and infrastructure, created by Microsoft, for building,
  deploying and managing applications and services through
  a global network of Microsoft-managed datacenters.
  It provides both platform as a service (PaaS) and
  infrastructure as a service (IaaS) services and supports
  many different programming languages, tools and frameworks,
  including both Microsoft-specific and third-party software
  and systems. Windows Azure is Microsoft's competing product
  to Amazon's AWS cloud computing platform, Google App Engine,
  and other systems.</p>
</div>
<button id="windowButton">See Details</button>
<script>
  $(document).ready(function() {
    $("#window").kendoWindow({
      width: "600px",
      title: "About Windows Azure",
      close: onClose
    });

    var onClose = function(){
      $("#windowButton").show();
    };

    $("#windowButton").on("click", function(){
      $("#window").data("kendoWindow").open();
      $("#windowButton").hide();
    });
  });
</script>
```

You can see the Kendo UI Window widget being created over the HTML element with an `id` value of `window`. The button with the ID of `windowButton` is wired up to open the Window widget and the event handlers hide this button while the Window widget is open and then show it again when the Window widget is closed.

The markup inside your `div` will be the markup inside the Window widget when it appears. This means that all of your styles and layouts are still shown properly in the same way as the rest of your page; there is no disconnect. The following is how this code looks when rendered on the page. Notice that the content of the Kendo UI Window widget is not yet shown, it must first be activated through an event; in this case that event is clicking on the **Show Window** button:

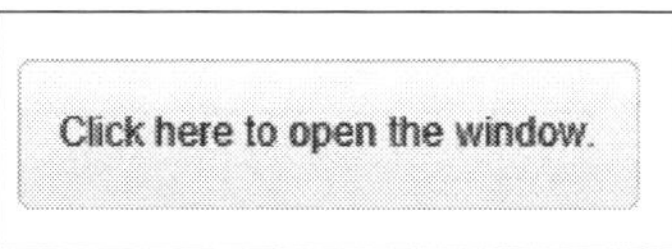

This is how the Kendo UI Window widget looks when it is activated:

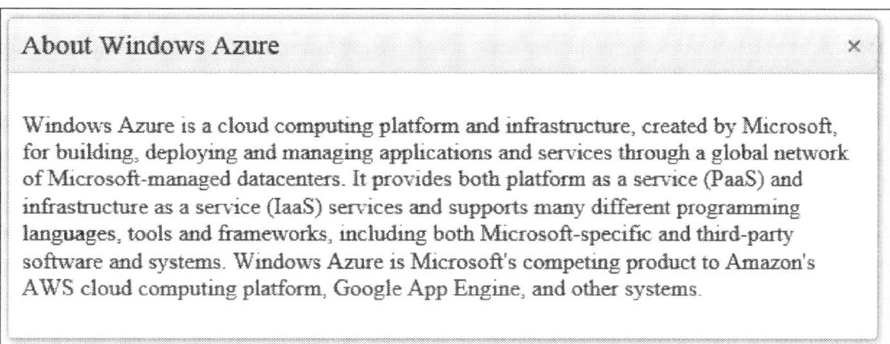

Customizing Window actions

The Kendo UI Window widget adds some default functionality to all windows that it creates. There is a button at the upper-right corner of the window, which is used as a close button, there is a title bar to give the purpose of the window content clear to the user, and the window is resizable if a user clicks one of the edges with a mouse and drags it. The buttons that appear in the upper-right corner of the Window widget can be customized for your web page and specific needs.

As you see, the only button that appears by default is the close button. However, there are three other buttons that can be added very easily: `Refresh`, `Minimize`, and `Maximize`. These buttons already have default functionality attached to them. The `Refresh` button will refresh the content inside the Window widget if it has been loaded from a remote source. The `Minimize` button will reduce the size of the Window widget to just the title bar. The `Maximize` button will enlarge the Window widget so that it takes up the entire web browser's screen size. After you click either the `Minimize` or `Maximize` buttons, a new special button appears for the sole purpose of restoring the Window widget back to its original position and size. Here is the code you need to use in order to enable these actions in your Window widget:

```
<script>
  $(document).ready(function() {
    $("#window").kendoWindow({
      width: "600px",
      title: "About Windows Azure",
      actions: ["Minimize", "Maximize", "Close"],
      close: onClose
    });

    var onClose = function(){
      $("#windowButton").show();
    };

    $("#windowButton").on("click", function(){
      $("#window").data("kendoWindow").open();
      $("#windowButton").hide();
    });
  });
</script>
```

Here is how the Window widget appears with these actions enabled:

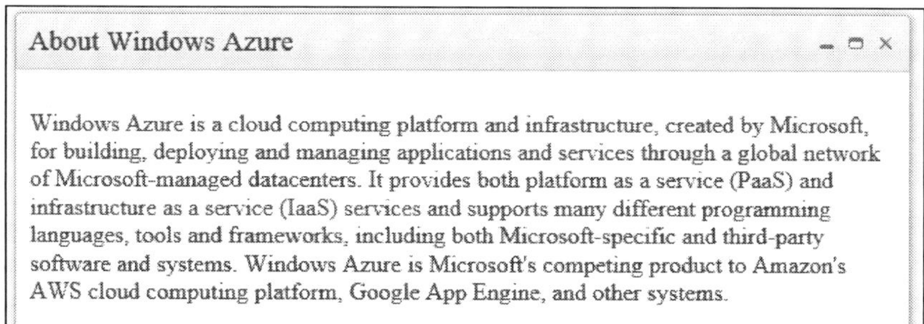

Here is a minimized Window widget, note that the `Minimize` button has been changed to the button which will restore the original size and shape of the window:

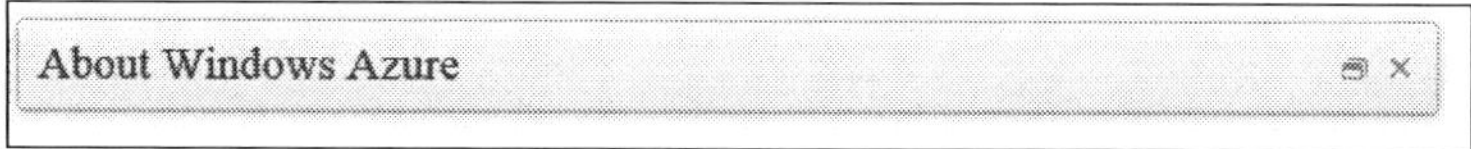

Here is a maximized Window widget in the next screenshot. Note that the `Maximize` button has been changed to the button that will restore the original size and shape of the window:

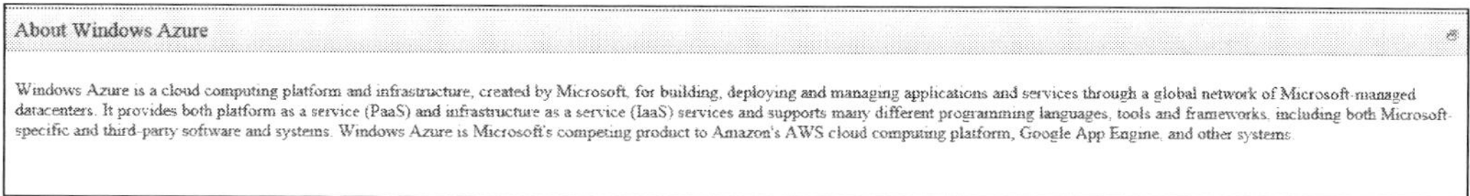

Loading content with AJAX

All of the examples you have seen so far have displayed local content in the Window widget, or content already embedded in the web page. This is only useful in limited scenarios. The Window widget is much more flexible when it can load content from external sources, such as other web pages in your overall site. To make this work, you need to configure the Window widget with a content source. You can see an example of this in the following code sample:

```
<script>
  $(document).ready(function() {
    $("#window").kendoWindow({
      width: "600px",
      title: "Rams's Ten Principles of Good Design",
      content: "OtherPage.html",
      close: onClose
    });

    var onClose = function(){
      $("#windowButton").show();
    };

    $("#windowButton").on("click", function(){
      $("#window").data("kendoWindow").open();
      $("#windowButton").hide();
    });
  });
</script>
```

With this enabled, the Window widget will load and display this external content as soon as it is activated. This has the added benefit that the loaded content is not downloaded until necessary, so the page will load somewhat faster. Here is a Window widget that has loaded external content in this way:

Using the animation effects

When the Window widget is activated on the page, it animates onto the screen with some pleasant effects. By default, it will use the zoom effect which makes the Window widget appear as if it zooms in from a very small object into the full size. The other available effects are the toggle effect, the expand effect, and a choice of whether or not the Window widget animation should start as semi-transparent. The following code sample shows the animation effects as they are configured by default:

Note that no special animation configuration is included. The only way to run the default animation is to leave the animation configuration element out of the setup.

```
<script>
  $(document).ready(function() {
    $("#window").kendoWindow({
      width: "600px",
      title: "About Alvar Aalto"
    }
      close: onClose
    });
```

```
      var onClose = function(){
        $("#windowButton").show();
      };

      $("#windowButton").on("click", function(){
        $("#window").data("kendoWindow").open();
        $("#windowButton").hide();
      });
    });
  </script>
```

To enable the toggle animation, change the code so that it appears like the following code sample. The toggle animation is actually the absence of a special animation, so that the Window Widget appears or disappears immediately instead of going through a graphical transition.

```
  <script>
    $(document).ready(function() {
      $("#window").kendoWindow({
        width: "600px",
        title: "About Alvar Aalto",
        animation: {
      open: {
        effects: ""
      },
      close: {
        effects: ""
      }
      }
        close: onClose
      });

      var onClose = function(){
        $("#windowButton").show();
      };

      $("#windowButton").on("click", function(){
        $("#window").data("kendoWindow").open();
        $("#windowButton").hide();
      });
    });
  </script>
```

To enable the expand animation, change the code so that it appears like the following code sample. The `reverse` configuration property is used to reverse the animation for the `close` effect.

```
<script>
  $(document).ready(function() {
    $("#window").kendoWindow({
      width: "600px",
      title: "About Alvar Aalto",
      animation: {
    open: {
      effects: "expand:vertical"
    },
    close: {
      effects: "expand:vertical",
      reverse: true
    }
    }
      close: onClose
    });

    var onClose = function(){
      $("#windowButton").show();
    };

    $("#windowButton").on("click", function(){
      $("#window").data("kendoWindow").open();
      $("#windowButton").hide();
    });
  });
</script>
```

The transparency effect can be used with any of these animation effects, and it is enabled or disabled separately. The following code sample shows how to enable or disable the animation. The only difference from the previous example is the extra string value `fadeIn` at the end of the `effects` property values.

```
<script>
  $(document).ready(function() {
    $("#window").kendoWindow({
      width: "600px",
      title: "About Alvar Aalto",
      animation: {
    open: {
      effects: "expand:vertical fadeIn"
```

```
      },
      close: {
        effects: "expand:vertical fadeIn",
        reverse: true
      }
      }
        close: onClose
      });

      var onClose = function(){
        $("#windowButton").show();
      };

      $("#windowButton").on("click", function(){
        $("#window").data("kendoWindow").open();
        $("#windowButton").hide();
      });
    });
  </script>
```

Using the Window widget events

The Kendo UI Window widget provides a set of events that fire in response to various user events. Since there a number of these, I will list them here with brief descriptions for each one:

- `Activate`: This event fires when the Window widget animation completes after opening
- `Close`: This event fires when the Window widget is closed
- `Deactivate`: This event fires when the Window widget animation completes after closing
- `Dragend`: This event fires when a user finishes dragging a Window widget with a mouse
- `Dragstart`: This event fires when a user starts to drag a Window widget with the mouse
- `Error`: This event fires when a Window widget encounters an error while loading remote content through AJAX

- `Open`: This event fires when a Window widget opens
- `Refresh`: This event fires when the remote content within a Window widget is refreshed from the remote source
- `Resize`: This event fires when a Window widget is resized by a user with the mouse

Using the Window widget API methods

The API methods allow us to execute functionality on the Window widget on demand in our JavaScript code. See the following brief description on what sort of options we have when calling API methods:

- `Center`: Calling this method returns the Window widget to the centre of the screen.
- `Close`: Calling this method closes the Window widget.
- `Content`: Calling this method either gets the current content of a Window widget when called with no parameters or sets the content of a Window widget when provided new content as a parameter.
- `Maximize`: Calling this method maximizes a Window widget.
- `Minimize`: Calling this method minimizes a Window widget.
- `Open`: Calling this method opens a Window widget that is closed.
- `Refresh`: Calling this method refreshes the content of a Window widget from its remote source through AJAX. This method only works for Window widget objects that have an AJAX content property set.
- `Restore`: Calling this method restores a Window widget from the minimized state back into the normal size and position.
- `SetOptions`: Calling this method sets the configuration options of a Window widget.
- `Title`: Calling this method either gets or sets the title of a Window widget
- `ToFront`: Calling this method brings a Window widget to the front of other elements on the page
- `ToggleMaximization`: Calling this method either maximizes a Window widget that is not currently maximized or returns a maximized Window widget back to its original size and position.

Summary

In this chapter, we learned how to use the Window and Upload widgets. These widgets give you the power to create scalable and interactive web pages that your users will appreciate. Most importantly, these widgets provide ready-made solutions to very common web development problems so that you can focus on your code instead of solving repetitive problems.

In this book, we have seen a full array of the different Kendo UI Web tools that are available for developing powerful web pages. As you have seen in every chapter, these widgets are very friendly to use and offer a wide range of configuration options to be tailored to your specific needs and situation. Not only this, but Telerik has an active community of developers that can assist with implementation details through web forums and blogs and even paid support, if necessary. I hope you have enjoyed learning about the powerful tools available from Telerik in the Kendo UI Web framework. These tools will lower the overall time investment and effort involved in delivering rich web pages, and that is something most of us can happily appreciate.

11
Web API Examples

Many of the widgets that we explored in the previous chapters are most useful when paired with more advanced server-side code. For example, many web applications use databases and work with files. While the previous chapters showed the client-side code, such as HTML and JavaScript, that is necessary to use these widgets, they did not focus on the ASP.NET server-side C# code that many real-world applications utilize. To demonstrate how to use the Kendo UI Framework with these types of scenarios, this chapter will show some specialized examples of using the Kendo UI Framework with the ASP.NET Web API and with the Entity Framework.

> If you are unfamiliar with the ASP.NET Web API framework, you can visit `www.asp.net/web-api` for some good examples, videos, and walkthroughs.

Getting familiar with the ASP.NET Web API

The most recent release of the ASP.NET MVC Framework, MVC 4, included templates for a new feature known as **Web API controllers**. These controllers are specialized HTTP communication endpoints and allow for the creation of RESTful API services. A RESTful API service is a HTTP web service that allows clients to communicate using standard HTTP verbs (`Get`, `Post`, `Put`, `Delete`, and `Patch`) in order to perform operations on the server.

> Traditionally, ASP.NET has had the ability to create web services as SOAP endpoints (as opposed to REST endpoints). SOAP web services use XML schemas and are very good at serializing and deserializing strongly-typed objects and have been widely adopted in production systems. Compared with RESTful services, SOAP services are very verbose and brittle, as a change to the schema is required to implement any new features. Additionally, the explosive growth around JavaScript has made RESTful services more appealing to developers since they can be easily accessed through HTML `script` blocks and common JavaScript code.

RESTful web services are becoming more and more common on the Internet. Many popular web-based services expose public RESTful APIs to enable integration with mobile apps, web-based dashboards, and other software projects. This widespread adoption is due largely in part to the equally widespread adoption of **JavaScript Object Notation (JSON)** for serializing and deserializing objects. JSON makes it simple for any web client to interpret data from any web server without requiring specialized or proprietary licenses or algorithms.

A RESTful web request is very simple and you use them every day, if you did not already know it. Every time you type a URL into a web browser, you are issuing an HTTP GET request to the server at that URL address. Likewise, most web pages that include forms use the HTTP POST verb to post that data back to the web server to be saved. This may also jog your memory back to some of our code samples in previous chapters. Do you remember seeing the `[HttpGet]` and `[HttpPost]` attributes on some of the controller action methods? These attributes indicated to ASP.NET that only a specific type of HTTP verb (either a GET or a POST) is allowed for that action method. This does have security implications of course, but it is actually more useful for determining which method the server should use depending on which HTTP verb the client sent along with the request. In other words, a controller could have five different action methods with different HTTP verb attributes for each one, as shown here:

```
[HttpGet]
public ActionResult Get(int objectId = 0)
{
  ...
}

[HttpPost]
public ActionResult Post(Object postedObject)
{
  ...
}
```

```
[HttpPut]
public ActionResult Put(Object objectToPut)
{
  ...
}

[HttpPatch]
public ActionResult Patch(Object objectToPatch)
{
  ...
}

[HttpDelete]
public ActionResult Delete(int objectId)
{
  ...
}
```

The problem with the preceding code is that it creates a separate route for each of the different functions for the page. If this page were accessible from the route `http://mysite.com/movies`, we could use `http://mysite.com/movies/get/25` to see data for a specific movie, but we would have to use a completely different route in order to add a new movie or to delete a movie, such as `http://mysite.com/movies/put`. This may not seem like such a big problem for a website where URLs can be embedded in forms and links without much interaction from the user, but this is a big problem for developers trying to create a program to access the API from remote code.

The ASP.NET MVC Web API solves this problem by creating special controllers solely for the purpose of creating RESTful services. In a standard MVC controller, each action method creates a new route (or URL) that ultimately generates some web content inside a view. In a Web API controller, however, each action method specifies a single HTTP verb for the same route (or URL). In other words, a Web API controller serves only a single HTTP endpoint; it only operates for a single route. For an API developer, this is perfect. A single HTTP endpoint, such as `http://mysite.com/api/movies`, can respond to all of the HTTP verbs appropriately without having to use different URLs for each operation.

Inside of the API controller, each of the HTTP verbs gets one or more action methods for serving that specific type of request. The route to the controller defaults to the controller's name. So a controller called `MoviesController.cs` would default to the route `http://mysite.com/api/movies`. This is as far as the route goes; the only difference now between requests to this endpoint is in which HTTP verb the request includes and which parameters are passed in as arguments. The following is the default code generated by the ASP.NET Web API template for an API controller:

```
// GET api/values
public IEnumerable<string> Get()
{
  return new string[] { "value1", "value2" };
}

// GET api/values/5
public string Get(int id)
{
  return "value";
}

// POST api/values
public void Post([FromBody]string value)
{
}

// PUT api/values/5
public void Put(int id, [FromBody]string value)
{
}

// DELETE api/values/5
public void Delete(int id)
{
}
```

Notice that the names of the action methods are the names of HTTP verbs. This is not an accident, it is required that the action method names either match an HTTP verb name or begin with an HTTP verb name. So an action method can either be called `Get` or it could be called `GetMovie`. Also notice that there are two different versions of the `Get` action method in this controller. Just like in a standard controller, the same action method can be listed multiple times as long as the signature for each method is unique. In this case, it allows us to have a standard `Get` method that does not require any parameters and a more specialized `Get` method that returns information for a specific record.

> You can visit http://www.asp.net/web-api/overview/web-api-routing-and-actions/routing-in-aspnet-web-api for a good overview of Web API routing rules and naming conventions.

You will also notice that these action methods do not have the HTTP verb attributes on them. For an API controller, these attributes are not required. There is a new attribute in the code sample, however. You can see it in front of the parameters for the `Post` and `Put` action methods: `[FromBody]`. This special attribute is used to assist the model binder in locating the parameter in the body of the HTTP request. It is not always necessary, such as when you are binding a complex object that the model binder can clearly see is made up of specific properties with specific names. For a simple string value as in this code sample, however, it needs to know that you intend to bind the HTTP request body to that input parameter. There is also an attribute (`[FromUri]`) to indicate that a parameter comes from the URL. Most of the time, these parameters will be unnecessary but they are available to help solve problems that the model binder is unable to solve on its own. It is worth some more research if you unfamiliar with it. The basic rules that Web API uses for model binding work like this:

- Simple types are taken from the URL (URI)
- Complex types are taken from the request body

Simple types include all of the .NET Framework primitive types, plus `DateTime`, `Decimal`, `Guid`, `String`, and `TimeSpan`. For each action method, at most one parameter can read the request body. If you try to mark more than one parameter with `[FromBody]`, you will either get a runtime error or null values.

> You can visit http://blogs.msdn.com/b/jmstall/archive/2012/04/16/how-webapi-does-parameter-binding.aspx for more information on parameter binding with Web API.

Another important concept to understand about API controllers is that they do not return views like standard controllers do. Rather than generating HTML markup for a web browser to display, API controllers generate raw data that is intended for specialized client code, such as JavaScript, to consume. The format of this data is something that you do not have to worry about. Notice how the action methods in the previous code sample simply return string values without using the `Json()` method that we have seen in some of the previous chapters. We do not need to tell the API controller how to format its data because it will auto-negotiate the correct format with the client during the communication process. The most common format is JSON, but some clients may prefer XML or other data types that the ASP.NET framework understands how to serialize.

> You may be interested in knowing how this auto-negotiation works. Here is the answer: it is based largely on the `Accept` header from the client during the API call. You can even create your own content types to extend the API framework for customized scenarios. See this page for more information: `http://www.asp.net/web-api/overview/formats-and-model-binding/content-negotiation`.

Since API controllers are not designed to render web pages with markup, you will need to create normal controllers for your web pages as you are used to doing. To interact with the API controllers, it is very common to utilize JavaScript, especially jQuery, to access the API endpoints with a specific HTTP verb to accomplish whatever task your page is designed for.

Getting familiar with Entity Framework Code First

Most applications use a database to store information. Most databases, however, store information in a way that does not exactly match up with server-side object oriented programming. This is a very common problem and has given rise to the field of **Object Relational Mapping (ORM)** systems. Many of these exist, but Microsoft has created one specific to the .NET framework known as the **Entity Framework (EF)**. It is basically a framework designed to more easily write code that stores information in a database but still behaves like an object oriented system. If you have downloaded the sample content for this chapter, go ahead and open the `Chapter 11` solution now to follow along. Otherwise, create a new ASP.NET MVC 4 project and choose the **Web API** template when asked.

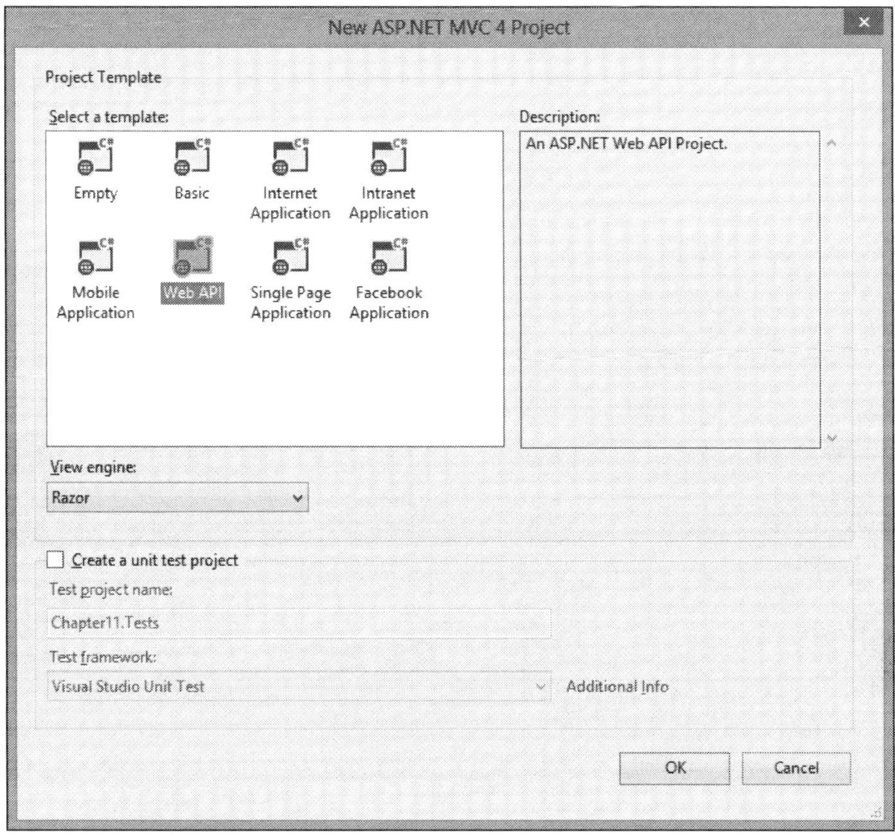

The particulars of the Entity Framework are numerous and there is not enough space here to explore them. We will go through a basic example of how to utilize the Entity Framework Code First model so that we can show this in the examples for this chapter. In order to use the Entity Framework, you must first install it into your Visual Studio project through NuGet. You can do this by right-clicking the project in the Solution Explorer in Visual Studio and choosing **Manage NuGet Packages...**, as shown here:

On the next screen, you should make sure that you are viewing the **Online** catalogue. Type the text `Entity Framework` into the search box and choose **Install** when it appears in the results window. Once installed, it will display a green check mark indicating that it is ready for use:

This will install all of the necessary components of the Entity Framework into your Visual Studio solution. We will be using a feature of the Entity Framework known as **Code First**. This feature allows us to create classes, or entities, for our data first before the database even exists. The biggest benefit from this model is that it guarantees that the database will be designed and the data will be stored in accordance with our object oriented architecture.

If you have not already done so, now is a good time to download the sample content for this chapter. All of these examples and files will already be present there, so you can follow along with working code.

For the sake of illustration, we will create our entity classes in the `Models` folder inside of our Visual Studio project. Create a class called `Movie.cs` in the `Models` folder like this:

```
public class Movie
{
  public int Id { get; set; }
  public string Name { get; set; }
  public int ReleaseYear { get; set; }
  public int Rating { get; set; }
  public int Rank { get; set; }
}
```

The Entity Framework will infer from the properties here that the `Id` property should become the primary key inside the database. Now that we have our model, we need to tell the Entity Framework that we want to make a database that includes it. Create another class in the `Models` folder and call it `MoviesContext.cs`, as shown here:

```
...
using System.Data.Entity;
...

public class MoviesContext : DbContext
{
  public DbSet<Movie> Movies { get; set; }
}
```

This code informs the Entity Framework that we want a `DbContext` context that includes a `DbSet` of `Movie` entities. Let's go ahead and add some movies to our database, so that we can make use of them in our examples. To get started, we need a page where we can type in the movie data and have the web server save that data to the database.

Create a `MoviesController` controller with these options selected; it will automatically scaffold action methods and views with basic operations for managing the `Movie` entity that we just created.

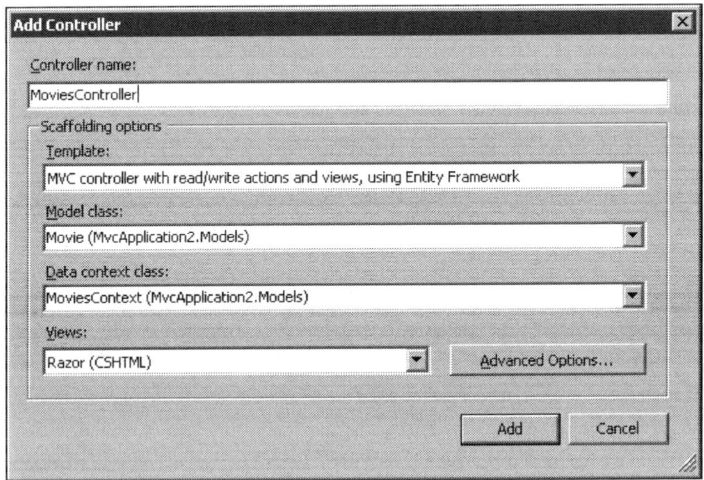

If you cannot find your `Movie` entity or the `MoviesContext` class, try building your project and trying again.

Now go to the `Movies/Index` page and create some movies. The first time you run the project, it may be very slow. The reason for this is that Entity Framework is creating your database on-the-fly in the background from the model and the context that you provided earlier. By the time you see the web page, the database will be up and running. You can see how I have created a few in the following screenshot. Create at least ten so that the examples have some data later in the chapter.

Index

Create New

Name	ReleaseYear	Rating	Rank	
Eternal Sunshine of the Spotless Mind	2004	84	1	Edit | Details | Delete
Safety Not Guaranteed	2012	71	2	Edit | Details | Delete
Star Trek	2009	80	3	Edit | Details | Delete
Go	1999	72	4	Edit | Details | Delete
Wonder Boys	2000	74	5	Edit | Details | Delete
The Game	1997	77	6	Edit | Details | Delete
The Ghost and the Darkness	1996	67	7	Edit | Details | Delete
Heat	1995	83	8	Edit | Details | Delete
Cowboys & Aliens	2011	61	9	Edit | Details | Delete
The Fugitive	1993	78	10	Edit | Details | Delete

Although there is a lot more to learn about the Entity Framework, this brief example has taken you all the way from a single class to a fully working database. We will be using this movies database in the rest of the examples for this chapter. If you are not familiar with the Entity Framework and would like to learn more, I recommend inspecting the `MoviesController.cs` class that we just created with Visual Studio to see how it created the default actions; you can then visit `www.msdn.com` for the official documentation on the topic.

Getting familiar with OData

The ASP.NET Web API framework supports data queries through a syntax known as **OData**. OData is a query language that is compatible with HTTP URLs so that it can appear in URL query strings. It provides two very powerful benefits to API action methods that are used to return lists of data. First, it automatically translates the OData query language into an actual data query on the data inside of your API action method. This is amazingly powerful and may be hard to believe until you can actually see it. Basically, it is a search engine for free. Second, the OData features allow the queries to occur on the server. This means that the server can query the data source for the specific elements that match and then return the result back to the client. The client does not have to query the full set of data and then filter on its own. This is a huge performance improvement and also simplifies both client and server code.

There are four ways by which you can enable the OData query features for your API controllers. Each providing more fine-grained control than its predecessor.

- Enable query support globally through `WebApiConfig.cs`
- Add the `[Queryable]` attribute to specific API action methods
- Inherit from `ODataController` instead of `ApiController`
- Inherit from `EntitySetController` instead of `ODataController`

The first option will globally enable query support for any `ApiController` action method with an `IQueryable` return type. To enable this, open the `WebApiConfig.cs` file inside of the `App_Start` folder and un-comment the line of code with `config.EnableQuerySupport()`:

```
// Uncomment the following line of code to enable query support
   for actions with an IQueryable or IQueryable<T> return type.
// To avoid processing unexpected or malicious queries, use the
   validation settings on QueryableAttribute to validate
   incoming queries.
// For more information, visit
   http://go.microsoft.com/fwlink/?LinkId=279712.
config.EnableQuerySupport();
```

The second option will enable query support for specific action methods that you decorate with the [Queryable] attribute. This gives you more configuration choices than the previous option because the [Queryable] attribute has many properties that you can configure to fine-tune its behavior. An action method decorated with this attribute looks like the following:

```
// GET api/values
[Queryable]
public IQueryable<string> Get()
{
  return new string[] { "value1", "value2" }.AsQueryable();
}
```

The third option involves inheriting your controller class from ODataController instead of ApiController. This will enable the full OData support that the Web API offers and also requires some more configuration to be done, so that the OData engine understands the **Entity Data Model (EDM)** for the entities that it is exposing.

```
ODataModelBuilder modelBuilder = new ODataConventionModelBuilder();
modelBuilder.EntitySet<Movie>("Movies");
Microsoft.Data.Edm.IEdmModel model = modelBuilder.GetEdmModel();
config.Routes.MapODataRoute("ODataRoute", "OData", model);
```

The preceding code needs to run as the web application starts, so it should be placed either in Global.asax or in one of the App_Start classes, such as WebApiConfig.cs. It reads the same type of entity model as the Entity Framework and loads this into an OData route so that Web API understands how each part of the model is related, what the primary keys are, and so on. This enables more advanced scenarios such as property navigation. For more information on this, you can visit http://www.asp.net/web-api/overview/odata-support-in-aspnet-web-api/getting-started-with-odata-in-web-api/create-a-read-only-odata-endpoint for an introduction.

The fourth option is similar to the previous option, but it enables more OData functionality automatically that the ODataController class would have to do manually. It still requires the ODataModelBuilder class as in the last option. The URL just listed also covers information on this topic.

For our examples in this chapter, we will be using the [Queryable] attribute to enable query support for specific action methods. I encourage you to explore this technology more on your own, it is a powerful and extensible framework that can provide huge productivity boosts to your code. To learn more about OData, you can visit www.odata.org.

Using DataSourceRequest with Kendo Grid

As we saw in the first chapter, the Kendo Grid widget is designed to allow a rich set of features such as paging, filtering, and sorting. We saw previously how this can be driven on the client side through JavaScript and the Kendo `DataSource` object. The Grid widget becomes even more powerful, however, when connected with server-side functionality to help drive its features.

The Kendo UI Framework for ASP.NET MVC includes a special object to help facilitate this functionality within standard MVC controllers. It does not require the Web API or OData, although you could use them if you want to configure the Kendo `DataSource` by hand. In this example, we will learn how to use the `DataSourceRequest` object and how it helps drive the functionality of a Kendo Grid widget.

First, add a new action method to the `MoviesController` class that we created earlier.

```
public ActionResult MoviesGrid([DataSourceRequest]DataSourceRequest
request)
{
  return Json(
     db.Movies.ToDataSourceResult(request), JsonRequestBehavior.
AllowGet);
}
```

You should notice right away the special attribute in the signature of the action method called `[DataSourceRequest]`. This attribute comes from the `Kendo.Mvc.Extensions` namespace, so you will need to include that in a `using` statement at the top of the controller. This attribute is necessary for the Kendo UI Framework to properly understand the communication between the Grid widget and this server-side action method. It is also important that the `[DataSourceRequest]` attribute is decorating a `DataSourceRequest` object and that the return value from this action method is passed through the extension method called `ToDataSourceResult(request)`. These special methods drive the Kendo functionality for data binding, sorting, paging and filtering.

With this code in place, add a new action method to the `KendoController` called `Grid`, which will be the action method we use for the view.

```
public ActionResult Grid()
{
  return View();
}
```

Create a view for this method and place the following Razor code inside it:

```
@using Kendo.Mvc.UI;

@{
    ViewBag.Title = "Grid";
}

@(Html.Kendo().Grid<Chapter11.Models.Movie>().Name("moviesGrid")
    .Columns(columns =>
        {
            columns.Bound(p => p.Name);
            columns.Bound(p => p.ReleaseYear);
            columns.Bound(p => p.Rating);
            columns.Bound(p => p.Rank);
        }
        )
    .Pageable()
    .Sortable()
    .Filterable()
    .DataSource(dataSource => dataSource
        .Ajax()
        .PageSize(5)
        .Read(read => read.Action("MoviesGrid", "Movies"))
    ))
```

As you have seen before, this `Html` helper method from the Kendo UI Framework generates a Grid widget on the view page. We have configured the columns and enabled the Grid to be `pageable`, `sortable`, and `filterable`. The significant part for this example is that we have set the `DataSource` object to point to the `MoviesGrid` action of the `Movies` controller, which we set up earlier with the special Kendo attribute and objects. When we run our project and navigate to this new view, we get a Kendo Grid widget like the following, which has working paging buttons, filter buttons, and sortable column headings:

Name ▲	Release Year	Rating	Rank
Cowboys & Aliens	2011	61	9
Eternal Sunshine of the Spotless Mind	2004	84	1
Go	1999	72	4
Heat	1995	83	8
Safety Not Guaranteed	2012	71	2

1 2 — 1 - 5 of 10 items

Unlike in *Chapter 1, Interacting with Data: DataSource, Templates, TabStrip, and Grid*, however, this Grid widget is asking the server to calculate the sort order, the pages, and the filtered results. It does this by sending special data instructions to the server that are interpreted by the special Kendo attribute and objects. To see these data instructions, you can turn on the Internet Explorer developer tools by pressing the *F12* key while the website is running. In the toolbar that appears, click on the **Network** tab and then click **Start Capturing**. After clicking these buttons, click on one of the Grid functions, such as the page arrow or one of the column headings. You will see some activity in the developer toolbar, which means that the Grid is communicating with the server through JavaScript AJAX calls. Double-click on the first item in the list that shows the address **/Movies/MoviesGrid**, as shown here:

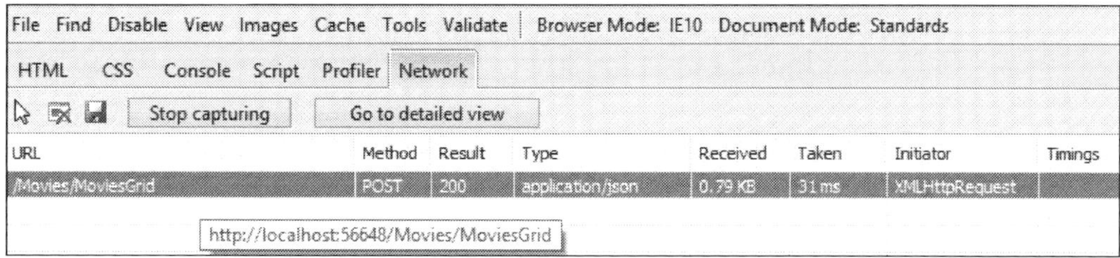

Double-clicking this item will open up a detailed description of the HTTP request. Click on the **Request body** tab to see what the Grid sent to the server:

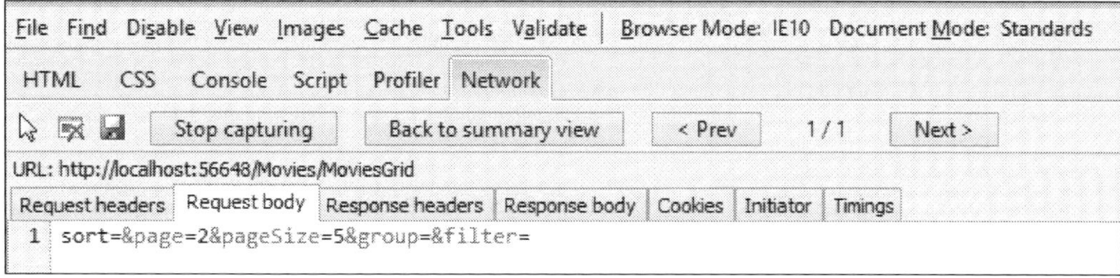

You can see here that the Grid has asked for page number `2` with a page size of `5` records. This is how the Kendo Grid communicates with the server, through the HTTP request body.

Driving the ListView with Web API

Similar to the Grid widget, the ListView widget is able to utilize the `[DataSourceRequest]` attribute to help drive special functionality for its operations. In this case, we will not simply be querying the data from the server, but also editing it with the Web API.

Create an action method for our ListView example in the `KendoController` class, as shown here:

```
private MoviesContext db = new MoviesContext();

public ActionResult ListView()
{
  return View(db.Movies);
}
```

Then add a view for this action method and add the following HTML markup inside:

```
@using Kendo.Mvc.UI;

@model IEnumerable<Chapter11.Models.Movie>

@{
    ViewBag.Title = "ListView";
}
<script type="text/x-kendo-tmpl" id="template">
    <div class="movie-view">
        <dl>
            <dt>Name</dt>
            <dd>${Name}</dd>
            <dt>Rating</dt>
            <dd>${Rating}</dd>
            <dt>Rank</dt>
            <dd>${Rank}</dd>
        </dl>
    </div>
    <div>
```

```
        <a class="k-button k-button-icontext k-edit-button"
            href="\\#"><span class="k-icon k-edit"></span>Edit</a>
        <a class="k-button k-button-icontext k-delete-button"
            href="\\#"><span class="k-icon k-delete"></span>Delete</a>
    </div>
</script>
<h2>ListView</h2>
```

This basic HTML and Kendo template will be used to build the page once the data has been retrieved. You can see how the template is simply showing each element of a `Movie` object and then providing the edit and delete buttons. Next, add the following MVC Razor code at the bottom of this view to wire everything together:

```
@(Html.Kendo().ListView(Model)
    .Name("moviesListView")
    .TagName("div")
    .ClientTemplateId("template")
    .Editable()
    .DataSource(dataSource => {
        dataSource
            .Read(read => read.Action("MoviesGrid", "Movies"))
            .Update(update => update.Type(HttpVerbs.Post)
              .Url("/api/MovieApi"))
            .PageSize(5)
            .Model(config => config.Id("Id"));
    })
    .Pageable())
```

Here, we have created a Kendo ListView, specified the ID of the template to use when rendering it on the page, marked it as editable, and specified the data source. Inside of the data source, we have indicated where to retrieve the data to display (the `Read` method) and where to send updated data (the `Update` method).

Next, we need to create an editor template for the `Movie` object, so that this ListView can edit our `Movie` objects. Make a new folder under the `Views/Shared` folder called `EditorTemplates`. Then, add a view to the `EditorTemplates` folder and call it `Movie.cshtml`.

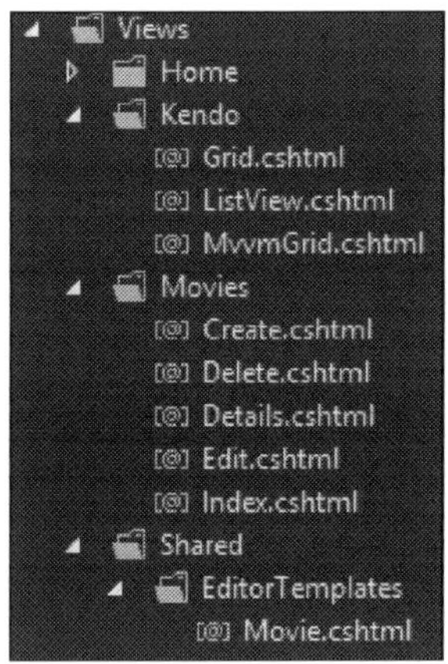

Open the `Movie.cshtml` view file and add the following code there:

```
@model Chapter11.Models.Movie

<div class="movie-view">
    <dl>
        <dt>Name</dt>
        <dd>@Html.EditorFor(model => model.Name)</dd>
        <dt>Rating</dt>
        <dd>@Html.EditorFor(model => model.Rating)</dd>
        <dt>Rank</dt>
        <dd>@Html.EditorFor(model => model.Rank)</dd>
    </dl>
    <div>
        <a class="k-button k-button-icontext k-update-button"
            href="\\#"><span class="k-icon k-update"></span>Save</a>
        <a class="k-button k-button-icontext k-cancel-button"
            href="\\#"><span class="k-icon k-cancel"></span>Cancel</a>
    </div>
</div>
```

This view will be used by the ListView widget when the **Edit** button is clicked on a `Movie` item. The following is how the page looks by default (when viewing the movies). You can see the different elements of a move item and the buttons used to edit or delete it:

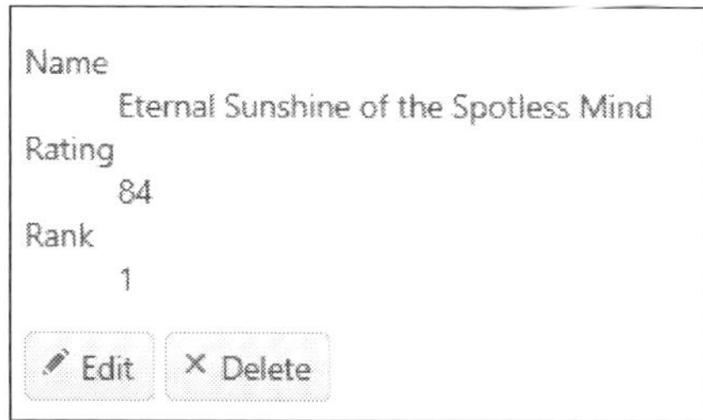

This is how a movie item is rendered when you click on the **Edit** button. See how the fields are now rendered as we specified in the `EditorTemplate` folder for the `Movie` data type.

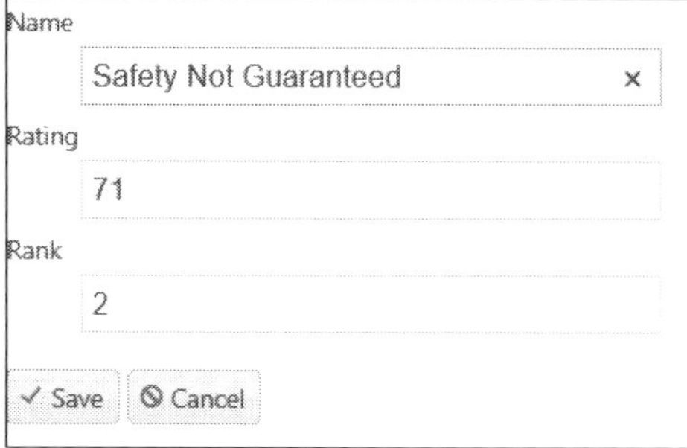

Since we have wired this up to the Web API, we can observe the changes being sent to the server for processing if we set a breakpoint in Visual Studio inside the API method that is being called. You can see that I have done this in the following screenshot:

```
namespace Chapter11.Controllers
{
    public class MovieApiController : ApiController
    {
        private MoviesContext db = new MoviesContext();

        public string Post(Movie movie)
        {
            return movie.Rating.ToString();
        }
    }
}
```

With Visual Studio set this way, the program will stop when an update is made and you can inspect the data to observe what is happening. For a production application, you would want to use the Entity Framework to edit the `movie` object and save the changes to the database.

Summary

In this chapter, we have seen how to use the Web API for some more realistic scenarios involving two of the Kendo widgets that deal with managing data. We also quickly explored the ASP.NET Web API fundamentals as well as Entity Framework and OData. These tools, used together, can be a very powerful set and can create nearly any custom solution that you need.

The examples we just saw, both use a special attribute that Telerik has provided to help with model binding and server-side paging and filtering. It is nice to make use of special helpers like this when they are available. I encourage you to continue to explore these technologies on your own and see how you can create your own custom solutions on your own web pages.

Index

Symbols

A

E

F

L

M

N

O

P

Q

R

S

T

U

V

W

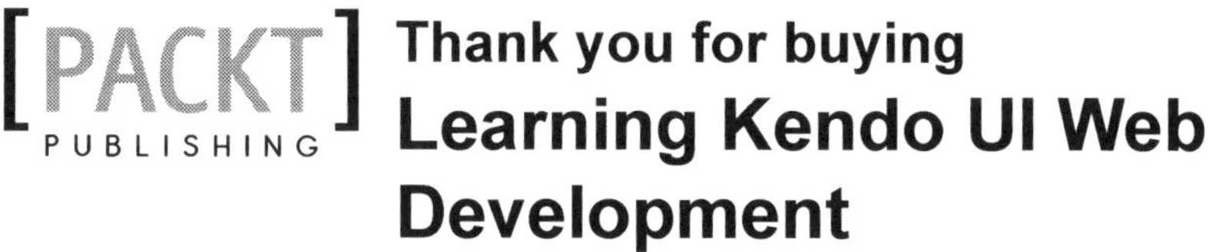

About Packt Publishing

Packt, pronounced 'packed', published its first book "*Mastering phpMyAdmin for Effective MySQL Management*" in April 2004 and subsequently continued to specialize in publishing highly focused books on specific technologies and solutions.

Our books and publications share the experiences of your fellow IT professionals in adapting and customizing today's systems, applications, and frameworks. Our solution based books give you the knowledge and power to customize the software and technologies you're using to get the job done. Packt books are more specific and less general than the IT books you have seen in the past. Our unique business model allows us to bring you more focused information, giving you more of what you need to know, and less of what you don't.

Packt is a modern, yet unique publishing company, which focuses on producing quality, cutting-edge books for communities of developers, administrators, and newbies alike. For more information, please visit our website: `www.packtpub.com`.

Writing for Packt

We welcome all inquiries from people who are interested in authoring. Book proposals should be sent to `author@packtpub.com`. If your book idea is still at an early stage and you would like to discuss it first before writing a formal book proposal, contact us; one of our commissioning editors will get in touch with you.

We're not just looking for published authors; if you have strong technical skills but no writing experience, our experienced editors can help you develop a writing career, or simply get some additional reward for your expertise.

jQuery Mobile Web Development Essentials

ISBN: 978-1-84951-726-3 Paperback: 246 pages

Learn to use the touch-optimized, cross-device, cross-platform jQM web framework for smartphones and tablets

1. Create websites that work beautifully on a wide range of mobile devices with jQuery mobile
2. Learn to prepare your jQuery mobile project by learning through three sample applications
3. Packed with easy to follow examples and clear explanations of how to easily build mobile-optimized websites

---

Learning jQuery, Third Edition

ISBN: 978-1-84951-654-9 Paperback: 428 pages

Create better interaction, design, and web development with simple JavaScript techniques

1. An introduction to jQuery that requires minimal programming experience
2. Detailed solutions to specific client-side problems
3. Revised and updated version of this popular jQuery book

Please check **www.PacktPub.com** for information on our titles

WordPress Mobile Web Development: Beginner's Guide

ISBN: 978-1-84951-572-6 Paperback: 332 pages

Make your WordPress website mobile-friendly and get to grips with the two hottest trends in web design— Mobile and WordPress

1. Learn how to build mobile and responsive websites using WordPress
2. Get to grips with the best mobile plugins and understand how they interact with your site
3. Learn how to make your own WordPress theme or site responsive, including layout, images, navigation and more

---

jQuery Tools UI Library

ISBN: 978-1-84951-780-5 Paperback: 112 pages

Learn jQuery Tools with clear, practical examples and get inspiration for developing your own ideas with the library

1. Learn how to use jQuery Tools, with clear, practical projects that you can use today in your websites
2. Learn how to use useful tools such as Overlay, Scrollable, Tabs and Tooltips
3. Full of practical examples and illustrations, with code that you can use in your own projects, straight from the book

Please check **www.PacktPub.com** for information on our titles

24262479R00163

Made in the USA
San Bernardino, CA
21 September 2015